Henry S. Sanford

Diplomacy and Business in Nineteenth-Century America

Henry S. Sanford (Courtesy of Library of Congress)

HENRY S. SANFORD:

Diplomacy and
Business in
Nineteenth-Century
America

Joseph A. Fry

University of Nevada Press
Reno, Nevada
1982

Nevada Studies in History and Political Science No. 16

Studies Editor
WILBUR S. SHEPPERSON

Editorial Committee
DON W. DRIGGS   ANDREW C. TUTTLE
JEROME E. EDWARDS   THOMAS C. WRIGHT

Library of Congress Cataloging in Publication Data
Fry, Joseph A., 1947–
Henry S. Sanford: diplomacy and business in nineteenth-century America.
Nevada studies in history and political science; no. 16)
Bibliography: p.
   1. Sanford, Henry Shelton, 1823–1891.   2. United
States—Foreign relations—1861–1865.   3. United States—
Foreign relations—1865–1898.   4. Diplomats—United States
—Biography.   5. Businessmen—United States—Biography.
I. Title.   II. Series.
E415.9.S16F79   1982   973.09'94 [B]   82–8360
ISBN 0–87417–070–2   AACR2

University of Nevada Press, Reno, Nevada 89557 USA
© Joseph A. Fry 1982. All rights reserved
Printed in the United States of America

For
Mom and Dad

CONTENTS

PREFACE AND ACKNOWLEDGMENTS

HENRY SHELTON SANFORD'S diverse diplomatic and business career has attracted the attention of scholars for more than seventy years. Though several historians have studied individual episodes or facets of his career, none has undertaken the comprehensive biography that his life warrants.[1] This study is meant to fill that void.

Over the second half of the nineteenth century, Sanford's diplomatic activities consistently influenced or symbolized the primary trends in United States foreign policy. His service as secretary of the American legation and chargé d'affaires in Paris and his Latin American business projects reflected the intense nationalism, filibustering tendencies, and economic expansionism of the 1850s. From his base as United States minister resident to Belgium during the 1860s, he was variously involved in the surveillance of Confederates, the preclusive buying of war materiel, the dissemination of Union propaganda, and the offer of a Union command to Giuseppe Garibaldi. The study of these endeavors is necessary for a complete view of Civil War diplomacy; collectively they made Sanford one of the Union's most important diplomatic representatives. Following the war Sanford became the most influential individual in the formation of United States policy toward the Congo. He helped stimulate American interest in the Congo during the 1870s and 1880s, engineered United States recognition of Leopold II's African International Association in 1884, and was a crucial member of the American delegations to the Berlin West African Conference of 1884–1885 and the Brussels Antislavery Conference of 1889–1890. His African involvements demonstrate the economic expansionism, the assumptions of cultural superiority, and the influence of individuals in the United States' Gilded Age diplomacy. In advocating a more assertive, purposeful, and interventionist foreign policy, Sanford served as a harbinger of what Robert L. Beisner has labeled the "new diplomacy" of the 1890s.[2]

Sanford's domestic business pursuits also command attention. During the 1870s and 1880s he launched several "New South" business ventures, including the rental of a South Carolina sea-island cotton plantation (1868) and the purchase of a Louisiana sugar plantation (1869). While both of these speculations furnished a telling commentary on Sanford's deficiencies as a businessman and the hazards of late-nineteenth-century agriculture, his contributions to the development of central Florida and the state's emerging citrus industry were much more lasting and significant. In 1870 Sanford bought a virgin tract of 12,547 acres along the St. Johns River in Orange County, Florida, and he subsequently founded the town that bears his name and established a slaughterhouse, sawmill, country store, and hotel. Although these projects, together with his Florida Land and Colonization Company, boosted the area's growth and development, his most notable Florida activity came with the establishment of Belair, a 145-acre citrus grove. In the twenty years after 1870, he poured thousands of dollars into this private "experiment station," and the knowledge generated there earned Sanford the apt designation as the "founder" of the modern Florida citrus industry.

I have received indispensable help from many people and institutions. I owe my greatest professional debt to the late Dr. Edward Younger, who suggested Sanford as a subject worthy of study and guided the writing of my dissertation. Dr. Younger was a superior graduate instructor and scholar, a southern gentleman in the very best sense of the term, and most of all a good friend. Norman Graebner read the dissertation and offered perceptive suggestions for its revision. Charles P. Cullop and James E. Dow first aroused my interest in history; Thomas R. Ross nurtured that interest, and both he and Dr. Cullop have aided me in numerous ways over the past fifteen years. Alan B. Bromberg, Paul E. Burns, Brent Tarter, and Thomas C. Wright each read the entire manuscript with great care; their suggestions were invariably thoughtful, occasionally painful, but always appreciated. Joyce Nelson typed several drafts of the manuscript with both skill and good cheer. Finally, I am pleased to thank Robert Laxalt, director of the University of Nevada Press; Nicholas M. Cady, assistant director and editor; and Wilbur S. Shepperson, editor of the Studies in History and Political Science, for their support throughout the publication process.

While thanking all of the libraries cited in the bibliography, I would like to express special appreciation to Robert L. Volz and his staff at the University of Rochester Library, Elizabeth Alexander and her personnel at the P. K. Yonge Library of Florida History at the University of Florida, the Manuscripts Division of the Library of Congress, and the interlibrary loan divisions of the University of Virginia and the University of Nevada, Las Vegas, libraries. For permission to quote, I am indebted to: the City of Sanford, Florida (Sanford Papers), the American Geographical Society (Charles P. Daly Papers), the Adams Manuscript Trust (Adams Papers), the Houghton Library at Harvard University (Charles Sumner Papers), the University of Vermont (George P. Marsh Papers), University of Rochester (William Henry Seward Papers and Thurlow Weed Papers), and the P. K. Yonge Library of Florida History (George W. Parsons Diary and T. Frederick Davis, "A Narrative History of the Orange in the Floridian Peninsula").

Research grants from both Virginia Polytechnic Institute and State University and the University of Nevada, Las Vegas, greatly facilitated my work. The two UNLV grants were particularly crucial; they enabled me to purchase essential microfilm materials and to make my final research trip to Florida.

Most importantly, I wish to thank my family. My mother and father have devoted their lives to me. Although I can never repay what they have given, it is a pleasure to acknowledge it. While working on this study, my son Bryan's vitality, curiosity, and zest for life constantly reminded me that books, while important, must always remain secondary. Finally, my greatest thanks go to my wife Sandy. She postponed her own graduate work so that I could pursue a doctorate, supported us during those years, helped me research and write the dissertation, and allowed Henry Sanford to be a part of our household far longer than either he or I could rightfully have expected.

CHAPTER 1

THE FORMATIVE YEARS, 1823-1849

ON OCTOBER 18, 1861, Benjamin Moran, assistant secretary of the United States legation in London, retired to his cluttered basement desk and vented his ire toward a colleague in the diplomatic corps. The vitriolic secretary fulminated that "of all the impertinent intruders we have ever had in Europe in an official life in my time, the most insolent is Mr. Henry S. Sanford, our present Resident Minister at Brussels." Sanford, whom Moran had earlier described as a "bouncing, ill-mannered yankee," had "offended almost all of his colleagues by meddling in their duties."[1] Echoing Moran's unflattering assessment, Adam Gurowski, a State Department clerk, sarcastically confided to his diary:

> What a devoted patriot this Sanford in Belgium is; he has continual *itchings in his hand* to pay a *higher price* for bad blankets that they might not fall into the hands of the secesh [sic] agents; so with cloth, so perhaps with arms. *Oh, disinterested patriot!*[2]

Sanford's post-Civil War activities proved equally offensive to other contemporaries. One late-nineteenth-century Floridian described him derisively as a "pompous northern gentleman" who swaggered into Orlando brandishing a "heavy gold-headed cane" and "dressed in the most correct styles of the day, with a high hat and spotless linen."[3]

Others rendered diametrically opposing assessments. Thurlow Weed answered Moran and other detractors by explaining that "Mr. Sanford's great activity, resulting from his temperament and his enthusiasm for the Union cause, was sometimes mistaken for officiousness." Had the public been better acquainted with Sanford's diplomatic efforts during the Civil War, Weed was confident that his old friend would have received general commendation.[4] The distinguished George P. Marsh agreed, informing Secretary of State William Henry Seward in 1861 that "continued intercourse with Mr. Sanford impresses me more and more favorably with respect to his character as a man and as a diplomatic agent."[5]

Edwin D. Morgan, former governor of New York, provided an additional perspective. Morgan acknowledged that Sanford had many enemies, but he attributed this primarily to "jealousy," since:

> He [Sanford] has the best house, the best furniture, the finest horses and carriage, the best servants, the best table, and perhaps I may say, the most attractive and accomplished wife of any of the United States Representatives at Foreign Courts. . . . I have seldom known a more able, scrupulous, and careful person than Sanford, in dealing with any matter in which the Government of the United States is concerned.[6]

And finally, a second Floridian, S. O. Chase, Sr., who eventually acquired Sanford's Florida citrus groves, touted his pleasant personality and his ability to mingle easily with all classes of people.[7]

Such conflicting evaluations confirm that Henry Shelton Sanford was a complex, multifaceted personality. Forceful and energetic, intelligent and learned, cultured and charming, Sanford was also ruthlessly ambitious, exceedingly vain, naively optimistic, frequently overzealous, and consistently undisciplined. Many of these traits became apparent during his first twenty-six, formative years. Even more importantly, it was during this period that he developed a fondness for Europe's aristocratic society and decided to pursue a diplomatic career.

Sanford was born in Woodbury, Connecticut, on June 23, 1823. Both his father, Nehemiah Curtis Sanford, and mother, Nancy Bateman Shelton Sanford, were from old New England stock. Nehemiah was a direct descendant of Thomas Sanford, who had arrived in America before 1634; Mrs. Sanford traced her lineage to Thomas Welles, the first colonial governor of Connecticut, and Daniel Shelton, a pioneer resident of Shelton, Connecticut. Described as a man of "sterling integrity," Nehemiah provided his family an upper middle-class existence from the proceeds of his mercantile business and served in the state senate during the 1830s.[8] Henry, the couple's only child, inherited much of his drive and energy from his father, whom he later characterized as "a man much above mediocrity, selfmade both in fortune and mind."[9]

Young Henry spent his first thirteen years among the rolling meadowlands surrounding the family's Woodbury estate. While benefitting from the instruction of private tutors, he spent much time alone and often longed for the company of other children. As he later recalled, "Loneliness in heart led me in early boyhood to find companionship in the thinking of others & early & late I would devote my hours in pouring over books." He especially enjoyed wandering in "the field of fiction," accompanied by gallant knights and lovely ladies.[10]

In 1836 the elder Sanford moved his family to Derby, Connecticut, a bustling little village on the east side of the Housatonic River, fifteen miles north of Long Island Sound. Nehemiah joined his brother-in-law, Edward N. Shelton, in establishing a tack factory in the new commercial-manufacturing village of Birmingham on the opposite bank of the Housatonic. Living in Derby and working in Birmingham, the Sanford family were solid fixtures in both communities. Nehemiah was "highly influential" among his 2,500 neighbors, and at his death the stores and factories of both communities closed as a token of respect.[11]

In Derby Henry studied the classics with Reverend Joseph Scott, rector of St. James' Episcopal Church of Birmingham. He also received his introduction to the business world. In May 1837, at the comparatively tender age of fourteen, he embarked alone on a two-month trip to Michigan to inspect his father's land holdings. After examining several tracts, he left funds with agents in Kalamazoo and Detroit for the purchase of additional property.[12]

Upon his return from the Great Lakes, Henry entered the Episcopal Academy at Cheshire, Connecticut, in September 1837. Because of the state's poor public schools, those parents with sufficient means often enrolled their children in private academies. At the thirty-six-year-old academy, Henry and his sixty schoolmates imbibed large doses of traditional academic fare: Latin, Greek, philosophy, and the classics, along with more modern courses in English, history, and French.[13]

Henry's Cheshire compositions reveal an active and logical, but not an original or brilliant mind. Several papers, dealing with honesty, generosity, and resolution as a prerequisite to success, and with the equality of opportunity in America, demonstrated that he had fully absorbed the prevailing ethic of his day. He ably articulated the maxim that man was the master of his fate and that success depended upon personal worth and determination. That a young man from a prosperous, Episcopalian, Whig family in conservative Connecticut should subscribe to these values was hardly surprising. That he could advise his son some forty years later to "Work hard, play hard, excel in whatever you do. . . . Always strive to do what is right . . . do nothing mean or tricky—be manly, open, truthful, [and] Godfearing" demonstrated that portions of these early lessons were enduring.[14]

In 1839 Sanford graduated from Cheshire and entered Washington College (now Trinity College) in Hartford, Connecticut. Founded in 1824 by Connecticut's Protestant Episcopal Church, the young college had introduced numerous innovations. Bishop Thomas C. Brounell, the first president, stressed a "policy of practicality," initiated courses in surveying and natural sciences, maintained a greenhouse and arboretum, and provided for a two-year degree program. Despite these innovations, the strong hand of tradition remained pervasive. As a candidate for the freshman class, Henry was required to pass examinations in English, Greek, and Latin grammar, Sallust, Virgil, Cicero, and the Gospels of Luke and John. Once admitted, he faced a curriculum heavily weighted toward the classics. The schedule was spartan, and the code of behavior strict. Each school day found Henry and his eighty classmates up for morning prayers by six o'clock and in bed by ten in the evening. According to the college catalog, "misdemeanors," such as playing cards or dice or attending a party without permission, and "high offenses," such as indecent language or "being concerned in any bonfire," would occasion strict punishment. If caught lying on his bed during study hours, he was subject to a one-dollar fine, and "festive entertainment in the city of Hartford or its vicinity" was forbidden. Henry was required to deposit all his private funds with the college bursar, who supervised his account with "parental discretion." In reality, these rules were "rather laxly enforced," which was probably fortunate for Henry. Judging from his subsequent behavior, he was almost assuredly among the mischievous boys who tortured the faculty with practical jokes and surreptitiously frequented local taverns.[15]

Although Henry was making satisfactory progress, an eye affliction forced him to withdraw from Washington during his sophomore year. He would suffer life-long problems with his eyes, and a pair of jaunty pince-nez soon became a permanent fixture atop his nose.[16] Before he could begin a therapeutic sea voyage recommended by his doctor, Henry was further shaken by the death of his father in early 1841. The two had been very close, and Henry later wrote that "I have never felt so completely desolate as after his death[.] It seemed as if the prop on which I had placed my utmost dependence had been suddenly taken from me." When, by August 1841, Henry had become "thin & weak" and was "quite miserable in health & spirits," he embarked on the prescribed sea voyage, his first of more than seventy-five transatlantic crossings.[17]

Arriving in Lisbon, Portugal, Henry was fascinated by the busy marketplace, where he observed women balancing heavy loads on their heads and men sporting huge moustaches; however, he was most impressed by the plight of the poor. He concluded that Portugal had only two classes, the nobles and their serfs: "It's either extremely rich or miserably poor." This dichotomy, he smugly concluded, developed naturally from the "horrors of Despotic Government." The young traveler enjoyed his first European trip immensely. Bolstered by a steady diet of fine fruits and tasty Portuguese wine, he returned to Derby on New Years Day 1842, "a new man—fat & hearty."[18]

Henry spent much of the subsequent six years in travel through the United States and Europe. He toured throughout western Europe in 1842–43 and 1845, managed two expeditions to the American Midwest, and spent long periods in New York City. Although his recurrent asthmatic ailment provided the rationale for these trips, his lack of direction and his hedonistic bent were more responsible. Financially secure and intellectually curious, he indulged in all the pleasures available to an intelligent and wealthy young man on the continent. Through study and social intercourse, Sanford learned German, French, Spanish, and Italian and simultaneously became an enthusiastic devotee of the aristocratic life style of Europe's upper classes. As his longtime French friend Jules Levita subsequently claimed with much accuracy, Sanford became "European by intellect, knowledge, artistic and socialistic taste."[19]

As his ability to endure the rigors of extensive travel suggests, Sanford enjoyed an active outdoor life. Although his chronic asthma periodically curtailed his activity, he relished fishing and bird shooting, and in the summer of 1846 even went buffalo hunting in Minnesota. Together with his Indian guide, he spent most of July and August of that year riding horseback on the northern plains. He thrilled at the "adventure" and "danger" of avoiding hostile Indians and braving the elements, but his description of the hunt was most compelling:

> ... dashing into the herd in search of a fat-cow with my horse at full speed. She was soon found and shot down and I on the ground beside seizing the horns of the struggling animal and giving the coup de grace with my knife and then with some of the choice bits cut out & strung over my horn was soon galloping back to find a place for camp and supper.[20]

He also sought opportunities for exercise on his sea voyages. On one Atlantic crossing he climbed about the rigging so frequently that his hands "passed the period of *blistering.*" Since this benefitted only his arms, he also began "pulling & hauling" ropes and sawing wood. While he found these pastimes healthful, Henry considered them socially degrading. The hauling of ropes, he complained, was done "in company with a parcel of dirty greasy sailors who if you helped them over once or twice would be given to consider you one of them & treat you accordingly." Similarly, by aiding the ship's carpenter he risked "compromising [his] *dignity.*"[21]

By his early twenties, Henry had grown into a striking figure. Six feet one inch in height, he had chestnut hair and hazel eyes, a high forehead with finely arched eyebrows, high cheek bones, a long straight nose, and a sensitive mouth.[22] As befitted such a handsome young man, Henry was "passionately fond of ... young ladies' society" and was "continually getting into scrapes of a tender nature." Indeed, he relished his reputation as a ladies' man. His college friend, Gilead A. Smith, characterized him as "Sanford the Invincible, the Alcides of the Housatonic"; his cousin, Sarah C. Sanford, marveled, "You must have hands and *your heart* full if you are obliged to beaux all the ladies in Birmingham"; and he subsequently earned the title of a "fast man" among his European acquaintances.[23]

One of Smith's many gossipy letters to Sanford provides a revealing commentary on both blithe young bachelors. A young lady had asked Smith if his friend Sanford "were not *very warm.*" She continued, "I have always suspected he was and have given him much credit for the propriety and apparent virtue of his conduct at home, when I knew he was dying to gratify his passions." Smith replied, "Anne, you must be well aware that all men have passions & I presume that Henry like myself could hardly resist the temptation of sleeping with a pretty girl" if the opportunity arose.[24]

Henry's behavior disturbed his mother. Religious, protective, and domineering, Nancy Sanford found her only son's social life unpalatable. She advised him in 1845 to "shun vice and disappation *[sic]* . . . it will ruin your body and soul, and will not afford you happiness." His prolonged stays in Europe and growing proclivity for continental society also drew her ire. Lamenting his fascination with "court society and nobility," she rebuked him for his selfishness: "Let not *self* be the *spring of action,* you have *too long bent everything* to your pleasure." She recommended discipline, marriage, and a quiet life near her in Derby. Her blueprint for Henry's life even included his ideal mate—Janie Howe, the daughter of a local doctor. For a time, Henry viewed Miss Howe similarly. They became engaged in 1846, but Henry's feelings cooled during his European sojourns, and he broke off the relationship in the fall of 1848. His mother was crestfallen and loudly bemoaned "how much" he had "lost."[25]

Although financially secure and untroubled by the minor problems of everyday existence, Henry grew increasingly restive. Aware of his potential and driven by a gnawing ambition, he realized that he might "be a man of more than ordinary calibre *by trying.*" Between journeys, he decided in the fall of 1846 to direct his energies into the tack business owned jointly with his uncle. Working with Uncle Ed proved unsatisfactory, and Henry soon felt stifled: "I am in his estimation a sort of cypher, and its *[sic]* what 'I,' [Uncle Ed] will do, will buy, will sell, etc. If I attempt to do anything he thrusts himself & opinions in the till. I can hope neither to gain respect from the workmen or anyone else concerned, but everything must cluster around him."[26]

Sanford's discontent derived from more than the prospect of "playing second fiddle & on a very minor key." He and Uncle Ed also disagreed about the operation of the business. Ten years Henry's senior, Edward N. Shelton was a much more cautious, systematic, and prudent businessman. He flatly rejected Henry's suggestions to give some customers preferred rates, to cheat "in the weight in the large sizes," and to take orders that the company might not be able to fill. Shelton also carefully checked on prospective buyers and dealt only with clients he was confident would pay promptly. As Nancy Sanford pointed out some years later, Henry more closely resembled her other brother, Philo S. Shelton, who lacked "cautiousness."

Realizing that manufacturing tacks with Uncle Ed would be neither satisfying nor harmonious, Henry sold him his share of the factory in December 1847.[27]

Soon thereafter he also assigned Uncle Ed his power of attorney and entrusted the canny New Englander with his general financial affairs. The young man's fortune was impressive. Following the disposal of the factory, his stock, real estate, and other receivables totaled $50,000. This included his partnership in a Birmingham general store which earned him more than $7,200 from 1846 through 1850. Moreover, at Shelton's behest, he expanded his stock portfolio after 1847 to include investments in the Manufacturers Bank of Birmingham, the Erie Railway, and the Delaware and Hudson Canal Company.[28]

Despite his apparent financial security, Sanford was anxious about the future and suffered through periods of intense self-analysis during the mid-1840s. He was harshly critical of time he had "misspent & frittered away." He confided to his diary that he had ample ambition "to look forward to anything"—even the presidency. Yet he also understood that "Everything to be done requires exertion and to climb over the heads of your neighbors & equals in rank requires it constantly & arduously." Echoing his mother's strictures, he convicted himself of lacking self-discipline and scorning purposeful activity. In his most acute moment of self-perception, he admitted trusting too much to "impulse." This was particularly true in business, where he judged his "greatest failing" to be "not having sufficiently an opinion of my own, not thinking enough."[29]

Not yet twenty-four years old, Sanford sailed again for Europe in 1847 determined to remedy these shortcomings. Declaring his intention to "do something useful for [his] country," he initiated a study of European languages and governmental institutions. He had just arrived in Paris and begun these tasks when an irresistible diversion appeared. Ralph Ingersoll, a fellow Connecticut resident and newly appointed United States minister to Russia, invited Henry to accompany him to St. Petersburg as temporary attaché. Henry jumped at the chance. Ambition and the potential entry into Europe's aristocratic society dictated his decision. The position would, he predicted, provide a "stepping stone" to "some future advancement" and "acquaintance & friends . . . that can put me on a high stand in any capital in Europe."[30]

Although he found St. Petersburg a social wasteland, the diplomatic service proved exhilarating. He thrilled at encountering *"living*

Politics instead of abstract *dead* men." "It gives me," he enthused, "an acquaintance with the chief men of Europe—those who wield its destinies." His six months in St. Petersburg fulfilled his expectations concerning possible advancement. In route to the Russian capital, he and Ingersoll stopped in Berlin where Sanford met Andrew Jackson Donelson, the American minister. The following year Sanford parlayed this acquaintance and his experience as attaché into an appointment as acting secretary of legation under Donelson. By 1848 Sanford had decided on a diplomatic career and was scanning the horizon for a permanent secretaryship.[31]

His decision for a "public" career also led him to study law at the University of Heidelberg from October 1848 through April 1849. Evincing his European inclinations, he announced that he was going to "experiment" by pursuing a "good scientific education such as is followed by those fitting themselves for public life" in Europe. He acknowledged that this kind of training might count for little in America, but he was determined to keep "drudging away" toward his doctor of laws, which he received *cum laude* in May 1849.[32] Although Sanford took great pride in this degree, it is difficult to assess its value. At least one of his friends held it in contempt. William Pennington warned Sanford:

> Don't attempt to gull me with long-winded stories about 'such study as never entered the brain of man.' I am not quite so green as you appear to think me still. I always told you that for $250 I would get you a Degree in any Branch you might desire, without your ever putting your foot within 3000 miles of Heidelburg or Germany.[33]

His mother denounced his decisions and reeled off a succession of reasons why Henry should not aspire to a "political" career. He had set his sights too high and was engaged in "Castle Building"; a career based on political preference was too uncertain; the demands would overtax his health; European "Court life" had little "affinity" for "our republican institutions"; she was lonely and wanted her only child to live near her. In sum, Nancy Sanford contended that Henry should return to Derby and pursue a more relaxed, more stable, more respectable calling such as medicine or farming.[34]

Her arguments had no effect on Henry, whom she characterized as "head strong" and "impatient of restraint."[35] He was intent upon breaking free from the last vestiges of parental restraint—upon establishing a lifestyle and career of his own choosing. Soon after Zachary

Taylor's inauguration, the young office seeker set sail for home to mount a "push for the Secretaryship at Paris." Upon landing in New York on June 6, 1849, Sanford hurried to Washington to press his claim. He secured interviews with President Taylor and Secretary of State John M. Clayton but found them unencouraging and decided against personally soliciting the secretaryship. Altering his strategy, he journeyed on to Connecticut and began recruiting the support of numerous influential Whigs.[36]

His two uncles, Edward N. Shelton and Philo S. Shelton, were the keys to aligning the necessary political backing. Uncle Ed enlisted the aid of Connecticut's leading Whigs. Governor Joseph Trumbull headed the list of state officers who petitioned Taylor on Sanford's behalf, and Connecticut's two United States senators, Roger S. Baldwin and Truman Smith, also endorsed Sanford's candidacy. Smith, who had been a "personal friend" of Henry's father, was especially important. One of Taylor's earliest backers, he had helped organize an important pro-Taylor congressional clique and had worked tirelessly for "old Rough and Ready" at the Whig National Convention in Philadelphia. From his post as chairman of the Whig Executive Committee, he had then coordinated the successful campaign, thereby placing both the president and the party in his debt.[37]

Sanford's support reached well beyond Connecticut. Through his Uncle Philo of Boston, the aspiring diplomat drew on the considerable influence of Thurlow Weed. Shelton had earned the respect of Weed and others through his work on behalf of the Massachusetts Whigs. The hulking New Yorker considered Shelton " 'all in all' the most elevated, efficient and reliable Whig in the whole Union," and he deemed it "all together just" that Sanford be appointed as compensation for his uncle's "invaluable service." At Shelton's behest, Weed recruited his protégé, William H. Seward, into the Sanford camp and requested Attorney General Reverdy Johnson to intercede with Clayton. Added to the efforts of these upstate New Yorkers were the endorsements of Vice-President Millard Fillmore and two prominent New York City merchants, Charles H. Russell and Moses Taylor.[38]

Even this impressive support did not assure Sanford's appointment. Mid-nineteenth-century ministers virtually dictated the choice of their secretaries, and William C. Rives, Taylor's nominee for the French mission, had planned to take his son along as first assistant. Clayton had initially agreed to Rives' request, but on June 12 he informed the veteran Virginia politician that the cabinet had decided "such an appointment would be inexpedient." Rives retained the right to designate his principal subordinate, but the selection could not come from within his family. Annoyed at Clayton's reversal, Rives disgustedly replied that Sanford or any of the other candidates were likely to be "more an encumbrance than a help."[39]

With the younger Rives eliminated, Sanford's primary competition came from Allyne Otis, the son of the late Massachusetts figure, Harrison Gray Otis. On July 14 Rives advised Clayton that he preferred Otis; but two days later, under heavy pressure from Truman Smith, he reconsidered and requested that the choice be temporarily postponed. Rives then wrote his friend Ralph Ingersoll of New Haven inquiring about Sanford. In 1847 Ingersoll had made Sanford his attaché in St. Petersburg, and his frank but favorable reply decided the matter. He described Sanford as well educated, of a congenial disposition, fluent in French and German, and in "all respects well principled." Ingersoll concluded that Sanford was a man "of gentlemanly habits, though rather too rapid in his manner and conversation," and was far "superior" to the usual secretarial appointee. After pondering the matter for still another month, Rives notified Clayton on August 17 that Sanford was his choice. His systematic and energetic efforts rewarded, the brash, young New Englander eagerly anticipated both his official duties and Parisian society. Still only twenty-six, Sanford stood on the threshold of a diplomatic career which would span forty years.[40]

CHAPTER 2

DIPLOMACY AND BUSINESS, 1850–1860

SANFORD'S DIVERSE ACTIVITIES in the 1850s illustrate the period's most prominent diplomatic themes. While serving as chargé d'affaires in Paris, he joined "Young America" in celebrating "republican simplicity" and ostensibly denigrating the trappings of European monarchy. Over the second half of the decade he actively promoted economic and territorial expansion in Latin America. His business and legal projects embodied both the United States' isthmian focus and the nation's arrogance in dealing with her southern neighbors.

Having settled on a diplomatic career, Sanford was constantly alert to possibility for advancement. While in Paris he acquired the experience necessary for a more prestigious appointment and cultivated people who could provide crucial political backing. Ambition was the key both to his response to Secretary of State William L. Marcy's dress circular in 1853 and his subsequent applications for diplomatic positions with the Democratic administration of James Buchanan. His persistence, experience, and political contacts finally paid dividends in 1861 when Abraham Lincoln appointed him minister resident to Belgium.

Sanford began his "various and arduous" duties as secretary to the American legation in Paris in August of 1849. Since Franco-American relations were largely uneventful during the first half of the 1850s, his days were crammed with necessary, but routine tasks. During his years in Paris, he wrote more than 11,500 pages of dispatches and prepared more than 10,000 passports. Requests from American travelers and expatriates for entrance to Napoleon's receptions, for passes to the National Assembly, and for invitations to the many court-sponsored *fêtes* seemed endless. The number of travelers once grew so large that Sanford wondered if "All America [was] giving itself air in Switzerland." Maintaining the legation's books and documents and commissioning diplomatic messengers further absorbed his time. He even inherited such unlikely tasks as communicating the latest French method of "drying lettuce" to the State Department and forwarding a gold snuff box from the Grand Duke of Tuscany to an American naval officer.[1]

He conscientiously attended to his diverse responsibilities. Gilead A. Smith, his old college friend, wrote that he was "delighted to hear the unanimous compliment" that American tourists paid to Sanford's "courtesy and attendance to them when in Paris." Although Sanford derived much satisfaction from such reports, he periodically complained that his duties were confining, time-consuming, and expensive; that his "time was no longer [his] own"; and that opportunities for intellectual "self-improvement" were practically eliminated. In fact, he found time to study language in the mornings and was usually able to leave the office each day by four. Still the volume and breadth of his tasks forced him to employ a full-time copyist, and when absent from the legation, he had to hire a clerk to serve in his stead. Though he had harbored no illusions that his salary of $2,000 per annum would suffice, he found that his annual expenses approached $4,000, and by the time of his departure in 1854 he had amassed more than $5,000 in debts.[2]

Sanford's insolvency was related directly to his enjoyment of Paris. In contrast to Bret Harte, who would denounce the French capital as a "wicked place . . . steeped in iniquity and dissipation," Sanford joined most mid-nineteenth-century American visitors in their admiration of the diverse and exciting city. Where else could one find such popular cafés and boutiques; such elegant shops and restaurants; such magnificent architecture as the Tuileries, Versailles, and Notre Dame; or such unrestrained night life as in the Jardin Mabille on the Champs Elysées? He quickly became a fixture in the American community of Paris. Numbering a few hundred by the 1850s, the expatriates often entertained and visited one another. They collectively supported an American chapel and tailor and together with British residents patronized an English-language newspaper.[3]

While lamenting his lack of time and money for Parisian society, Sanford actually enjoyed an elegant and expensive lifestyle. He delighted in the lavish French society, which he considered "extremely important for a man to frequent." When not attending balls, concerts, and receptions, he escorted Americans visiting Paris. These activities were not simply intrinsically enjoyable; they also provided a "foundation to build upon at home in [the] shape of friends in every position." Thurlow Weed, Stephen A. Douglas, and Truman Smith were among the "principal people" whom Sanford either met or became better acquainted with during these years. Disdaining less pretentious quarters, he leased a house in one of Paris' fashionable areas and bought furniture, a library, a carriage, and four fine horses. In February 1851 he sponsored a "Ball" at his house for more than 250 American expatriates, and the following year he initiated the formation of a Circle of Conversation for resident Americans.[4] Nor did he ignore the fair sex. As he jokingly remarked to his friend Bancroft Davis, "I am, of course, public property here, and . . . engaged to each young lady in turn who comes to Paris." Referring to Sanford's many flirtations, Colin Ingersoll pointedly asked: "Do you expect that you'll ever be a Minister if you go on this way?"[5]

Henry's mother and his two uncles, Edward and Philo, were appalled at his extravagance. Puzzled over whether her son was "intoxicated" by his position or just plain "cracked," Nancy Sanford wrote in 1851, "I cannot express how much I have been grieved and pained that you should not live more . . . in accordance with the station you fill." Uncle Ed agreed and prophetically warned Henry that he was "acquiring habits that you cannot well shake off." Shelton conceded that Henry could support his indulgence while still single but feared that would change dramatically when he had a family.[6]

Henry ignored their warnings. He protested that his mother took insufficient "pride" in his accomplishments and office; rather than "encouraging" him she sought to impede his progress. His declaration of independence was unmistakable: "I have, since I have been in Europe known what I was about, & it has required considerable firmness on my part not to yield to the suggestion[s] . . . continually made to me in my plans & way of living by you. You know perfectly well that had I followed your opinions & advice I should be far off from being what I now am." He was after all twenty-eight, not fifteen, and she would have to trust his judgment.[7]

Sanford believed that American diplomats could perform a useful service by reporting on the government machinery of the countries to which they were assigned. Despite his routine duties and active social life, he completed two such treatises during his years in France. The first was a study of European penal codes, and the second was a thorough recounting of the administrative changes in France from the Revolution of 1848 through 1853. The two works were combined and printed as a senate executive document by the Thirty-third Congress in the spring of 1854.[8] Sanford composed a number of other such descriptive accounts during his years abroad. Collectively these documents reveal an orderly, logical mind, a thorough knowledge of several foreign languages, and a wide acquaintance with European legal institutions; but like his compositions at Cheshire Academy, they disclose little original, creative genius. Sanford was intelligent and energetic, but not brilliant.[9]

With the victory of Franklin Pierce and the Democrats in 1852, Rives tendered his resignation. He urged Sanford to do likewise, but his ambitious young assistant demurred. Sanford desired the distinction and opportunity of serving as chargé d'affaires until the Democrats sent over Rives' successor. He hoped that his interim performance might prompt the new administration to retain him as secretary. Following Rives' departure in mid-1853, Sanford expected only a three-month tenure as chargé; however, the Pierce administration's initial sluggishness extended his control of the most important United States mission on the continent to nearly eight months. Not until early January 1854 did the new minister, John Y. Mason, arrive.[10]

It was during this interim that Secretary of State Marcy issued his curious dress circular. The custom requiring United States representatives to don an ornate diplomatic uniform for formal European court functions had long rankled Marcy and many other Americans. Convinced that the United States was creating a new and better society, these ardent nationalists demanded that their representatives' dress reflect the idealized American qualities of republicanism and simplicity.[11] In his circular of June 1, 1854, Marcy withdrew all prior instructions concerning diplomatic uniform. Although he technically left the mode of attire to the discretion of the individual diplomats, he strongly encouraged his subordinates to adopt "the simple dress of an American citizen."[12] Symbolizing the "Young America" furor of the period, Marcy's circular received a warm public reception. Editorial comment was overwhelmingly laudatory, and letters expressing hearty approval poured into the State Department from all areas of the country. The *New York Herald* predicted that "all the country from Cape Cod to California will cry amen."[13]

After momentary hesitation, Henry Sanford cried amen. His "own inclinations" were to discard diplomatic uniform for the plain black suit commonly worn as evening dress in the United States, but Napoleon III and Eugenie's "system of rigorous etiquette" made him apprehensive. To avoid difficulties, he obtained an interview with Edouard Drouyn de Lhuys, the French foreign minister. Sanford stressed that he intended no disrespect of the French Court and that his altered dress would signify no "change in the sentiments of the Government and people of the United States towards France." Drouyn de Lhuys replied that Sanford's intentions would neither elicit complaint nor jeopardize Franco-American relations. Thus assured, Sanford wore his black suit to the *fête* of August 15, which included Napoleon's reception of the diplomatic corps, a dinner given by the foreign minister, and a *soirée* at the Tuileries. He was pleased by Napoleon's "marked attention" and "friendly tenor of conversation" and was confident he had occasioned no offense.[14]

Thereafter, Sanford donned his citizen's dress of black coat and white tie on all occasions, both festive and formal. While this led some to dub him the "Black Crow," he continued unperturbed, relishing the notoriety.[15] He gloried in such comments in the Parisian journals as: "The most conspicuous figure at the court ball last evening was Mr. Sanford, the American Chargé d'Affaires, *Simplex Munditiis.*"[16] Sanford enjoyed this attention, but his course also reflected careful calculation. Still hoping to remain as secretary under the new Democratic administration, he recognized that close adherence to Marcy's directive could enhance his position. Such was the opinion of one of his Democratic friends who wrote, "I cannot help chuckling over the fact that a Whig appointment has first illustrated the republican simplicity of Marcy's instructions and that the new Democratic ministers can only imitate your costume." Nelson M. Beckwith, one of Sanford's closest American friends in Paris, agreed and punned, "Who next will have the pluck to follow? Or rather who will dare not to follow suit?"[17]

The new minister, John Y. Mason, arrived on January 8, 1854, and quickly indicated he would not follow suit. Fifty-four years old, fat and ruddy, Mason had long supplemented his income from land and slaves by serving in various official positions, including cabinet posts under Tyler and Polk. Jovial and good humored, but lacking in social graces and somewhat indolent, Judge Mason's primary concern was to maintain an adequate supply of Virginia hams and tobacco. He was particularly fond of chewing tobacco and could find but one feature lacking in the magnificent Tuileries—it had no spittoons. After consulting with Drouyn de Lhuys and several Americans in

Paris, Mason concluded that continuing Sanford's precedent would impair his diplomatic usefulness. He acknowledged that Sanford stood "well in society generally" but contended that his conspicuous disregard for court etiquette had rendered his interactions with the government less "agreeable."[18]

On January 18 Mason confronted his Whig subordinate and confirmed Sanford's fear that the administration planned to appoint a new secretary. Though disappointed, Sanford accepted the news calmly and graciously replied that he had no desire to obstruct either Mason's or the president's intentions. Mason then stated that he planned to reintroduce traditional diplomatic attire. Sanford was indignant. He interpreted Mason's decision as a personal and official affront and warned the veteran Virginian politician that he would not accompany him to court; instead he would resign and force the State Department to choose between them.[19]

Mason held firm, and on January 23 he wore his more formal garb to a ball at the Tuileries. Sanford immediately fired off his letter of resignation to Secretary Marcy. He contended that Mason's decision made his further official intercourse with the French court "impractical." Sanford argued that since his actions had conformed completely with Marcy's instructions, contrary conduct by his new superior must convey "the apparent disapprobation of the Government." Two officers at the same legation following different practices could only cause embarrassment; therefore, duty dictated his resignation.[20]

Sanford admitted to Bancroft Davis that he would likely "be accused of an *artful dodge* to prevent . . . being turned out" but asserted that Mason's course left him no alternative. While his actions derived partially from principle, expediency was the primary consideration. He was sure his resignation would "put" him "well before the country at home." In fact, he speculated to Uncle Ed, "I could not go home under better auspices nor expect to gain much more in reputation or credit."[21]

The usually amiable Mason was incensed. Sanford especially irritated the old judge by not allowing him to read and approve his letter of resignation. Mason cogently contended that since Sanford was soon to be relieved his resignation over the matter of dress was hypocritical. In mid-March, after most American papers had endorsed Sanford's course, Mason complained bitterly to Marcy that Sanford was "full of self-conceit, and places such an estimate on himself that he recognizes no superior."[22]

As Rives observed, Sanford's resignation placed the Pierce administration in a "dilemma."[23] Marcy's ambiguity had led to the difficulty: while strongly urging the adoption of citizen's dress, he had left the final decision to the discretion of individual ministers. This made it possible for both Sanford and Mason to act in accordance with the circular, but only Sanford's actions had elicited bipartisan approval in the United States. Although Marcy agreed philosophically with Sanford, he could hardly disavow his newly-appointed Democratic minister.

Marcy sought to escape from this dilemma by approving the conduct of both Sanford and Mason. Although he dutifully supported Mason, his annoyance was ill concealed. The secretary privately lamented the "awkwardness" of the incident since "the course pursued by Mr. Sanford in doffing his uniform was so generally approved in this country as to amount to a public judgment in its favor." Marcy accepted Mason's estimate of the situation but regretted that Mason had complied "with the exactions of an etiquette so uncongenial with the views and feelings of this country."[24]

Sanford dismissed Marcy's reply to his resignation as a "labored effort" skirting Mason's basic "contradiction of the circular." Yet the letter's tone was more sympathetic than Marcy's treatment of Mason. Marcy commended Sanford's official conduct, particularly in regard to the sensitive dress problem, expressed "regret" that Sanford and Mason had not agreed, and pointedly corrected Sanford's "erroneous impression" that Mason's decision had signaled official "disapprobation." How, asked Marcy, could this be the case when both men had acted under the identical circular? Pointing lamely to the discretionary nature of the directive, Marcy contended that the department could not have prevented this development.[25]

Sanford's reply succinctly outlined the impossibility of his remaining in Paris. Even if the secretary had not intended to disavow his actions, French observers would naturally draw that conclusion. How could two diplomats interpret the same instructions correctly yet follow courses "directly, if not absurdly, in contrast . . .[?] The more natural conclusion would be that both had acted capriciously . . . or else that the inferior officer had misunderstood his Government & was disapproved by it." Since either appearance would severely hamper his usefulness, resignation was the only alternative. Despite its cogency, Sanford's argument was semantic and irrelevant; the Pierce administration had already decided to replace him.[26]

On April 4, 1854, Sanford concluded his tenure in France and soon thereafter returned to the United States. His five years in Paris had been his longest continuous residence in one place since the age of fourteen. He had ably met his responsibilities as secretary and had acquired valuable experience which would help make him a contender for future appointments. As chargé he had become the focal point of one of the more bizarre diplomatic incidents of the 1850s. Marcy's dress circular and the flap over court costume vividly illustrated the country's swaggering nationalism. Sanford's response to Marcy's instructions and to Mason's decision to readopt diplomatic costume derived in part from nationalistic fervor, but calculating ambition was a more important motive. This first significant diplomatic post had demonstrated many of the characteristics that marked his later endeavors. Energetic, capable, and aggressive, Sanford had a proclivity for becoming embroiled in controversy, both official and private.

On his return to the United States in the spring of 1854, Sanford found the nation approaching the midpoint of a paradoxical decade. Perhaps no year better illustrated the outwardly contradictory themes running through the 1850s—an increasingly divisive sectionalism and a heady, aggressive nationalism. Even before Sanford embarked from Paris, Stephen A. Douglas had introduced the explosive Kansas-Nebraska Bill in the Senate. Its passage in May produced Northern outrage at the repeal of the Missouri Compromise and raised the possibility of slavery being extended north of 36°30'. Anti-Nebraska groups sprung up in the North, and the Republican party formed in June to oppose the extension of slavery. This growing sectionalism was accompanied through much of the decade by the militant, impulsive nationalism embodied in Marcy's circular. Eighteen fifty-four was also the year of the abortive, but nevertheless suggestive, Ostend Manifesto, in which America's ministers to Great Britain, France, and Spain urged the United States to seize Cuba from Spain. The following year William Walker and the fifty-eight "immortals" sailed from San Francisco on their initial filibustering journey to usurp control of Nicaragua's government.

Like Walker, the notorious "grey-eyed man of destiny," Sanford focused most of his attention on Latin America during the second half of the 1850s. He was primarily concerned with the prosecution of his Uncle Philo S. Shelton's claim against Venezuela. The problem resulted from Shelton's attempt to exploit guano deposits on Aves Island, a small, uninhabited Caribbean isle 600 miles north of Venezuela.[27] Shelton's exploring expedition, under the command of Nathan Gibbs, had located the island in April 1854.[28] Following Gibbs' return to Boston, a member of this original exploring party defected, offering both his services and knowledge of Aves to Lang and Delano, a competing Boston firm. Both groups raced to claim the island, reaching Aves within an hour of one another on July 15. To avoid violence, the rivals divided the island and commenced work, and as of mid-December 1854, the Shelton employees had shipped approximately 7,200 tons of guano to Boston.

By November 1854 the Aves operation had attracted the attention of other northern speculators, and the following month the Philadelphia Guano Company dispatched John D. F. Wallace to Venezuela. On December 21 José Tadeo Monagas, the Venezuelan dictator, granted Wallace the right to extract guano from all islands under Venezuelan sovereignty. Monagas then dispatched naval vessels to Aves on December 21 and 23, and on December 30 the *Trece de Diciembre's* crew expelled both groups of American workers.

Shelton immediately appealed to the State Department for aid. Arguing that Aves had been a "derelict," unclaimed island prior to Gibbs' discovery, Shelton declared damages of $341,000: $28,500 actual losses and $312,500 potential profits on 25,000 tons of guano at $12.50 per ton.[29] Soon thereafter, he retained Henry Sanford to prosecute his claim. Sanford began his work for a 5 percent commission on any settlement, but by 1862 he had acquired title to the entire claim.[30] His efforts tranformed this comparatively trivial incident into a serious diplomatic issue which jeopardized relations between the United States and Venezuela. Only after more than one hundred trips to the State Department, three voyages to Caracas, and a thirty-year campaign did he gain a final settlement.

Secretary of State Marcy originally accepted Shelton's contention that Aves had been derelict. When Charles Eames, the United States minister to Venezuela, presented the Shelton claim, the Monagas government countered with a document dated December 13, 1854, and signed by both Gibbs and the Lang and Delano representative prior to their expulsion from Aves. Written entirely in Spanish, this *permiso* temporarily allowed the Americans to remain on the island and committed both groups to place their arms "at the disposition and under the flag of Venezuela, to which the island belongs." On

June 14, 1855, Marcy demanded an explanation. Before proceeding, he had to "be satisfied that this agreement was made under duress." If this were not the case, the failure to disavow Gibbs' action would "seriously" imperil any claim for damages.[31]

Sanford replied in a long letter over Shelton's signature. He argued that Gibbs' agreement resulted from a combination of duress and fraud. The armed military personnel aboard Venezuela's naval vessel constituted the duress, and Gibbs' inability to read Spanish facilitated the misrepresentation of the note. Sanford correctly contended that the facts of occupation and discovery, not the permit, were the determinants of ultimate sovereignty. Since Aves had long been abondoned and "derelict," the American occupation irrevocably established Shelton's ownership. Sanford and Shelton buttressed their claim with depositions from the workers present at Aves in December 1854. The secretary had hardly finished sorting these materials when Sanford forwarded a long memorial treating the relevant legal points. Especially interesting was his contention that, as an agent, Gibbs had no legal authority to alienate Shelton's title to the island or its guano.[32]

Sanford reinforced these private efforts by cultivating public and political support. He had earlier published Shelton's May 14, 1855, letter demanding action from Marcy in the New York papers, and he privately printed his legal memorial under the inflammatory title of "Venezuelan Outrage Upon United States Citizens and Property at Shelton's Isle."[33] He and his uncle also enlisted influential persons in their cause. Shelton contacted his old friend Thurlow Weed, and Sanford communicated with both Weed and William H. Seward, the powerful New York senator. In a vivid forecast of their subsequent tactics, Shelton requested Sanford to ascertain if "the administration could be screwed up to the point of enforcing such a claim if some of their friends were *let in* as shareholders."[34]

Sanford was incensed when these efforts failed to stimulate forceful action from the State Department. He charged that Eames owned an interest in the rival Philadelphia company and had failed to protect Shelton's interests. Rather than prod Eames to action, Marcy had wasted time in drafting "hypocritical epistles" to the aggrieved Americans. The secretary's neglect was, according to Sanford, "a d . . . d small business." When confronting a country such as Venezuela, he fumed, "prudence" was a "most rascally virtue" and "timidity worse than stupidity."[35]

Frustrated by his dealing with the State Department, Sanford took his case directly to President Franklin Pierce and Congress. In an interview with Pierce on December 20, 1855, Sanford requested permission to outfit an expedition to expel the Venezuelan garrison from Aves. Pierce vetoed this bellicose suggestion and was similarly unresponsive to subsequent appeals during the spring of 1856.[36] Sanford also memorialized Congress. On April 19, 1856, he repeated his interpretation of the case and complained that the State Department had ignored his uncle's January 1855 petition. He implored Congress to correct this injustice by recognizing Shelton's "exclusive ownership" of the island. Sanford simultaneously sent letters to a number of congressmen and senators exhorting them to act on the memorial. To one he pleaded melodramatically, "Our dishonored flag should be sustained—our outraged citizens should be protected."[37]

In February Sanford augmented these actions with his first trip to Caracas, where he found the chances for a prompt settlement "distant" and "slim." Both the corruption and bankruptcy of the Monagas regime precluded payment of the claim.[38] The trip was not, however, devoid of results since he recruited several strategically placed Venezuelans who thereafter kept him informed of developments and ultimately facilitated a settlement. He also harassed and badgered Eames into heightened activity. Sanford smugly reported that the minister, whom he described as a "vain, weak, avaricious [sic] man," was "laboring under considerable excitement & seems convinced that he is to be turned out and by my instrumentality!" Eames in turn threatened the Venezuelan government, and when no satisfactory response was forthcoming, he requested his passport and sailed for the United States in June 1857.[39]

Sanford also hurried back to Washington to get the recently installed Buchanan administration "screwed up to [the] proper pitch." On August 10 he presented a revised strategy to Lewis Cass, the new secretary of state. Sanford suggested that an agent be sent to Venezuela with a letter demanding that subsequent debate be limited to the amount of the indemnity. If the Venezuelan "pigmies" refused, Cass should suspend diplomatic relations and resort to force. Sanford cited section five of the guano-island bill of August 1856 as the authority for this drastic step. This law empowered the president "to employ the land and naval forces of the United States to protect the rights of said discoverers . . ."[40]

Neither President Buchanan, who maintained close personal control over the State Department, nor Secretary Cass required prompting to reach the "proper pitch." Harassed by the country's reaction to the pro-Southern Dred Scott decision and his failure to reject Kansas' proslavery Lecompton Constitution, Buchanan hoped that an active, aggressive foreign policy might help to divert attention from the growing domestic tensions. Since the president and Secretary Cass were especially concerned over the United States' position in Central and South America, they enthusiastically adopted Sanford's idea of sending an open letter to Venezuela. In a brusque note Cass termed the facts of the case beyond dispute and demanded that Venezuela promptly agree to a suitable indemnity. If Venezuela failed to surrender within thirty days, the United States would break diplomatic relations. When Cass presented this note to the Venezuelan chargé in early December, the *New York Times* fancied that it spied a "speck of war on the horizon, Venezuela-wards."[41]

As tensions mounted between the two countries, Sanford made a second trip to Venezuela. Arriving in January 1858, he renewed his private contacts and his pressure upon Eames but made no headway with the Venezuelan government. His spirited prosecution of the case had aroused hostility among both Venezuelan authorities and significant elements of the public. He ruefully admitted that his name seemed "about as popular with the gov't as that of Walker in Nicaragua." When the Monagas regime remained intransigent, Sanford concluded that perhaps the only "sure way of securing claims" was "the holy cause [of] Revolution!"[42] While Sanford played no role in the bloodless coup that followed his departure for the United States in February 1858, General Julian Castro's rise to power marked a major turning point in the Aves case. By admitting the propriety of reparations and calling for an equitable settlement, the Castro government complied with Sanford's basic demands.[43]

Sensing victory, Sanford formulated a more realistic claims figure. In January 1857 he and Shelton had increased the original claim of $341,000 to $655,390. Although they attributed the additional $314,-390 to more careful estimates of equipment and guano losses and the injury to Shelton's credit, Shelton had admitted privately that he would accept $40,000 "*net* money." Sanford further revealed the exaggerated nature of these figures when he sent a "compromise" proposal of $150,000 to Cass on August 10, 1858. He also combined the Shelton claim with that of Lang and Delano. The competing Boston firm had initially claimed $639,412 in damages, but Sanford reduced this to $50,000 in September and urged Cass to present the $200,000 cumulative figure "forcibly" as an "ultimatum."[44]

Working from these figures, Sanford held a December meeting in New York City with an official Venezuelan representative, Dr. Maurice Berrisbeitia, who was on his way to a diplomatic post in Europe. He informed Sanford that his government would offer only $95,000 for the Shelton claim and $25,000 for that of Lang and Delano. Sanford tentatively agreed to these reductions, and each of them reported the understanding to his respective government. Negotiations were then transferred to Valencia, where Edward A. Turpin, Eames' successor, successfully wrested an official agreement from the Venezuelan government. Signed on January 14, 1859, the Aves Convention awarded the claimants a total of $130,000 to be paid in installments from June 1859 through December 1863.[45]

Obtaining a convention was not, however, equivalent to collecting the funds. Soon after Turpin concluded the pact, the Federal Revolution struck Venezuela, sustaining the pattern of internal strife, corruption, and bankruptcy that plagued the country through much of the nineteenth century. By March 1863 Venezuela was $75,000 in arrears on the promised payments.[46]

Despite these persistent reversals, Sanford doggedly dunned his Venezuelan debtors. His rapport and influence with the State Department increased dramatically following the Lincoln administration's inauguration. William H. Seward, the new secretary of state, was a personal friend; and after Sanford's appointment as minister resident to Belgium in 1861, he exercised critical leverage in Europe. Generally adopting Sanford's suggestions, Seward maintained a steady diplomatic pressure on Venezuela. In March 1862 he granted Sanford a leave of absence from his post in Brussels for a third trip to Caracas. The following spring he forwarded to Secretary of the Navy Gideon Welles Sanford's request that a warship be employed to coerce Venezuela. Although the navy secretary cared little for either Seward or Sanford, whom he described as "one of Seward's pets," he agreed to dispatch the *Vanderbilt* under the command of Rear Admiral Charles Wilkes. When combined with Sanford's opposition to a Venezuelan loan pending in Europe, this gunboat diplomacy produced another pledge to pay—this time guaranteed by a lien on Venezuela's export duties.[47]

Before any of the promised payments were collected, revolution again intervened. In June 1863 a new clique headed by Juan Crisostomo Falcón and Antonio Guzmán Blanco seized power. When

Falcón dispatched Guzmán Blanco in August to procure a European loan, Sanford at last gained the leverage to force a settlement. He helped Guzmán Blanco obtain advantageous interest rates and arranged for Baron Abraham Oppenheim, a German financier, to underwrite the loan. In return Guzmán Blanco agreed to pay the Aves claim from the £1,500,000 loan he negotiated on October 31, 1863, with the General Credit and Finance Company of London.[48]

The Venezuelan Assembly ratified the loan on January 14, 1864, and it took another nine months to conclude the details. When the General Credit Company dictated that the Venezuelan customs revenues be freed of all valid liens, the Falcón government capitulated and ordered Guzmán Blanco to pay Sanford. The two men conferred in London during August and September of 1864, but the Caracas government had already issued so many anticipatory drafts against the loan that Guzmán Blanco could not make a full cash payment. Instead he offered to give Sanford one-half the sum in specie and one-half in Venezuelan bonds and personally guaranteed compensation for any loss Sanford incurred in disposing of the bonds. Sanford agreed, and on September 12, 1864, nearly ten years after the expulsion at Aves, he received a total payment of $162,487.75. Sanford quickly sold the bonds, but the rapidity of their depreciation produced a loss of nearly $20,000.[49]

Sanford refused to accept this loss. Over the ensuing twenty years he tried vainly to collect upon Guzmán Blanco's "solemn" promise. Through the remainder of the 1860s, he sporadically prodded the State Department and communicated with United States ministers in Caracas. Compared to his relentless activity of the 1850s and early 1860s, Sanford's efforts lagged during the 1870s and 1880s. His primary interests were focused elsewhere, but he remained alert for an opportunity to collect the claim. This opportunity appeared in 1889 when the United States and Venezuela established a joint commission to settle all outstanding claims. Sanford immediately submitted his claim for $19,709 plus interest. He gathered all the relevant post-1864 correspondence and buttressed this with a statement from Guzmán Blanco acknowledging the validity of the claim. The Venezuelan politico had just fallen from power and therefore readily admitted the debt he had artfully avoided over the previous two and one-half decades. On August 26, 1890, the commission awarded Sanford the $19,709 but disallowed his request for interest. Payments continued until 1904, thirteen years after his death.[50]

Sanford's prosecution of the Aves Island case vividly illustrated the arrogant, domineering tone and pressure for economic expansion that characterized the interaction of the United States with her southern neighbors during the 1850s. Sanford had converted a minor altercation into a major diplomatic confrontation between the United States and Venezuela. Although he had worked in the nonviolent world of legal and political maneuver and had found his weapons in the tightly argued brief and well-placed bribe, Sanford exhibited many of the same traits which characterized William Walker and his cohorts. His single-mindedness, perhaps even fanaticism, his ruthless aggressiveness, his vast energy, and his unquestioning assumption of American superiority combined to make him a "legal filibusterer." When combined with his talent for covert lobbying and his ability to perceive crucial junctures and act decisively, these qualities ultimately enabled him to collect the vastly inflated indemnity of over $162,000.

Sanford's Latin American involvements stretched well beyond the Aves case. He twice traveled to Central America as a special agent for United States railroad companies and actively solicited two Latin American diplomatic appointments from the Buchanan administration. His first special assignment was with the Honduras Interoceanic Railway Company, the brainchild of Ephraim G. Squier. Formerly chargé d'affaires to Guatemala and Central America during the late 1840s, Squier had obtained a charter from the Honduras government providing exclusive transit rights for seventy years, a liberal land grant, free access to usable raw materials, and an eight-year deadline for completion of the road. After failing to enlist sufficient American capital willing to challenge the Panama Railroad, Squier organized a French-English-American company in 1855. In April 1857 the firm undertook a final "locating" survey to establish the proposed route's feasibility and thereby secure the backing of the British government and facilitate a public sale of stock. By late summer it appeared that the survey would do more harm than good. The rugged terrain, widespread cholera, and an early rainy season had badly disrupted the schedule; and there were public charges of immoral conduct by the chief engineer.[51]

Squier sought to rectify these difficulties by dispatching Sanford to Honduras as the company's special agent. Sanford had met Squier while serving in Paris and had invested about $2,000 in the venture.

Authorized to make all necessary changes, Sanford arrived in La Union, Honduras, on September 25 and immediately marched off for the interior to survey the suveyors. The man who had so recently delighted in cruising about Paris in the finest carriages now found himself astride a mule lumbering through the Central American jungle. He half-jokingly reported that he carried the two items essential to all Honduran travelers—a hammock and a coffee pot.[52]

Sanford found matters in a muddle. The survey party's situation was desperate, its organization chaotic, and its relations with the Honduran government tenuous. Sanford's report to Squier summarized the project's plight: "A pretty business, I have had of it in your lovely Honduras! It's the worst scrape, all in all, I was ever in." Sanford met each problem head on. He ensured the survey's funding by drawing on private resources and exercising personal influence to have the company's drafts accepted in Panama; he dictated organizational reforms including a clear division of labor, a system of requisition slips and receipts, and required monthly reports; he dismissed those men who were ill or disinclined to work and forbade further use of intoxicants; and he met with both the president and the vice-president of Honduras and secured their pledge that the company's charter would be faithfully observed.[53]

Sanford departed for New York on November 8 confident that he had rescued the mission and the company. Never inclined to minimize his own importance, Sanford informed Squier that he had "saved the expedition from certain ruin . . . My coming was opportune . . . a week or so more and there would have been a regular stampede!" This self-adulation proved ill-founded. The survey ultimately exceeded its budget by $130,000; no public sale of stock was attempted; and the charter's eight-year span elapsed. After two attempts at reviving the project in the 1860s, Squier abandoned his dream.[54] James S. Mackie observed that Sanford's loss of between $2,000 and $6,000 had been a "bad affair even for a man with $17,000 a year."[55]

During the spring and summer of 1858, Sanford mounted the first of two unsuccessful campaigns to obtain a diplomatic appointment from the Buchanan administration. He desired the potentially important position of special commissioner to Paraguay. Over the previous four years a number of minor incidents had disturbed relations between the United States and Paraguay. The Paraguayan government had harassed and arrested an American citizen, a Paraguayan shore battery had fired upon an American vessel, and Paraguay had

refused to exchange a Treaty of Friendship, Commerce, and Navigation previously ratified by both countries. Infuriated, President
James Buchanan decided to send a diplomatic mission and secured
a congressional allocation of $10,000 for an accompanying naval
squadron.[56]

Sanford hoped that leading this special mission would give public
"recognition" of his fitness for office and disperse the "cloud thrown
over him" by the court dress wrangle.[57] He drew strong backing
from a group of prominent Connecticut and Rhode Island Democrats headed by Senator Philip Allen of Rhode Island and a contin-
gent of influential New York merchants led by Moses Taylor. C. S.
Brady, a Providence businessman with interests in Paraguay;
Thomas J. Page, the naval officer slated to command the accompanying squadron; and James S. Mackie, Sanford's close friend in the
State Department, added their endorsements. The New York merchants' petition to Buchanan accentuated the themes of Sanford's
campaign. It emphasized his diplomatic experience and knowledge
of Spanish and pointedly referred to his treatment during the diplomatic costume affair:

> He has served the country with distinction abroad retiring from the
> office voluntarily, when not sustained by our government in a course
> which the whole country approved and his appointment would be to
> the world, a recognition, and approval of that course, which the late
> administration failed to give.[58]

Encouraged by this support and reports of Buchanan's "favorable
impression," Sanford optimistically predicted in July that he would
be offered the mission "within ten days."[59]

When the "miserable considerations of party politics" intervened,
he learned differently. His opponents circulated the explosive charge
that he was a "Black Republican," and on July 23 C. S. Brady
relayed Buchanan's concern that Sanford was not an active administration supporter. Sanford quickly posted letters to Buchanan and
John Appleton, the assistant secretary of state, denying that he was
either a "Black Republican" or an "abolitionist." He rhetorically
assured Buchanan that had he not been an administration supporter
he could not have applied for the appointment.[60] In truth, Sanford's
desire for the appointment was much stronger than his partisan
political convictions. He had been out of the country for most of the
previous ten years and had never taken an active role in domestic

politics. Still, his family and nominal political affiliations had been with the northern Whigs, most of whom were becoming Republicans. Anyone who counted William H. Seward, Truman Smith, and Thurlow Weed among his most important political benefactors was naive to believe that either feigned neutrality or vocal support for the Buchanan administration would constitute the political credentials necessary for a diplomatic assignment. And in fact, when it became more expedient to do so in 1860, Sanford would make an explicit commitment to the Republican party. In so doing, he joined other conservative Whigs who valued the Union over antislavery measures.

Buchanan desperately needed to reunite the Democratic party after the Lecompton debacle, and he could ill-afford to waste even a minor appointment on an ex-Whig with close ties to several prominent Republicans. When Secretary of the Navy Issac Toucey of Connecticut decisively opposed Sanford, Buchanan chose James B. Bowlin, a former Democratic congressman from Missouri and minister to Colombia under President Pierce. Mackie conveyed the inside assessment: "The President and 1st Lt. A[ppleton] were both for you, but . . . Toucey opposed you on political grounds."[61]

Practical politics also played its usual role in Buchanan's nomination of George W. Jones as minister to Colombia. Jones had defied the Iowa General Assembly and the majority of his constituents by voting for the proslavery Lecompton constitution, and Iowa's Democratic party caucus had retaliated by blocking his renomination as United States senator. When Jones' senatorial term ended in March 1859, Buchanan rewarded his friend's loyalty by proffering the South American post. Surprisingly, Jones declined the nomination and started home to Dubuque. While urging him to reconsider, Buchanan solicited alternative recommendations from the Panama Railroad Company and the Pacific Mail Steamship Company, the business groups most interested in United States–Colombian relations. Both companies endorsed Henry Sanford, and one informed observer considered him the nearly unanimous choice of New York's commercial community. This business support resulted from Sanford's and his Uncle Edward's association with the New York mercantile community, especially Moses Taylor and Charles H. Russell. Sanford's successful prosecution of the Aves case had also enhanced his reputation as a Latin American trouble shooter. Although this endorsement by firms with investments of $10 million in Colombia rekindled Sanford's optimism, Jones reconsidered and accepted the position.[62]

Having failed to secure Sanford's appointment as minister, the Panama Railroad Company sent him to Bogotá as its private agent in January 1860. His primary objective was to gain an extension of the company's monopoly from forty-nine to ninety-nine years. He was also to head off a potential threat from the Chiriquí Company, whose organizers had tentatively sold their right-of-way through the province north of Panama to the United States Navy Department in January 1860. To facilitate his work, the Panama Company provided Sanford a £100,000 credit with Baring Brothers, and David Hoadley, the firm's president, urged him to expend these funds in any fashion he deemed "expedient." Sanford was to receive his expenses and approximately 10,000 acres of land on Manzanilla Island at the eastern terminus of the road.[63]

He arrived in Bogotá on March 9, 1860, and had his first interview with President Mariano Ospina two weeks later. He found widespread opposition to any extension of the contract: The press denounced modification of the agreement, and in late April the Colombian Senate unanimously forbade the sale of further concessions to railroad companies. Although a revolution had begun in February, he was unable to exploit it as he had done in the Aves case. The revolt gained strength through the summer, but the beleaguered Ospina spurned Sanford's conditional offers of assistance.[64]

Sanford dismissed his mission as hopeless in early September and commenced a harrowing return to New York. After traveling by mule from Bogotá to Honda, he was forced by marauding rebels to descend the Magdalena River aboard a makeshift raft. His trip, originally projected as an easy three-month assignment, had stretched into a fruitless nine-month ordeal. Though he had failed to attain his goals, Sanford petitioned the company for additional compensation to cover his time and $6,500 in expenses; on December 15, 1860, the directors granted him $10,000.[65] These Central American escapades were neither so profitable nor so revealing as the Aves prosecution. Nevertheless, Sanford's activities again placed him in the mainstream of the nation's Latin American diplomacy, with its isthmian and economic emphases.

Sanford arrived back in the United States on the eve of the 1860 presidential election. In less than a month after Abraham Lincoln's victory, all the deep South states but Louisiana had seceded. Many Northerners simultaneously began advocating concessions or at least reassurances for their Southern neighbors. Most conspicuous in the call for Lincoln to deliver a soothing "Union speech" was the Democratic *New York Herald.* The eastern business and commercial establishment vigorously endorsed compromise plans, and from the Republican party itself numerous ex-Whigs, such as Sanford's old friends, Thurlow Weed, William H. Seward, and Truman Smith, favored a conservative stance.[66] Sanford, a prosperous ex-Whig with strong ties to the conservative wing of the Republican party and the New York commercial community, rather naturally aligned himself with those desiring compromise. In collectively describing Northern conservatives, one contemporary rendered a vivid portrait of Sanford: They are "men who are well to do, worldly speaking . . . usually found in warm parlors . . . remarkable for good feeding . . . sleek and comfortable . . . also they pay attention to the price of stocks."[67]

Hoping to promote some settlement short of war, Sanford joined the growing procession to Springfield, Illinois. He sought to elicit a public statement or letter from the president-elect, who had not made an important speech since his appearance at the Cooper Institute in February 1860. On November 8, 1860, Sanford met with Lincoln and emphasized the necessity of allaying Southern fears. He also presented his host with a letter from their mutual friend, Truman Smith. The former Connecticut senator stressed that Lincoln's administration should be "moderate, impartial, just, and conservative," and he implored Lincoln to correct the numerous popular misconceptions and "compose the public mind."[68]

Lincoln's reply to Smith and Sanford was "private and confidential." Declining to issue a public statement, he declared his views unchanged from earlier speeches, which were available for anyone to read: "To press a repetition of this upon those who *have* listened is useless; to press it upon those who have *refused* to listen, and still refuse, would be wanting in self-respect and would have an appearance of sychophancy and timidity." Although Sanford had failed to secure a public statement, he came away "convinced that no right of the South will be imperilled under" Lincoln. He assured William C. Rives that there was nothing in Lincoln's speeches that his Virginia friend "would have objected to in 1856" and that the "nigger question" would be settled peacefully.[69]

Soon after his return to the East, Sanford entered the debate raging over the nation's future. On December 15, 1860, he wrote to the

Albany Evening Journal an extended letter which he subsequently published as a pamphlet entitled, "Free Cotton and Free Cotton States." He advocated Union-sponsored cotton growing in Central America as a means of undermining the South's near-monopoly of the valuable commodity. Unlike William Walker's "pro-slavery raids," which sought to force the peculiar institution on an unwilling people, "this *legitimate Filibusterism* by the peaceful arts of trade and agriculture would be welcomed as a boon by the Central Americans." The keys to his plan were the creation of a "*Free Cotton League*" and the recruitment of Oriental labor.[70] Though widely discussed at the time, Sanford's project has assumed its rightful niche in obscurity. It was deficient in three critical respects. There were no Northern capitalists willing to fund the essential Free Cotton League; Sanford had ignored the alarming suicide and mortality rate among Chinese workers on the Panama Railroad; and it was unlikely that the Central American states would have welcomed a bizarre coalition of Yankee capital and Oriental labor.

As the country anxiously awaited the inauguration of its first Republican president, Sanford worked as a Washington lobbyist and angled for a diplomatic appointment. In mid-December he moved to Washington for the winter, leased a house, and assumed an active role in society. He retained his association with the Panama Railroad Company and also affiliated with the Pacific Mail Steamship Company. Although the February 25 *New York Times* characterized him as a "gentleman of high character and liberal means, who entertains his friends for social purposes only, and is incapable of becoming the lobby-agent of any company whatever," he actually labored throughout the winter promoting the two companies' private claims bills.[71]

These business pursuits did not alter his primary objective—a diplomatic appointment. With this in mind, he regularly entertained many influential Republicans. Included among the frequent guests at his fashionable dinner parties were Truman Smith, Henry B. Anthony, William H. Seward, and Frederick W. Seward.[72] Gideon Welles, a fellow Connecticut native who was soon to become secretary of the navy, was puzzled by Sanford's social flair. He wrote his wife that Sanford was:

A very extraordinary Connecticut friend, evidently a man of large fortune . . . [who lives] in quiet costly English style with his French cook, costly and rare wines, etc. . . . He gives dinner parties every day, I believe, but only to four or five persons at a time and they the very first persons in society. To me he is a great deal of mystery.[73]

Sanford encountered a highly competitive field in his quest for office. After picking his way through the crowded White House, Seward had noted incredulously that "the grounds, halls, stairways, [and] closets are filled with applicants."[74] By now a veteran office-seeker, Sanford extended his campaign well beyond calculated social activity. He also recruited many influential backers as he had done in 1849. Among the more important politicians supporting his candidacy were Oregon Senator Edward D. Baker, and former Connecticut Senator Truman Smith, both old friends of Lincoln and Seward; Connecticut Senator Lafayette S. Foster; Rhode Island Senator Henry B. Anthony; and Michigan's two senators, Kinsley S. Bingham and Zachariah Chandler. To these political figures, Sanford added a "strong basis of New York Capital." From the Wall Street of the day came an impressive petition signed by Charles H. Russell, William H. Aspinwall, J. J. Astor, Jr., and Moses Taylor. Though this array of backing bolstered Sanford's cause, his old friends, Thurlow Weed and William H. Seward, provided the decisive influence.[75]

Sanford had originally envisioned returning to Europe as minister to France, but he lacked the political capital necessary to corner such a prominent mission. Correctly assessing his situation, Sanford ingeniously formulated a diplomatic mission specifically tailored to his qualifications and commensurate with his political influence. As Lincoln's inauguration approached, appointees of the tainted Buchanan administration retained control of the crucial American missions to Paris and London. Furthermore, the South had already begun sending representatives abroad. Sanford anticipated that the new administration might favor the prompt dispatch of a trusted Republican to present the Northern position and to correct any misrepresentations by Buchanan's ministers. Since he had diplomatic experience and was thoroughly familiar with European governments, languages, and society, Sanford saw himself as a natural choice for such an assignment. According to his plan, he would reside temporarily in Paris until the arrival of Lincoln's permanent minister to France; he would then continue on to Brussels and assume the post of minister resident to Belgium.[76]

He presented the plan to Weed, who agreed to its viability and vigorously supported it with Secretary of State Seward. Seward in turn carried the day with President Lincoln. On March 20, 1861, Sanford wrote excitedly, "The game has finally been brought down! My name goes in today as Minister to Belgium." Charles Sumner steered the nomination rapidly through the Senate; and before the month had ended, Sanford was bound for Europe, his instructions embodying the very mission he had formulated in January.[77]

Even in the hour of Sanford's most distinguished appointment, portents of his future political difficulties were evident. As with all nineteenth-century diplomatic assignments, well-placed political support had been crucial. Still, Sanford was "not a politician by trade," and this together with his linguistic abilities, social skills, education, prior experience, and familiarity with Europe, led several observers to conclude that his appointment might presage a professional "diplomatic service." Indeed he embodied the qualifications demanded by the *Nation, Atlantic Monthly,* and *North American Review* for a reformed diplomatic corps.[78] Having consciously prepared for a diplomatic career, Sanford took satisfaction in comments such as that of the *New Haven Palladium,* which argued that he "was selected for his mission with more reference to his peculiar fitness for it than for any other reason. He is a man of pure character, high-minded and honorable, and in all respects an accomplished gentleman and able diplomat."[79]

Politics, however, remained central. Even as the *Palladium* endorsed Sanford's character and ability, it noted that some people had found fault with his appointment because he had "not been long and intimately identified with the Republican party." The *Palladium* dismissed this objection but regretted that his appointment should be credited to the "account of Connecticut when Mr. Sanford is a citizen of the Republic."[80] A professional diplomatic corps was far in the future; despite his qualifications and eight years of creditable service in Belgium, Sanford would ultimately find that his lack of a solid, geographical political base and a proven record of service to the party would prevent him from continuing his diplomatic career.

CHAPTER 3

SEWARD'S MINISTER TO EUROPE, 1861–1865

ON MARCH 26, 1861, Sanford departed from a nation rent by sectional strife and engulfed by nervous expectancy. By the time of his arrival in Paris on April 15, war had erupted with Beauregard's attack on Fort Sumter three days earlier. The ensuing four years proved to be the most exciting and satisfying of Sanford's life. From his first weeks in Europe, it was apparent that his energy and drive far surpassed those required by his duties in Belgium. Since his "little court" was "afraid to do anything without the approval of the great powers,"[1] Sanford was not involved in the urgent and critical problems that harassed American ministers to Great Britain and France. This freed him to undertake several broader, European assignments, including propaganda dissemination, secret service work, arms purchases, and the attempted recruitment of Giuseppe Garibaldi for the Union army. He relished these duties. In November 1861 he exulted, "Times are getting lively over here. I am in my clement." And Seward allegedly remarked, "That man Sanford during the first year of the war was the Minister of the United States in Europe."[2]

Seward's March 26 instructions to Sanford summarzied the Union's diplomatic position. He directed Sanford "to counteract by all proper means the efforts" of Confederate agents. Characterizing the conflict as "merely a domestic" disturbance rather than a clash between two sovereign states, Seward warned that the North would tolerate no interference, either "directly or indirectly", by foreign powers. In an appeal to European self-interest, the secretary emphasized that European commercial and manufacturing prosperity was directly linked to the "undisturbed activity of the American people." By aiding the South and promoting "disharmony," Europe could only disrupt the transatlantic economy and injure herself.[3]

Since William L. Dayton, Lincoln's minister-designate to France, had requested a month to conclude urgent business at home, Secretary Seward instructed Sanford to oppose Confederate activity in Paris until Dayton's arrival. Sanford was then to assume his duties in Brussels. After reaching Paris on April 15, Sanford began renewing his diplomatic and social acquaintances; but Charles J. Faulkner, the incumbent United States minister, obstructed his access to the French government. Faulkner, a Virginia Democrat who subsequently served on Stonewall Jackson's staff, had previously presented United States arguments against recognition of the Confederacy in a "half-hearted and evasive manner" and for nearly a week "found it inconvenient" to present Sanford officially to Antoine E. Thouvenel, the French foreign minister.[4]

When Sanford obtained an official interview on April 24, he delivered Seward's request that France neither receive the Confederate envoys nor allow Southern ships access to her ports. Thouvenel assured Sanford that, while the "Government of France felt no sympathy" for the Confederacy and had "no intention of giving aid or countenance to the Revolution," he did plan to meet the Confederate commissioners unofficially. He also confirmed earlier reports that Great Britain and France had agreed to consult and adopt a joint course regarding the American war. While professing concern for the "integral maintenance of the North American Union," Thouvenel reminded Sanford that the United States had been "conspicuous" in recognizing revolutionary governments all over the world. Should the situation warrant, France would be prepared to recognize the Confederacy.

Sanford rejoined that the United States had traditionally recognized "*de facto* governments" which had clearly demonstrated their viability. The South had not met this criterion. Turning to economic matters, he stressed that French trade with the South constituted only a small percentage of her overall American commerce. The North, not the South, was the greater consumer of French products, and encouraging the Confederacy would inevitably disrupt commerce and injure the French economy.[5]

Sanford could not prevent France from recognizing the Confederacy's status as a belligerent. Confronted by the South's intention to commission privateers and the North's proclamation of a blockade and resolve to treat Southern privateers as pirates, both France and Great Britain acted to clarify their positions as neutrals and to protect their maritime interests.[6] On May 11 Thouvenel directed Henri Mercier, the French minister in Washington, to inform Seward of France's decision to recognize Southern belligerency. The Union protest, which continued throughout the war, was first voiced by Sanford in his second major interview with Thouvenel on May 12. In apprising Sanford of French intentions, the foreign minister emphasized that France had "no desire to give any countenance to the Confederate States." The French position derived solely from the need to protect the "commercial interests involved."[7]

Sanford's response anticipated that of Seward in Washington and Charles Francis Adams in London. He expressed "painful surprise" that France had joined Britain in a decision that would "encourage the Insurgents and prolong the struggle." The South would hail this "moral support" as the first step toward ultimate independence. France's haste in extending recognition was equally disturbing. Only fifteen days had passed since Lincoln issued his blockade proclamation, and the South had yet to demonstrate its viability on the battlefield.[8]

This interview ended Sanford's official duties as interim minister, but his intermittent and meddlesome presence in Paris continued. Even before Dayton's arrival, Sanford had written disparagingly of the new minister. Referring to Dayton's inability to speak French, Sanford judged that the portly New Jersey politician would "be, when I am not here, utterly helpless"; and he later embellished this criticism: "How little he [Dayton] will be able to do here actively or usefully in directing public or social or official opinion!"[9] Confident of his superior abilities as a linguist and diplomat, Sanford subsequently visited Paris often. He hoped by upstaging Dayton to be promoted to the more prestigious French post. Ambition was not, however, his only motivation; he was also wholeheartedly committed to furthering Union interests. Writing in 1864, Gideon Welles, Lincoln's secretary of the navy, incisively evaluated Sanford's conduct: "Sanford . . . is fond of notoriety, delights to be busy and fussy, to show pomp and power . . . not that he is mischievously inclined, but he seeks to be consequential, wants to figure and to do."[10] His motives were complex: a compelling desire for fame and notoriety, a driving ambition for advancement, and a sincere devotion to the cause.

By October 1, 1861, the peripatetic Sanford had made sixteen trips between Brussels and Paris, five trips to London, two trips to Liege, and one to Italy. This initial flurry characterized his regime over the next eight years as minister to Belgium. Writing to Seward in 1864, Sanford unabashedly proclaimed the importance of his frequent trips around the continent: "I have . . . received no official advices touching the progress of the war. If you send such to Messrs. Dayton and Adams, I would be gratified by a duplicate. I am in the way of seeing more people having influence in public affairs in Europe than both their legations." Seward assented. Earlier the same year, the secretary had curtailed the absence of United States ministers from their posts, but he pointedly excepted his envoy to Belgium. To Sanford he wrote: "You need not consider yourself as being restricted . . . from repairing at any time to points in Europe which you may deem your presence necessary, or likely to conduce to the public interest."[11]

Sanford's numerous and detailed reports were even more extensive than his travels. In voluminous dispatches and hurried personal notes, Sanford penned his impressions of the European political and diplomatic scene. Cognizant of Sanford's intimate acquaintance with Europe and her people, Seward assured Sanford that he was always pleased to receive his "intelligent speculations and opinions" and often solicited their continuation.[12]

Soon after his arrival, Sanford prodded Seward to launch a Union propaganda effort in Europe. After only four days in Paris, he correctly surmised that Confederate and pro-Southern publications would actively seek to "prejudice" the European people against the North. He recommended cooperation with the opposition Liberal party in France and subsidization of articles in key English and continental papers.[13] When Dayton in France, George P. Marsh in Italy, and Navy Department secret agent William Walker echoed this appeal, Seward sent John Bigelow to Paris as consul-general. Bigelow, a lawyer and former editor of the *New York Evening Post,* was charged with developing a favorable French press.[14]

In the interim between his initial requests and Bigelow's arrival in mid-September, Sanford helped fill the breach. He vigorously combated all the pro-Southern opinion encountered in his travels and edited an antisecession pamphlet for circulation in England. Following Bigelow's arrival, he aided the new consul-general by soliciting contributions from the wealthy American community in Paris. When Seward sent Thurlow Weed to promote the Union cause with the English public in November 1861, Sanford willingly cooperated with his old friend and benefactor. He provided Weed with funds from his secret service account and applauded Weed and Bigelow for their letters to sympathetic editors and their courting of friendly journalists.[15]

Despite some successes, Sanford considered these efforts insufficient. He believed that the United States needed to supplement such tactics by acquiring control of a prominent European newspaper: "We *must* have an organ of our own to repel the attacks of the hostile press of England and France and to give light upon our affairs . . ." In December 1861 Sanford reported to Seward that he could enlist *L'Independence Belge,* a Brussels papers with a large and influential circulation, into his scheme. Should the secretary consider this project too ambitious, Sanford suggested an alternative: the establishment of a central news bureau in Paris to serve as a clearing house for funneling pro-Northern news releases to continental journals. During the remainder of the war, Sanford periodically reiterated his desire to purchase a controlling interest in the Belgian paper, and in the spring of 1863 he launched an abortive campaign to collect the necessary funds from Northern businessmen.[16]

Seward doubted the viability of Sanford's propaganda proposals from the beginning. Undoubtedly irritated by rumors that England was about to recognize the Confederacy, Seward's tone was unusually sharp on October 6, 1862. "How," he queried, "could we attempt to regulate the press of Europe when we cannot regulate our own? Where are the funds which would be necessary?" Two years later his conclusion was the same, but his rationale was more elevated. He contended that the Union should not "compromise" its "dignity by employing other than the customary diplomatic defenders in any part of the world."[17] Although Seward discouraged Sanford's far-reaching suggestions, he did not expressly forbid propaganda projects. After the spring of 1862, Sanford regularly extended "support" to sympathetic elements of the European press. In Belgium he provided materials for L. Jottrand's pro-Northern stories in Ghent's *L'Observateur,* and he employed "personal relations" and occasional monetary inducements to insure the aid of *L'Independence Belge.* After one such payment in May 1862, he

enthusiastically informed Seward, "We now have a pulpit to preach
from which reaches a large audience and I consider it a very important gain." Ambrose Dudley Mann, the Confederate commissioner
to Belgium, concurred with Sanford's evaluation: "There can be but
little doubt that *L'Independence Belge* the most popular perhaps, but
certainly not the most able, of continental journals, is under a peculiar influence in its violent hostility to the Confederate States . . ."
Like *L'Independence Belge,* the majority of the Belgian press favored
the North. This, together with Belgium's relative diplomatic unim-
portance, made more extensive press manipulation unnecessary.[18]

Like so much of his other work, Sanford's most important attempts to influence European public opinion occurred beyond the
Belgian borders. As the Union forces marched into the late summer
of 1862 still seeking their first decisive victory, Sanford increasingly
feared that France and England would attempt some form of intervention. Like subsequent historians, he recognized that the question
of European intervention would ultimately be decided on the American battlefields. Not realizing the symbolic significance of Antietam,
he wrote to Seward on November 24, 1862, "It is now for us to work
actively in the field; what we most need in Europe is a *great victory*
. . . We must convince Europe by deeds that we have the capacity as
well as the determination speedily to subdue our enemy."[19]

In the absence of such a victory, Sanford resorted to the purposeful
manipulation of the European press. He was apprehensive that Europe's "people & nations" were forming opinions regarding "our
affairs" that would persist "long after this war has passed." He hoped
to prod the theoretically pro-Northern working classes into forcing
a policy of inaction upon their governments. Convinced that the
common man exercised no significant influence over English policy,
which was "bitterly Southern," Sanford concentrated on France.
There, he opined, the will of the "people" could be decisive: "No
man in Europe is more easily swayed by the sentiments of the
masses" than Napoleon III.[20]

Near the end of August 1862, he travelled to Paris and retained
A. Malespine, a writer for the pro-Union *Opinion Nationale.* Having
spent seven years in the United States, Malespine possessed a knowledge of American affairs unequalled by any other French journalist.
In return for 500 francs per month, he agreed to leave no "article of
import unanswered" and to carry the fight "into the hostile camp."
Sanford, working closely with John Bigelow, maintained this association with Malespine through 1865. In addition to writing for the

Opinion Nationale, Malespine also composed numerous pamphlets, which treated the Northern interpretation of the war's progress, significant American speeches, revelations of Confederate shipbuilding in France, and criticisms of Napoleon's Mexican involvement. In May 1864 Bigelow even arranged for Malespine to furnish a weekly letter, ostensibly from New York, to the *Gazette de France,* a legitimatist organ generally opposed to republicanism.[21]

Though less optimistic about the chances of success in England, Sanford did not ignore the island kingdom when he thought the press might be used to stimulate the "chronic British suspicion of France." In the fall of 1862, he conducted a futile search in London for an English counterpart to Malespine. Disturbed by what he considered deliberate attempts by the London *Times* to misrepresent American affairs, he arranged in the fall of 1863 for the U.S. consul at Queenstown to send him coded telegrams containing the latest American intelligence. He then relayed these pro-Northern interpretations to friendly journals. Finally, the summer of 1864 found the tireless envoy soliciting material from Seward for a pro-Juarez journal in London.[22] While Sanford never received the financial support he requested for his public opinion work and the effect of his endeavors beyond Belgium is difficult to gauge, his persistent efforts revealed a dogged determination to further the Union cause.

Sanford displayed a similar commitment and even greater enthusiasm for the organization of a secret service network for the surveillance of Confederate agents. In May 1861 Seward had directed him to gather information concerning Confederate purchases and shipments of arms.[23] He responded by developing an octopus-like secret service network enveloping most of Europe's important textile mills, armories, shipyards, and ports. On July 4, 1861, he wrote excitedly to Seward:

> I am determined, if it is possible, to get at the operations of these 'Commissioners' through their own papers. . . . How it will be done, whether through a pretty mistress, or an intelligent servant, or a spying landlord is nobody's business; but I lay great stress on getting you full *official* accounts of their operations here![24]

Soon after his arrival in Europe, Sanford initiated the surveillance system by prodding Union consuls in ports along the European coast to ascertain Confederate shipments of arms and other contraband. He also urged Seward to replace consuls of dubious loyalty, such as those at Ghent and Genoa, with dependable Union men. He especially importuned the secretary to select an able man for the strategic Paris consulship, and his lobbying subsequently convinced Seward to establish a new consular post for the important Belgian industrial region around Liege and Verviers.[25]

Sanford also beseeched several fellow ministers to ferret out Confederate activities. He notified George P. Marsh that funds were available for the retention of a private detective: "If you find it necessary to have somebody employed to track or watch any Southern agent—do so & send to me for the pay." From Madrid, Sanford secured the assurance of Secretary of Legation Horatio J. Perry that the Spanish police would vigilantly attend to reports that the Confederates were issuing letters of marque in Barcelona. Deeming official channels of information inadequate, Sanford advised William Dayton to press French authorities for additional cooperation.[26]

To supplement the efforts of American diplomats, Sanford retained or authorized the employment of numerous private detectives and informers. He arranged special surveillance in Genoa and Toulon and secured confidential reports of Confederate arms procurement in Liege and Verviers. Dissatisfied with the performance of the Paris police force, he regularly employed one or two special agents to oversee Southern activity in the French capital.[27] Though these endeavors were characteristic, Sanford forcused his most extensive secret service work during 1861 on Great Britain.

By midsummer Sanford had correctly determined that the Confederates had centered their primary purchasing activities in Great Britain; he had also decided that effective scrutiny of Southern agents required a private surveillance organization, independent of the British police system. With the aid of Freeman H. Morse, United States consul at London, he employed Ignatius Pollaky to coordinate the Federal network in England. Pollaky, a London private detective, demanded £100 for thirty to forty days of "close work." On June 29 Morse admitted that since he knew little about Pollaky there was "some risk in dealing with him." "But," he continued, "it is a 'risky business' anyway and I think we better engage him at once." Sanford agreed and consummated the arrangement. On September 24 Pollaky informed Sanford that the system was "established whole & everywhere."[28]

After identifying the principal Southern agents, Pollaky and his men monitored their activities. They bribed postmen to ascertain the names of Confederate correspondents and treated messengers at the "public house" in return for a glimpse of Confederate dispatches. Pollaky's sleuths also located many of the warehouses containing Confederate purchases and the docks from which the contraband goods began their transatlantic crossing. By examining the labels and trademarks of these newly purchased materials, the detectives learned which English companies were involved and began observing these firms.[29]

Although Morse complained in mid-September that Pollaky's services had yielded "no great discoveries,"[30] they were not completely devoid of results. Pollaky had provided Sanford with the names and addresses of seventeen Southern "conspirators" in London, including Captain James D. Bulloch, Major Edward C. Anderson, and Captain Caleb Huse. He had identified the London firms of Isaac Campbell and Company, Chandler and Company, and Boane and Company as the primary sources of Confederate arms during these first crucial months, and he had isolated the Liverpool house of Fraser, Trenholm and Company as the South's European bankers. Pollaky's detectives also forwarded descriptions of many ships and cargoes sailing for the South. This continued harassment of Confederate agents circumscribed their actions and forced them to take extraordinary precautions. In late July Huse, the most effective agent of the Confederate Ordnance Bureau, complained that "the ministers to England, France, and Belgium have been very active in their endeavors to discover what the agents of the Confederacy are effecting. They have agents employed for no other purpose . . ."[31]

Sanford was not yet satisfied. Characterizing Pollaky's work as little more than a "halfway" measure, he implored Seward in September to authorize a more comprehensive secret service system. Always the promoter, he contended that a "score of men of suitable capacity, employed in the business in England alone, with means and command . . . would be more effective upon the enemy than as many battalions in the field at home." He projected an English organization headed by a general superintendent and four immediate subordinates and manned by secret agents strategically placed throughout the British Isles. He envisioned at least one private agent in every important port and confidential contacts in all the country's shipyards and armories.[32]

After a number of closely observed Confederate ships had escaped during the fall of 1861, Sanford complained that it was of "little use knowing of the supplies and ships purchased by the Rebels unless we apply a remedy on the spot." He repeatedly beseeched Seward to

correct this defect by stationing a United States steamer off the
English coast to act on secret service information and intercept
Confederate shipments. Disregarding international law, he advocated the seizure of at least one vessel carrying contraband regardless of her flag—we can "discuss the matter with the English
afterwards." He was so disgusted that valuable supplies were escap-
ing that he contemplated other acts which could easily have occasioned a dangerous confrontation with the British. These included
sabotage by "accidental collisions or boiler bustings" and delaying
legal action by "libeling or getting up expensive suits." In November
Sanford even abortively attempted to scuttle the *Gladiator* by smug-
gling Captain Edwin G. Eastman and a select group of Union men
into her crew.[33]

Among Southern representatives abroad, Sanford most feared
Captain James D. Bulloch, the Confederate Navy Department's primary agent in England. Bulloch, described by Sanford as "prompt,
energetic, & wary," was a formidable adversary who successfully
matched wits and strategy with Union diplomats throughout the
war. Sanford directed Pollaky to concentrate "special attention" on
the wily Southerner, and in July Sanford informed Seward that he
was expending £150 per month on Bulloch alone. So dangerous did
Sanford consider the captain that he advocated arresting Bulloch on
"some charge or other" the moment he ventured onto the continent.
Since Bulloch had no diplomatic papers or immunity, Sanford hoped
that he *"might be sent home for Examination."*[34]

Sanford's English surveillance activities culminated with the observation of Bulloch and the *Fingal* in early October. Pollaky and
his men had learned that the *Fingal* was loading valuable materiel
at the Greenock docks, and Bulloch subsequently boasted that no
other Dixie-bound ship carried a cargo "so entirely composed of
military and naval supplies." Afraid that the steamer might be detained as a suspicious vessel, Bulloch avoided direct connection with
the *Fingal* until it had cleared Greenock and British customs. Six
days after the *Fingal*'s departure on October 9, he inconspicuously
took command at Holyhead as the ship steamed toward the Atlantic.
Under his direction, the *Fingal* reached Bermuda on November 2
and ultimately ran the blockade into Savannah.[35] While Sanford was
incensed that the *Fingal* had eluded his agents, he was even more
"vexed" that Consul Morse had spent $500 to duplicate Pollaky's
work. He complained to Seward that Morse had not only used
money earmarked for another purpose but had also failed to obtain

additional intelligence. Morse's expenditure exhausted Sanford's secret service funds and forced him to draw on his personal account for continued surveillance.[36]

Sanford was not the only American minister annoyed at this misunderstanding. Charles Francis Adams had instructed Morse to hire the additional agent, and he was outraged at Sanford's presuming to interfere with the dispersal of his legation funds. Adams had earlier grumbled at Sanford's "poaching a little in [his] manor," and on October 18 he protested to Seward that the department was "incurring unnecessary expense in a double system of investigation." He asserted that Morse rather than Sanford should direct these activities in Great Britain.[37]

In late October the British press began publishing accounts of a Federal "system of political espionage and terrorism [in which] . . . many persons . . . have been seized and searched, and in some cases imprisoned, immediately on their arrival at Boston and New York."[38] Every inch a prim and proper Adams, Charles Francis was personally appalled by these activities. More significantly, he feared that accounts terming him the director of the system would compromise his diplomatic usefulness and that Sanford's sabotage schemes might occasion an Anglo-American diplomatic crisis. On November 1, 1861, Adams bluntly demanded that Seward discontinue Sanford's operations in Great Britain.[39]

The following day Sanford, who was in London working to sabotage the *Gladiator,* visited the United States legation. The seething Adams informed his "startled" visitor that he considered the situation intolerable. Although Sanford agreed to end the "coarser part" of his operations and to limit his English activities to the observation of shipping movements, this did not placate Adams. He later confided to his ever-present diary:

> One of Mr. Seward's errors since he has been in the Government has been the extent to which he has placed confidence in this shallow and imprudent man. Mr. Sanford bore my remonstrance with a good deal of equanimity and left apparently very cordial. But I imagine he will never forgive me.

Adams' prophesy proved much more accurate than his appraisal of Sanford's character and ability.[40]

Seward responded to Adams' complaints by instructing Sanford to transfer supervision of the English surveillance system to Consul

Morse and to confine his future activities to the continent. Thereafter, Morse and Thomas H. Dudley, the United States consul in Liverpool, directed the operation. Both consuls continued several of Sanford's precedents, especially the hiring of private detectives and the forwarding of detailed descriptions of Confederate activities, ships, and cargoes.[41]

Although Seward had relieved Sanford of his English responsibilities, the episode had not diminished his confidence in his minister to Belgium. Seward privately assured Sanford on January 22, 1862, "I cannot tell you how much I prize your courage, your courtesy, and your energy." The secretary of state continued periodically to employ Sanford's "activity and vigilance" in countering persons and projects hostile to the Union.[42] The indefatigable Sanford maintained his contacts with United States consuls and other private sources of information throughout Europe, and he regularly provided precise descriptions of ships clearing continental ports for the South. He also renewed efforts to sabotage ships carrying supplies to the Confederacy. In the spring of 1862, he offered the pilots of both the *Melitia* and the *Memphis* the cost of their cargo plus a bonus to run their ships into the North's blockade. Neither negotiation proved successful.[43]

Sanford also continued to function as a clearing hourse for funds required by Federal representatives in their "unofficial" duties of influencing the European press and observing Confederate activity. Although Sanford was never specifically designated to act in this capacity, Seward often supplied him with credits to meet "extraordinary expenses" and allowed him considerable discretion in expending them. The government was fortunate to have a man of Sanford's wealth and inclination in this position; when official funds ran low, he drew so liberally on his personal fortune that by July 1863 he had spent more than $10,000 from his own pocket.[44]

After 1861 Sanford concentrated his most intensive surveillance efforts in Paris. He worked closely with his old friend Nelson M. Beckwith, a strong Union man residing in Paris, and with John Bigelow, United States consul-general in Paris. Although he corresponded extensively with both men, many of their endeavors were never recorded. Sanford made frequent trips to Paris, and he followed Beckwith's advice: "Don't write—keep to verbals. . . . You can't of course trust any of these people with a *line* of writing."[45]

Sanford's final important surveillance project began with Bulloch's transfer of Confederate shipbuilding efforts from Britain to

France. Until the spring of 1863, the legal technicalities of Britain's 1861 Foreign Enlistment Act had consistently frustrated Dudley and Adams' attempts to forestall Bulloch's purchases. The British Foreign Office's requirement of conclusive proof that a vessel was intended for belligerent use had allowed both the *Florida* and the *Alabama* to embark upon their careers as fearsome Confederate raiders. In April 1863 Lord John Russell, British foreign secretary, abruptly altered Britain's neutrality policy by seizing the *Alexandria* on the grounds that she was "apparently" intended for use against the North. When the judiciary disallowed the seizure in June, the crown immediately appealed the decision. Bulloch recognized that it was unlikely that either the *Alexandria* or the nearly completed Laird rams (iron-clad vessels designed to literally break the Northern blockade) would ever join the Confederate navy.[46]

While Russell based his decision on apprehension over the precedent being set by the *Alabama* and the *Florida,* concern over the European diplomatic situation, and the desire to demonstrate British good faith, Sanford had characteristically attempted to influence events. On June 9, 1863, he met with Jules Van Praet, minister of Leopold's household. After reviewing the *Alabama*'s construction and departure from England, Sanford warned that a similar escape by the Laird rams could lead to a "rupture" between the United States and Great Britain. Referring to Leopold's close relationship with his niece, Queen Victoria, Sanford suggested that the king use his "well-known influence in England" to prevent the sailing of the ironclads. Van Praet "listened attentively" and promised to convey Sanford's ideas to the king.[47]

The following day Sanford supplemented this interview by taking John Murray Forbes to see Van Pract and Belgian Foreign Minister Charles Rogier. Seward had sent Forbes and William H. Aspinwall to Europe in March 1863 to purchase potentially dangerous vessels then under construction in British shipyards, and in May the two Union agents had crossed over to the continent. Forbes presented Van Praet and Rogier with a detailed description and sketch of the rams, which left little doubt that they were actually armed vessels. Sanford later reported that Leopold had responded by sending a "strong letter to the Queen of England to urge the importance of not permitting the departure of the Ironclads ..."[48]

As prospects dimmed in Britain, Bulloch transferred his purchasing operations to France, where Napoleon III seemed ready to lend support. The emperor had previously suggested to John Slidell, the

Confederate representative in Paris, that the South might obtain
ships in France; and in early 1863 Lucien Arman, the country's
largest shipbuilder and a confidant of Napoleon, extended Slidell a
similar offer. When Arman assured Bulloch in March that the emperor knew and approved of his proposal, the South contracted with
Arman for four heavily armed cruisers similar to the *Alabama* and
two ironclads designed for river combat. Arman undertook the construction of the ironclads and two of the cruisers in his yard at
Bordeaux and subcontracted the other cruisers to J. Vouz in
Nantes.[49]

Rumors of these Franco-Confederate negotiations soon surfaced
in Paris. On July 9, 1863, Nelson Beckwith wrote Sanford that
Bulloch had reportedly contracted for the building of eight iron
steamers. Sanford relayed this intelligence to Seward and then hurried off to Paris to investigate personally. Two days in the French
capital convinced him of the need for an "immediate and thorough
investigation," and he "inaugurated the necessary steps."[50]

His initial "steps" included alerting the Federal consuls at Havre,
Nantes, and Bordeaux and helping John Bigelow to hire a private
detective. On July 18 Bigelow asked Sanford to come to Paris to meet
jointly with Beckwith and "fix upon a plan of operations that will
express our combined knowledge and wisdom." Implicitly deferring
to Sanford's facility in the field, he continued, "As I have but very
little experience in, and no taste for this kind of business, I feel that
I cannot take too many precautions at the outset." Soon thereafter
Sanford arranged for a detective to meet Bigelow at the Normandy
shore and begin investigating the Confederate contracts.[51]

By mid-August these efforts had produced encouraging but incon-
clusive results. The trio of Sanford, Beckwith, and Bigelow had thus
far concealed their suspicions and surveillance measures from William Dayton, whom all three held in low regard. Worried that their
efforts might fail, Bigelow urged Sanford to inform Dayton of their
work, if only on the chance "that he may know of some means which
has not occurred to us of getting on the tracks of these rogues." On
August 21 Sanford demurred and advocated further investigation.
When Sanford dashed to Paris three days later in an effort to have
the U.S.S. *Macedonia* intercept the *Florida* off Queenstown, Bigelow
again prodded him to tell Dayton of their information regarding
Bulloch's activities. That evening Sanford casually mentioned to
Dayton that he had reports of Confederate shipbuilding in France.
Dayton replied that he too had heard these rumors but that the

consul at Havre considered them false. When Sanford dropped the subject without revealing his knowledge to the contrary, Bigelow noted that "Sanford wants to beat Dayton in vigilance etc. on his own ground and unseat him as minister and get into his place."[52]

Bigelow frustrated this intention on September 15 when he announced that he had the "key to the whole business" and smugly advised Sanford to make no additional outlays for related information. In return for 15,000 francs, Bigelow had purchased from a clerk in J. Vouz's office in Nantes original documents demonstrating that the four cruisers and two ironclads had been ordered by the South and that the French government had authorized their armament. Dayton forwarded these documents to Drouyn de Lhuys, the French foreign minister, who on October 22 withdrew Arman's permission to arm the four cruisers. Still no one, not even Drouyn de Lhuys, was certain that the unarmed ships could be prevented from sailing. Not until May 1864 did the foreign minister quash all possibility of the Confederacy's obtaining the four cruisers. Bulloch and Arman belatedly succeeded in putting the ironclad *Stonewall* to sea in January 1865, long after the Confederacy's fate had been sealed.[53]

In the interim between October 1863 and Drouyn de Lhuys' final decision in May 1864, rumors persisted concerning the vessels' completion and sailing. During this period of uncertainty, Sanford continued to supply Bigelow with funds for activities calculated to prevent the ships' escape. Most importantly, Bigelow contracted with Pierre Antoine Berreyer, a distinguished French attorney, to prepare a brief using the captured documents, and in April 1864 Bigelow placed an article derived from Berreyer's brief in the *Opinion Nationale*. Sanford also maintained his periodic presence in Paris. In a series of interviews with Drouyn de Lhuys stretching from October 1863 through August 1864, he pressed the French minister not to foment a Franco-American crisis by allowing the ships to sail and elicited repeated promises that the vessels would not find their way to the Confederacy.[54]

The North's surveillance and espionage activities in Europe contributed substantially to the Union victory. The surveillance system harassed Southern agents, frustrated many of their purchases of guns and materiel, facilitated the capture of blockade runners, and helped frustrate the Confederacy's efforts to outfit a navy in Europe. Henry Sanford was among the first to recognize the urgent need for this system, and his influence with Seward was largely responsible for the sporadic, but crucial, replenishing of the secret service fund. Sanford was also more responsible than any other United States official for the form of the surveillance activities. Although not directly responsible for the critical discoveries of either Consuls Dudley or Bigelow, he had initiated the first monitoring system in England on which Dudley and Morse so ably built; and he had cooperated in all of Bigelow's secret service endeavors. Indeed, Sanford's work in the summer and fall of 1861 furnished the prototype and set the tone for the entire Northern espionage effort. He and other American diplomats continued throughout the war to hire private detectives, to shadow Confederate agents, and to channel voluminous information to the State Department concerning Southern activities in Europe. Only in his early inclinations to sabotage Confederate ships and flout international law did he set precedents not generally adopted.

Sabotage was not the only device Sanford advocated for denying war materials to the Confederacy. He also pushed for a broad-ranging Union program of preclusive buying, and his purchasing of arms and other supplies constituted another of his important pan-European assignments. Just as with the surveillance system, Sanford early recognized the potential importance of purchasing European arms. Soon after his arrival in 1861, he discovered that "Jews, speculators, & Southerners" were "scouring" Europe for arms, and from May through July he persistently exhorted Seward and the War Department to action. His argument for "immediate action" was based on two developments. First, the competition among Confederates, Northern state agents, and speculators was rapidly inflating arms prices. Second, there was a limited supply of properly rifled arms available. Most European countries were substituting rifled barrels and breech-loaders for the older smooth-bore muzzle-loaders, and the additional American demand was producing acute shortages.[55]

Despite Seward's endorsement, Sanford's appeals failed to impress Secretary of War Simon Cameron. Neither the bewildered Pennsylvania spoilsman nor his associates, Thomas A. Scott, assistant secretary of war, and Lieutanant Colonel James W. Ripley, chief of the Ordnance Bureau, perceived the potential for acquiring critically needed weapons for the Union while simultaneously denying arms to the nonindustrialized South. At the time of the firing on Fort Sumter, the North had approximately 350,000 shoulder arms, of which about 250,000 were serviceable and 28,000 qualified as first-class weapons (.58 caliber rifles or rifled muskets). By the end of May the Federal government had dispersed all its rifled arms; by midsummer all the smooth-bore muskets were in the field; and by fall Union arsenals were empty and the Springfield Armory's production had proven woefully insufficient.[56]

The South's situation was even more desperate. Beginning the war with approximately 160,000 usable weapons, no more than 1,800 first-class arms, and no munitions works or skilled labor force, the Confederacy depended almost exclusively on foreign arms through the first two years of the war and imported nearly 600,000 arms through 1865. Although arms and munitions were the Confederacy's most pressing needs, the South also relied on European sources for a myriad of other materials, ranging from cloth, leather, and blankets to zinc, tin, and saltpeter. According to Robert Bruce, the North's failure to grasp its opportunity for cornering the European arms market was "one of the costliest blunders of the war."[57]

Sanford's one attempt at arms procurement during the summer of 1861 intensified his frustration with the War Department. Traveling in Europe when the war began, General John C. Frémont had unilaterally contracted for $200,000 in arms, cannon, and shells and had lobbied successfully for this purchase with the Lincoln government. Prior to his departure from Paris, Frémont had also begun negotiations for an additional 10,000 arms, and on July 11 Secretary Seward instructed Sanford to procure and ship these weapons. Sanford closed the contract for these older model French arms on August 6, but his efforts went for naught. When Chief of Ordinance Ripley objected that the government could not manufacture ammunition for the caliber, Seward cancelled Sanford's mission. The secretary's revised instructions proved unnecessary. Sanford had already forfeited the contract when he discovered that the War Department had neglected to furnish him credits with Baring Brothers. Unencumbered by either the administrative or political pressures confronting Washington officials, Sanford was puzzled and exasperated by this confusion and indecision.[58]

Only after Beauregard's rout of the Union forces at Bull Run shattered Northern expectations of a short, painless struggle did Cameron consent to purchase foreign arms and materials. In late July the War Department dispatched Colonel George L. Schuyler with instructions to secure 100,000 rifled muskets with bayonets, 10,000 carbines, 20,000 cavalry sabres, and 10,000 revolvers. He was explicitly restricted to the purchase of first-class arms. Schuyler's mission was not, however, equivalent to a systematic or organized Union purchasing program.[59] Much to Sanford's dismay, the War Department not only authorized Schuyler as its agent but simultaneously contracted with numerous private dealers and permitted the states to pursue a similar policy. As Sanford observed, this "seesawing business" created ruinous competition among the various Union agents and further inflated arms prices. He was equally distressed by the department's failure to establish Schuyler's credits until nearly a month after his arrival in Europe and by the reluctance to purchase second-class arms. Both Sanford and Schuyler repeatedly protested that there were virtually no first-class weapons available at any price. And because he emphasized the preclusive aspect of the purchases, Sanford considered Ripley's objection to introducing arms of varying calibers as quibbling over "minor detail." He railed at the "hypocritical red-tapism" blocking purchases: "If our Government shows as much folly in the conduct of the campaign as it has displayed in the matter of foreign arms, we deserve to fail."[60]

Following the government's change of policy, Sanford was instructed to aid both Schuyler and Herman Boker and Co., one of the principal private firms contracting to deliver European arms to the War Department. Sanford had previously contended that the government should select "one agent" to supervise European purchasing activities, and in September he successfully lobbied for the position. Writing to Secretary Seward on September 27, he argued that "in these matters where prompt and efficient action seem so important, the Department" could avoid inevitable confusion and delay by entrusting control "to one of its representatives abroad." Sanford's blatant solicitation of the post was even more explicit in a note penned the same day to Seward's son, Frederick William. While professing his willingness to undertake any task—even "cleaning" the guns, he protested a joint assignment of arms procurement with Ministers Adams and Dayton. The former considered himself "much above such things," and the latter "though anxious to please" knew "nothing" of these matters.[61] Secretary Seward forwarded Sanford's official note to the War Department where it accomplished the ambitious envoy's objective. On August 28, 1861, Secretary Cameron had provided Schuyler, Dayton, and Sanford a joint credit of $1 million with Baring Brothers. Sanford's argument for sole authority proved convincing, and on October 14 the War Department transferred the $1 million to his sole control.[62]

In this position as coordinator of Union arms purchasing, Sanford actively cooperated with Schuyler. The colonel had arrived in London on August 8, and acting on the advice of Secretary Seward, had immediately established communications with Sanford. Throughout the fall Sanford put Schuyler in touch with French and Italian arms dealers and attempted to alleviate friction between Schuyler and other American agents.[63]

The most serious source of this friction was Gilead A. Smith, the representative of Boker and Co. and Sanford's old friend and Washington College classmate. Even before Cameron had directed Sanford to "aid the firm," Smith had written requesting information that might be translated into *"well divided profits."* Despite Smith's overtures and the charges of Sanford's critics, there is no evidence of impropriety in either his dealings with Boker and Co. or his independent arms purchases. Sanford attempted to eliminate direct competition between Smith and Schuyler, but Smith's desire to upstage Schuyler precluded coordinated activity. To his dismay, Sanford found himself caught in the middle of the competition he had admonished against.[64]

Delicately balancing his responsibilities, Sanford maintained his contacts with Schuyler and facilitated Boker and Co.'s purchases. From November 1861 through March 1862, he paid the firm over $280,000, accepted their deliveries, and arranged for transporting the materiel to the United States. Throughout these dealings, Sanford compensated the firm only after receiving certificates from the U.S. government inspectors approving the arms and bills of lading documenting that the cargoes were packed and ready for shipment.[65]

In addition to his work with Schuyler and Boker and Co., Sanford personally conducted extensive preclusive purchasing operations. Through his surveillance system he identified numerous Southern contracts, and during November he outbid the Confederates for two large arms shipments—one for 40,000 and the other for 72,000 weapons. In notifying Cameron of the latter purchase, Sanford contended that he had paid between $4 and $7 for guns regularly costing $17. When the seller of the 40,000 arms defaulted, Sanford threatened legal action and obtained a compromise agreement for 25,000 arms at 14½ francs per weapon, a reduction of 7½ francs. This compromise settlement also netted Sanford 11,000 sabres and 12,000 muskets at reduced rates. He reported that the cumulative saving amounted to $40,000. Later in December he secured several smaller contracts totalling over 30,000 arms and an agreement in Liege for all the Vincennes carbines deliverable by Christmas. He also considered purchasing all the available Enfield gun barrels in Liege but rejected the lot when the government inspector informed him they did not conform to the Union's Springfield standard. By March 1862 he had expended over $415,700 in these personal acquisitions.[66]

The most informed student of the Union's small-arms procurement has concluded that compared to Schuyler, Sanford obtained "many of the poor quality and even useless arms." Still, Sanford should not be too harshly censured. Acknowledging that the "gun business" was not his *"line,"* he systematically obtained the inspectors' clearances before finalizing contracts and quickly rejected the Enfield barrels that failed to conform to Union specifications. His instructions to government inspector Adam Rhulman regarding a lot of 20,000 Prussian muskets were typical: "These arms must be in *good condition fit to be issued to troops."* On another occasion he had Rhulman reexamine arms previously approved by another inspector in whom Sanford lacked confidence. Unlike Boker and Co., which also furnished substandard weapons, Sanford made no profits; and "whatever the critical evaluation of these foreign arms, it must be remembered that they filled a void which could not have been filled in any other way." Most importantly, although he recognized that first-class arms were preferable, he also grasped the importance of denying second-class weapons to the Confederacy.[67]

Sanford did not confine his preclusive buying to arms. In late October 1861 he discovered a large Confederate contract for French cloth and blankets. He asserted that intercepting these materials would mark "the greatest victory yet over the enemy. The winter clothing for 100,000 men taken out of their hands . . . would almost compensate for Bull Run." After seeking unsuccessfully to enlist the aid of Dayton and Schuyler, he turned to George Plumer Smith, an agent of the United States Quartermaster Department. Smith had contacted Sanford on November 5 and provided his minimum standards for cloth purchases, stating explicitly that *"grey* being the Rebel colors, is prohibited." Although the 200,000 yards of cloth in question were grey and did not meet Smith's quality criteria, Sanford believed that this lot could easily be dyed blue and was superior to many previous purchases. Even more crucial was the possibility of denying the Confederates badly needed winter clothing. On November 12 Sanford wrote Smith urging him to come immediately to

Brussels. He emphasized that his deposit of 5,000 francs would only secure the Union's option to purchase until the following evening.[68]

Smith came to the continent, examined the cloth, refused the contract, and left an account of the incident that plagued Sanford until his death. The quartermaster agent charged that Sanford had greeted him in London with the proposal that Smith use his credits to purchase the cloth, which after dyeing blue, they would resell to the government for a profit. Professing indignation, Smith claimed to have rejected this scheme.[69]

Sanford told a different story. He subsequently contended (in 1877) that he had referred Smith to Leon Gauchez, a Frenchman who had been serving as his intermediary in negotiations for the contract. The following day Gauchez reported that Smith had aborted the talks by demanding a large personal commission. Sanford also alleged that Smith had sought similar compensation from other purchases.[70]

Sanford's dismissal of Smith's accusation as a "tissue of infamous falsehoods" appears warranted. Smith's allegation that Sanford wanted to use Union credits to buy the cloth and then resell it to the same government is unlikely. Even if profiteering had been his objective, Sanford was far too smooth and clever to have suggested such an unworkable plot. But that was not Sanford's objective; rather than profiting financially from his position in Brussels, Sanford contributed sizable sums to the Union cause. Only four days before summoning Smith, he had written revealingly to his mother, "Were I not a Gov't officer I could make legitimately heaps of money. As it is I get half my expenses paid for [while] devoting my self & all my time to Gov't service." Smith also argued that Sanford's November 12 communication had been self-incriminating, but the note contains to hint of illegality. While the cloth was sub-standard, as Sanford acknowledged, Smith's subsequent assertion that Confederate inspectors had rejected it was untrue. Moreover, Smith weakened his charges by waiting eight years to lodge them. That he mentioned no wrongdoing on Sanford's part to Benjamin Moran in February 1862 is significant. Smith was an "old friend" of Moran, and they dined together in London on February 11. Had Smith conveyed anything negative about Sanford, Moran, who especially detested Sanford, would certainly have recorded it in his copious and caustic diary. Despite the doubtful veracity of Smith's account, he repeated it loudly and often, and his indictments seriously damaged Sanford's later attempts to secure diplomatic appointments.[71]

If Smith's story was flawed, so too was Sanford's. His counter-charges also surfaced long after the incident. In complaining of Smith's actions in November 1861, he simply stated that Smith had come to the continent, inspected the cloth, and refused to pay the "bonus" necessary to wrest the contract from the Confederates. Although Sanford was distressed at the lost opportunity, he mentioned no irregularities. His more fanciful version appears to have been concocted later in response to that of his attacker.[72]

As November 1861 drew to a close, Sanford made one of his frequent jaunts to Paris—this time to greet his good friend Thurlow Weed, who was then on a special Union mission to cultivate European goodwill. Although delighted to visit with Weed, Sanford was startled by the news of the *Trent* affair. Captain Charles Wilkes' removal of the Confederate commissioners, James M. Mason and John Slidell, from the British mail steamer produced a crisis in Anglo-American relations. Until news of the decision to release Mason and Slidell reached Europe six weeks later, Union diplomats operated in the shadow of imminent war with Britain, the world's greatest power.

Like the bulk of the American public, Sanford was initially "delighted" with Wilkes' work; it was the Union's "first show of action," of "force, spunk, vitality." In the immediate aftermath of the incident he assumed a belligerent public posture. From Brussels, Britain's minister reported that Sanford was affecting "a tone of indifference and boasting . . . in regard . . . to . . . a war with Great Britain," and Lord Palmerston, the British prime minister, subsequently portrayed him as "the most warlike of the American diplomatists." His early truculence was misleading; privately he quickly recognized that British preparations for war were "immense," that "feeling here [Belgium] as in France is strongly against us," and that the United States could not "afford . . . to fight over the traitors whose martyrdom would ensure an opening of the Southern blockade." As the bleak December days passed, anxiety over a possible war left him "sleepless and half sick." He soon began telling friends that the government should release Mason and Slidell, and he wrote wistfully to Seward: "My faith still is that the present excitement in England will be followed by reaction & that if you have managed to gain time, the common sense of the English will come to the rescue."[73]

While awaiting intelligence from the United States, he did his utmost to influence events. Upon learning in Paris of the seizure of the Confederate commissioners, he cooperated in the first attempt to moderate the European response to Wilkes' deed. Both he and John Bigelow predicted that the French would condemn Wilkes; and the two, together with Weed, Dayton, Archbishop John Hughes, and General Winfield Scott, composed a public letter over Scott's signature. The letter, written by Bigelow, emphasized the possibility that Wilkes had acted without authority and that the United States was not spoiling for war with Great Britain. It appeared in the French papers on December 4 and was reprinted throughout Europe. In complimenting Bigelow, Sanford termed the epistle "very opportune" and was confident it had done much "good."[74]

Sanford also endeavored to enlist French mediation in the Anglo-American quarrel. On his return to Brussels, he suggested to Baron Charles de Talleyrand-Perigord, the French minister to Belgium, that Emperor Napoleon III might serve as mediator. While underscoring that the United States desired peace, Sanford noted the importance of United States commercial power as a "counterpoise against that of England." Talleyrand agreed that maintenance of the United States' integrity would best serve French interests, and he relayed the request for mediation to Foreign Minister Thouvenel in Paris. In an important December 6 cabinet meeting, Touvenel advocated absolute neutrality but apparently did not mention Sanford's proposal. Had he done so, Napoleon's reply would certainly have been identical to that given Archbishop John Hughes on December 26, when he declined Hughes' appeal for mediation on the grounds that it would be unacceptable to England.[75]

With the death of Prince Albert, the British prince consort, Sanford sought to use Leopold I to temper British policy. Anticipating that Leopold would go to England to console Victoria, Sanford visited Jules Van Praet, the minister of the king's household, on December 16. He emphasized that the points at issue were more matters of form than substance and that an Anglo-American war would be harmful for all of Europe. By using his influence for peace, Leopold would be serving Belgium as well as the potential belligerents. When Leopold departed for London later in the month, Sanford was convinced that the old monarch went with "every disposition" to do his utmost for the "interests of peace."[76]

While hoping and working for peace, Sanford simultaneously continued the procurement and shipment of war materiel, some of which he purchased specifically out of fear of war with Great Britain. The most significant commodity in this category was saltpeter, an essential ingredient for the production of gunpowder. At the onset of the war the Union possessed 3 million pounds of saltpeter, but by the fall of 1861 supplies had fallen dangerously low. Acting on behalf of the Navy Department, Lamont DuPont had purchase 4½ million pounds in England; but before he could make shipment, the British government reacted to the *Trent* affair by banning further saltpeter exports. Sanford feared that with an Anglo-American war British sea power would also block Northern access to continental supplies, and Robert Bruce has since contended that conflict with the British would have inflicted "gunpowder starvation" on the Union.[77]

In early December 1861 Sanford solicited the opinions of Weed, Dayton, and Scott, and then acted on his own authority in purchasing over 400 tons of saltpeter worth approximately $140,000. He gathered these stocks from Hamburg, Antwerp, Bremen, and Havre and even narrowly missed smuggling an order out of London. Convinced that the English authorities had foiled this latter scheme by tampering with his mail, Sanford periodically employed an alias during the duration of the crisis. In a more significant precautionary move, he transferred the remaining £75,000 of the War Department's account with Baring Brothers to the Bank of Belgium in Brussels.[78]

Sanford also worked feverishly throughout December arranging transportation for the war materiel he and other Union agents had purchased. This was no easy task. On November 16 he had supervised the shipment of a large cargo of contraband aboard the *Congress* from Antwerp. The vessel encountered bad weather off the English coast, put in at South Hampton, and was detained by British officials. In early December the British consul at Antwerp blocked Sanford's plan to send goods aboard the English steamer *Estella.* Sanford promptly warned Boker and Co. to risk no shipments aboard vessels scheduled for an English stop and the possibility of falling "into the lion's mouth." After unsuccessfully offering $30,000 to charter a direct steamer from Hamburg to the United States, he persuaded the Hamburg-American Steamer Packet Company to bypass England with one of its regular runs, and on December 24 the *Saxonia* sailed from Hamburg with an 850-ton cargo.[79]

Faced with large quantities of goods still to be shipped and the undiminished threat of war with Britain, Sanford renewed his effort to charter a private steamer. His second attempt proved successful, and he dispatched the *Melitia* from Antwerp during the third week of January 1862. The vessel's freight included the last of his purchases—some 25,000 guns and 140 tons of saltpeter. To ensure its safe passage, he placed on board as a "supercargo" a handpicked crew under Captain Edwin G. Eastman.[80] After arranging shipment for late deliveries from Boker and Co. in February and March, Sanford ended his involvement in the procurement of war materiel. Early in 1862 Lincoln replaced Secretary of War Cameron with Edwin M. Stanton, a Union Democrat and former attorney general in the Buchanan administration. Freightened by the spector of national bankruptcy, Stanton sought closer control over purchases and expenditures. On January 29 he cancelled all outstanding orders for foreign goods and forbade future foreign contracts for any article produced in the United States.[81]

Sanford had played a central role in these European purchasing operations. He had quickly recognized the importance of the European arms market, and after the War Department belatedly acted on his suggestions, he functioned as the coordinator for Union purchases and shipments. In addition he personally purchased more than 125,000 arms and 400 tons of saltpeter. When combined with his propaganda and surveillance activities, his work in this area easily made him the most active Union diplomat in Europe. As if these diverse involvements had not been sufficient to occupy Sanford's time and energies, Secretary Seward assigned him another special mission during the summer of 1861.

As the last echoes of McDowell's troops fleeing the field at Bull Run resounded in Washington, Lincoln and Seward decided to offer Giuseppe Garibaldi a command in the Union army. The president and secretary of state chose Sanford as their envoy to the old Italian hero. J. W. Quiggle, an obscure American consul at Antwerp, had initiated the proceedings which Charles Francis Adams later described as a "strange medley of blunders." In writing to thank Henry T. Tuckerman for an appreciation of Garibaldi in the January 1861 *North American Review,* Augusto Veechi, a trusted comrade of the general, suggested that the conqueror of the two Sicilies might be induced to aid the Union cause. Rumors to this effect soon circulated in both American and European newspapers and prompted Quiggle to write Garibaldi inquiring of their validity. Garibaldi replied that if his presence were not required in Italy and the United States government requested his service, he would go to America. Quiggle forwarded this correspondence to Seward on July 5, 1861.[82]

Lincoln and Seward seized the opportunity of enrolling the famed Italian. Although influenced by the recent disaster at Bull Run, they were probably more strongly affected by Garibaldi's potential impact on American public opinion and military morale. By 1861 he was one of the world's most celebrated figures. Upon arrival in the United States in 1850, he had been warmly greeted as the "Modern Hannibal of Italy." The conquest of the two Sicilies increased American admiration for the dashing soldier; numerous 1860 Independence Day celebrations bestowed impassioned praise on the "Washington of Italy"; and his famed red-shirted legions were widely recognized symbols of freedom. Newly formed regiments in the Union army were proudly adopting the name "Garibaldi's Guards."[83]

On July 27 Seward confidentially directed Sanford to establish immediate "relations with the celebrated warrior for liberty." He was to tell Garibaldi that his services were "warmly desired and requested" and to proffer him the grade of major general. Seward further instructed Sanford to work in conjunction with George P. Marsh, American Minister to Italy, and he enclosed a letter of commendation for Consul Quiggle.[84]

Although pessimistic about the project, which one of his friends in the State Department aptly labeled a "wild goose chase," Sanford promptly undertook Seward's directives. He first wrote Marsh on August 13, informing him of Seward's instructions and requesting him to gather any information that might bear upon their mission. He then sent for Quiggle, gave him his letter from Seward, and showed him the secretary's July 27 dispatch. Sanford stressed the importance of secrecy to Quiggle, whom he later characterized as "a low besotted Pennsylvania politician with an eye to money-making and political capital." Quiggle pledged himself to secrecy, but Sanford remained apprehensive lest the consul break the project to the papers.[85]

Despite these precautions, American newspapers closely followed Sanford's activities. On August 14, the very day Sanford and Quiggle met, the *New York Tribune* reported that Garibaldi had offered his services to the Union and that the government had tendered him the rank of major general. American papers continued to cover the affair with keen interest until early October. As news of his efforts became known throughout Europe, the *Tribune* announced on September 24 that Sanford had indeed visited the famed Italian, and by October 2 Horace Greeley's paper was certain that Garibaldi had spurned the Union offer.[86]

As Sanford traveled to Turin by way of Paris, Quiggle anticipated his arrival with another letter to Garibaldi. Quiggle announced that

Sanford was authorized to offer "the highest army commission which it is in the power of the President to confer." Not realizing that this "highest army commission" was in fact the rank of major general, Garibaldi wrongly assumed that Sanford was empowered to tender the supreme command of the Union army.[87]

Upon his arrival in Turin on August 20, Sanford consulted with Marsh and sent a messenger with a confidential letter asking if Garibaldi wished to serve in the United States. Sanford and Marsh concluded that, with the Roman question nearing settlement, Garibaldi would soon be summoned to help restore order in southern Italy. It was, therefore, improbable that he would consider going to America. By sending an intermediary, Sanford hoped to avoid the adverse publicity which could result from his personally receiving the anticipated rebuff. Unfortunately, Joseph Artomi, the messenger entrusted with Sanford's letter, further confused the American offer. When confronted by the illustrious soldier, Artomi became flustered and told Garibaldi that Lincoln unquestionably wished to make him commander-in-chief.[88]

Garibaldi cleverly employed the United States offer as a device to force his Roman policy on King Victor Emmanuel II. Refusing to consider Italy truly united until Rome and Venice had been incorporated, he had advocated an immediate march on Rome. The more prudent king sought to consolidate recent victories and did not wish to challenge Napoleon III, then posing as the protector of the Church. Armed with the American invitation, the popular hero could threaten leaving Italy if the king denied his wishes. On September 3 Garbaldi began his power play by sending Caspare Trecchi to the king with an open letter and verbal instructions to obtain an answer within twenty-four hours. Garibaldi informed Victor Emmanuel that the United States had offered him the command of its armies. Did the king need him in Italy or should he go to America? On September 6 the king rejected Garibaldi's Roman policy and gave him permission to sail for America.[89]

Sanford learned of the king's answer from Colonel Trecchi, who was certain Garibaldi would quit Italy for America. In the face of the king's rebuff, Sanford considered acceptance of his offer as Garibaldi's only means of salvaging his self-respect. After discussions with Trecchi, Sanford feared that negotiations with the general might falter over the question of rank, and he and Marsh concluded that no time should be lost in clarifying any misconceptions. On September 7 Sanford went from Turin to Genoa and, under an

assumed name, chartered a small steamer to Garibaldi's island retreat at Caprera. He disembarked on the rugged windswept island
the next day. After walking a mile over a rough, rocky path under
the hot Mediterranean sun, he reached Garibaldi's humble stone
cottage. The famous Italian hardly looked like a potential savior of
the Union. While Garibaldi managed to leave his room for the first
time in four months, Sanford believed his "inflammatory rheuma-
tism still rendered him very much an invalid."[90]

As evening approached, the negotiations began. Garibaldi quickly
squelched any possibility of agreement by demanding far more than
Sanford, or even Lincoln, had the power to offer. Having been misled
by both Quiggle and Artomi, Garibaldi would accept no rank lower
than supreme commander. He further requested the authority to
emancipate all the slaves at his discretion. As Sanford reported to
Seward, the "Ex-Dictator of the Two Sicilies" had bid quite "high."
Sanford responded that he could offer only the rank of major general
with the command of a large army corps. This was the highest rank
the president could constitutionally confer. After Garibaldi rejected
it, Sanford suggested that the general and his entourage go to the
United States and make a final decision after acquiring a clearer idea
of the American situation. Garibaldi did not decline this offer so
peremptorily, but the next morning he again replied negatively. Since
he had not addressed any "formal or official demand of, or proposition" to Garibaldi, Sanford naively believed he had prevented the
United States from appearing to have unsuccessfully sought aid
abroad.[91]

This was not to be. Despite his efforts at secrecy, the general
outlines of Sanford's activities became known throughout Europe.
The Italian press's first notice of the offer on August 30 was actually
taken from the *New York Herald,* and Sanford's prediction that it
was "but a foretaste of what we've to undergo" proved accurate.
Alarmed at the prospect of their hero's quitting Italy, Garibaldi's
friends leaked the details in early September to arouse opposition
among the public. A vehement protest immediately arose from Italy's liberal press, and petitions circulated throughout the country
beseeching the general not to desert his native land.[92]

The publicity soon spread in garbled form to France and England
and was relished by those hostile to the North. In Paris the imperial
journals reported that the United States had tendered Garibaldi the
post of commander-in-chief, but that he had declined. John Bigelow
observed that this was "regarded as a confession of military incompe-
tence that has done us incalculable damage." London papers agreed.

The London *Times* of September 17 declared:

> As if despairing of native genius or enterprise, the President at Washington has actually sent to ask Garibaldi to accept the post of Commander-in-Chief, throwing into the bargain the emancipation of the slaves.

This, the *Times* concluded, constituted a sign of "American degeneracy" and a "confession of failure."[93]

Although vexed by these attacks, Sanford declined to issue a public explanation or disclaimer. He believed this should be done only by the "two principal parties in the transaction . . . Seward & G." Sanford had reached this conclusion in consultation with Nelson Beckwith, his old friend and confidant, who lived in Paris. Beckwith advised, and Sanford concurred, that any contradiction of stories like that in the *Times* would necessitate extensive and embarrassing explanations. Both men doubted the *Times* would publish a correction, and they feared that the British press would further criticize any such endeavor. Sanford and Beckwith chose instead to deny such newspaper reports verbally, both because of erroneous claims about the rank proffered and the less justifiable contention that Sanford had technically made no official offer to Garibaldi.[94]

Meanwhile, William L. Dayton aggravated Sanford's discomfort by compromising his policy of public silence. Like Bigelow, Dayton was appalled by European press attacks on the United States. After talking with Beckwith, who told him "the straight story" of Sanford's activities, Dayton retained James Mortimer, a *New York Herald* correspondent, and wrote Marsh asking him to give Mortimer details of the affair. Marsh denied the offer of the supreme command and referred Dayton and Mortimer to Sanford for further information. Without contacting Sanford, Dayton gave Mortimer's written denial to the Paris press. Enraged, Sanford complained to Seward of Dayton's failure to consult him on the matter.[95]

A number of observers blamed Sanford for the mission's failure and the accompanying publicity. John Hay, Lincoln's private secretary, later asserted that Sanford had "made the proposition entirely off his own bat, and without any authority from President Lincoln." Consul Quiggle charged him with divulging his mission at Turin and making himself conspicuous by chartering the private steamer to Caprera. Charles Francis Adams indicted him for allowing Quiggle to see the relevant instructions. According to Adams, Sanford thereby lost exclusive control of the project and enabled Quiggle to write his misleading letter to Garibaldi. Benjamin Moran, Adams' vitriolic secretary, critized Sanford most severly. He attributed the publicity to Sanford's "meddlesome impertinence" and dismissed him as a "forward twaddle."[96]

Others evaluated Sanford's work more positively. Marsh was very favorably impressed by his animated colleague. On September 4, before Sanford had gone to Caprera, Marsh wrote Seward:

> Continued intercourse with Mr. Sanford impresses me more and more favorably with respect to his character as a man and as a diplomatic agent. His experience and regular training in the different grades of diplomatic life have given him such readiness and efficiency in negotiation and his fine . . . natural and acquired qualities have fitted him to be eminently useful in his present or in higher positions of delicacy and confidence.

Nor did Marsh change his opinion after Sanford's abortive journey to Garibaldi's rocky retreat. Marsh ascribed the failure to Garibaldi's refusal to accept the offer rather than to any "error or indiscretion" on Sanford's part. Seward agreed. After considering the reports from Sanford and Marsh, he wrote Sanford that his execution of the mission had been "in all respects considerate and proper."[97]

Regardless of their evaluation of Sanford's performance, all responsible observers concluded that the United States' failure to lure Garibaldi to America was fortunate. Sanford considered Garibaldi incapable of the cooperative action so necessary to successful military operations; both his past career and present position demonstrated that he must be "all or nothing." Marsh, who had harbored apprehensions from the beginning over "this worse than *old woman* scheme," believed that Garibaldi would have aroused debilitating jealousy among American officers and created serious problems because of his attitudes on emancipation. From London and Paris, Adams, Dayton, and Bigelow concurred in these evaluations. Seward, despite expressing regret at Garibaldi's decision, also reconsidered the advisability of importing the famed Italian. The secretary implied as much to Marsh, and as Charles C. Tansill has observed, his "perfect equanimity" at the project's failure demonstrated no great disappointment.[98]

The *Trent* affair quickly ended public and official interest in the episode. It had caused the United States, Secretary Seward, and Sanford considerable embarrassment and had confirmed the views of pro-Southern groups in Europe who were ever-watchful for hints of Northern weakness. Some, like Adams and Moran, took occasion to criticize Sanford's abilities, but in fact the secrecy of his mission had been badly compromised from the beginning and was totally betrayed by Garibaldi's associates. Sanford did err in communicating his instructions to Quiggle, thus helping to foster Garibaldi's belief that he was to receive the supreme command. But regardless of this misunderstanding, the general's demands for emancipation presented an insurmountable obstacle. Garibaldi's ambitions centered on the capture of Rome, not Richmond, and he sought to use the American offer as a device for realizing this goal. Even if he had sincerely considered coming to the United States, he was neither physically nor temperamentally prepared to aid the Union. This bizarre, ill-conceived project was foredoomed to failure, with fortunate results for the North.

Sanford's special assignments were diverse and significant. Although they were not so crucial to Union diplomatic success as Adams' work in London, a proper understanding of Sanford's activities is necessary for a comprehensive portrait of Civil War diplomacy. Sanford made mistakes: He occasionally disregarded international law; he purchased low-quality arms; and he revealed his instructions regarding Garibaldi to Consul Quiggle. Still, his overall performance was commendable, and his roles in the Union surveillance system, purchasing operations, and propaganda activities were important contributions to Northern victory. Taken as a whole his activities qualified him as one of the Union's most tireless workers in Europe.

Ubiquitous and heedless of his colleagues' sensibilities, Sanford naturally alienated many of his fellow diplomats. Benjamin Moran referred to him as that "Legation on wheels"; Charles Francis Adams complained of Sanford's "poaching" on his "manor"; George P. Marsh characterized him as "able but overzealous and vain"; and William L. Dayton spoke of Sanford when grumbling about American "officials transiently in Paris" who heard groundless rumors and transmitted them to Washington.[99] Each of these appraisals was partially true; but only Marsh acknowledged that Sanford was capable and useful, which he most certainly was. Recognizing this, Seward, who was no mean judge of character, had made Sanford his "Minister" to Europe.

CHAPTER 4

SEWARD'S MINISTER TO BELGIUM, 1861–1869

ALTHOUGH Sanford's diverse special assignments were his most important work during the 1860s, he did not neglect his duties in Belgium. During the war years, he effectively presented Union policies, especially those treating the Maximilian affair in Mexico; and after 1865 he successfully negotiated several beneficial treaties. His eight year tenure in Brussels was also marked by the most significant personal event of his life—his marriage in 1864 to Gertrude Ellen du Puy. The newlyweds established a luxurious residence and opulent lifestyle and by the end of the decade had two children. Although Sanford easily supported this household from his investment income, his tendency toward hasty, ill-advised business speculation became apparent in the 1860s.

The ambition that had characterized his conduct as chargé in Paris remained prominent. Throughout his term in Belgium, he unsuccessfully angled for promotion to the more prestigious United States ministership to Paris. He also tried to persuade Congress and the State Department to upgrade the classification of the Belgian position from minister resident to envoy extraordinary and minister plenipotentiary. His service in Brussels ended in 1869 with the inauguration of Ulysses S. Grant's administration. Grant replaced Sanford in Belgium, and Congress rejected his nomination as United States minister to Spain.

Sanford did not allow his continental projects to interfere with his responsibilities in Belgium. He correctly perceived that Belgium was "afraid to do anything without the approval of the great powers"— that in "political matters" Leopold I could only lead his tiny kingdom in the "tracks" of her more powerful neighbors. Still, the Belgian court wielded considerable influence. Through purposeful royal matchmaking, Leopold had become the "father-in-law of Europe," with kinship ties to most of the ruling houses. Sanford contended that Leopold's "great age" qualified him as the "Dean" of European monarchs and that, with the exception of Napoleon III, the old Coburg prince exercised greater influence than any continental head of state.[1]

No friend of popular rule, Leopold had little sympathy for the Union. He disparaged the Northern cause as "rank Republicanism," and apprehension over the United States' emergence as a manufacturing rival led him to favor "two great Republics instead of one." During November 1862 he endorsed English and French mediation and argued that American rejection of such an offer should have led "naturally to the recognition of the South."[2] Despite the king's position, Sanford generally maintained a cordial and intimate relationship with the Belgian government. Sanford's fluent French and long experience in Europe enabled him to communicate directly and easily with both Leopold and his ministers.

While facilitating access to the Belgian court, Sanford's prior diplomatic experience simultaneously occasioned some awkward moments. On May 8, 1861, Sanford attended his first audience with Leopold I clad in the "citizen's dress" he had so defiantly sported eight years before in Paris. He soon discovered that he was the only American diplomat in Europe to have donned the plain black suit. Rather than appear brash he reluctantly reverted to a diplomatic costume. But to do so without contradicting his former position and thereby sacrificing either "principle or dignity" left Sanford in a dilemma, which he resolved by procuring a military title and with it the technical right to wear a uniform.[3]

After appeals to the Connecticut State Militia and Secretary of State Seward had failed, he presented the First Minnesota Infantry with a battery of three six-pound cannons. Minnesota Governor Alexander Ramsey reciprocated by making Sanford a major general in the Minnesota Militia.[4] Sanford gratefully accepted the title "General," which he retained through the remainder of his life. Beginning in March 1862 he graced formal Belgian occasions in resplendent attire:

[His] coat was a tight fitting, close-buttoned swallowtail of dark blue, covered before and behind with a mass of gold embroidery, which outshone the splendor of the Russian Ambassador. White cashmere trousers, with broad gold-lace bands, decorated his legs, while a cocked hat, adorned with startling white and orange plumes, was carried under his arm. A most elaborate presentation sword, pendant from an embroidered belt, jingled by his side.[5]

This remained his official dress until March 1867, when Congress passed Charles Sumner's resolution forbidding American diplomats to wear diplomatic regalia. Despite his own vacillating course, Sanford gloried in the congressional action. To Seward he wrote, "Excuse my onslaught on the diplomatic costume question—but while I am in no way the instigator or abbettor of the Joint Resolution, I have been the apostle (& martyr too), of the principle!" He promptly returned to the black suit, "a garb more in keeping with our institutions and usages." Although at a subsequent dinner at the royal palace, Sanford was the only one of seventy guests who did not wear an elaborate uniform, Leopold II greeted him with great respect—just as if he had worn "a coat like Joseph's: 'of many colors.' "[6]

Sanford's initial audience with Leopold I in May 1861 also set the tone for their discussions over the ensuing four years. While manifesting a "kind and cordial spirit," Leopold repeatedly advocated peace. The king often couched his "eternal refrain" in humanitarian terms, but Sanford interpreted this as pro-Southern since it would have ended hostilities even at the cost of dividing the Union. He treated all Leopold's suggestions for mediation "very curtly" and rejected any "arrangement theory" proposing mutual concessions. He likewise denied the inevitability of Southern independence and countered with Seward's argument that European interference would only prolong the conflict.[7]

Soon after Sanford's arrival in 1861, Seward instructed him to seek a Belgian-American agreement based upon the 1856 Declaration of Paris. The Congress of Paris had forbidden privateering and paper blockades; had proclaimed that, with the exception of contraband, belligerent goods would be considered neutral when aboard neutral ships; and had stated that contraband belonging to a neutral was exempt from capture. Seward had originally hoped to barter America's adherence to these principles for Europe's refusal to recognize Confederate belligerence. After England and France had declared their neutrality, he unrealistically thought this American offer might prompt their reconsideration. He also hoped to induce the European powers to outlaw Confederate privateering or close their ports to these Southern vessels.[8]

On June 4 Sanford presented Baron de Vriere, the Belgain foreign minister, with a formal note requesting agreement to the Paris standards. After two months and another note failed to elicit a substantive reply, Sanford concluded that Belgium would do "nothing till after the great powers have decided upon a course of action." When both France and Great Britain declined similar American offers, Sanford permitted his proposal to die a quiet death. In the interim, however, he had partially achieved Seward's objectives by securing an official proclamation denying privateers entry into Belgian ports, save in "cases of extreme danger by stress of weather." The government also warned Belgian subjects that any participation in privateering activities carried with it the risk of being charged with piracy.[9]

Leopold's persistent calls for peace did not derive solely from his hostility to republicanism or fear of United States economic power. Of more immediate concern was the American war's disruption of ordinary commercial patterns and the problems of Belgium's cotton industry. Among European countries only England and France suffered more acutely, and within Belgium distress was especially concentrated around Ghent, the country's principal cotton manufacturing center. By September 1862 nearly one-third of Ghent's 10,000 cotton operatives were unemployed, and another third were working part-time. Two years later Belgian cotton mills were still operating at only two-thirds of their pre-1861 capacity.[10]

Sanford sympathized with the Belgian difficulties, but he argued that only Northern victory would bring relief: "The peace & traffic [in cotton] . . . so much desired could only be obtained by the submission of the insurgents." He initially accepted the European explanation, which attributed the distress to the interruption of trade with the South and the resulting scarcity of raw cotton. Arguing from the scarcity rationale, Sanford urged Seward in April 1862 to open one or more Southern ports as quickly as they could be captured. This would simultaneously demonstrate United States concern for the neutrals' plight and funnel the coveted staple to Europe. Seward was impressed by Sanford's appeal, and when it was seconded by other Northern representatives in Europe, the secretary and President Lincoln opened New Orleans, Beaufort, and Port Royal in May 1862.[11]

During the fall and winter of 1862–63, Sanford made a number of trips to Belgian and French cotton manufacturing areas. These travels through Ghent, Rouen, Lille, and Alsace altered his perception of the "cotton crisis" and convinced him that the problem was abundance rather than scarcity. In an explanation that anticipated subsequent historians,[12] he contended that the European cotton industry's consistent over-production had glutted the world's markets and that a dearth of orders hampered cotton manufacturers much more seriously than their inability to obtain raw cotton. He also recognized that the French cotton industry's failure to modernize had put it at a serious competitive disadvantage relative to the British. Given the "accumulated" stock of goods in January 1863, Sanford argued that, even without the American supply, alternative sources of raw cotton should suffice "for many months if not for years to come." The decreased flow of raw cotton from America had actually benefitted the cotton magnates by allowing them to slow production and dispose of overstocked inventories of finished goods. Sanford speculated that a massive influx of Southern cotton could be detrimental to mill owners by compounding the problem of overproduction and inducing an abrupt price reduction. He also contended that the suffering among workers was overstated. Particularly in France, the "cotton crisis" was "greatly exaggerated," "falsely based," and largely "manufactured by the press" in cooperation with elements hostile to the United States. The "cotton famine" was, in short, "a humbug."[13]

Having scrapped the scarcity theory, Sanford also modified his views on the need to export Southern cotton. Since he projected that an influx of raw cotton would stimulate further overproduction and lower prices, he saw no reason on "grounds of humanity" for the United States to make inordinate sacrifices for this end. Moreover, he doubted that such measures would either secure the withdrawal of Europe's recognition of Southern belligerency or halt the flow of ships and contraband to the insurgents. Permitting Southerners to sell their cotton through captured ports would provide them profits easily converted into ironclads and military supplies. Instead, the North should frankly inform the Europeans that they could procure cotton only from within the "lines of our advancing armies."[14]

By the end of 1864, Sherman's irresistible advance through Georgia and Grant's entrenchment on the outskirts of Petersburg sounded the death knell of the Confederacy. Sanford took particular satisfaction in tracing Europe's gradual realization that the United States had become a formidable nation. As early as April 1863 he had noted that the resources called forth by the Union war effort were exciting "extensive comment," and Charles Rogier, the Belgian foreign minister, later expressed amazement at the North's ever-increasing strength. By January 1865 Sanford was sure this amazement had become apprehension in many quarters of Europe—an apprehension that, after disposing of the Confederacy, United States armies would be loosed on Canada or Mexico. With the end of the epic struggle, Sanford proudly reported that the United States was commonly characterized as a "great power."[15]

Events closed with a rush after April 15, 1865, when word of Richmond's fall reached Brussels. A week later Sanford basked in the glory of a torchlight parade by friendly Belgians expressing their congratulations, and in response to the "great cheers" of the crowd, he delivered a short speech from the legation balcony. His euphoria was short-lived. After a respite of only five days, the tragic news of Lincoln's assassination and the brutal attack upon Seward arrived. Sanford ascribed these horrifying acts to Confederate "plotters" and predicted that it would stimulate a "more friendly feeling towards us and the cause of the Union." Writing to Charles Sumner, he declared that he could "remember no event since the Revolution of 1848 which has so stirred up the people of every class." A month later, the close of the great American struggle was further symbolized in Brussels by the lonely departure of Ambrose Dudley Mann, Sanford's Confederate counterpart.[16]

With the war's end, Sanford's pace relaxed noticeably; by 1868 he was complaining that he had "nothing to do now. I am simply wasting a lot of money here, which in a great capital would be likely to tell in influence & that would be useful to our country."[17] Despite this disclaimer, he did have important matters to oversee, and one holdover issue especially commanded his attention. As early as March 1862 he had reported rumors that Leopold I's son-in-law, Archduke Ferdinand Maximilian, was being considered for the throne of Napoleon III's Mexican imperial venture. In September 1863, just a month after the French-sponsored Mexican regency council had offered Maximilian the crown, Sanford talked with Leopold's son, the Count of Flanders. The count professed opposition to Maximilian's accepting the Mexican throne and doubted that he would do so without English support. Sanford responded that the occupation of 800,000 square miles of Mexican territory was impossible and that the venture would inevitably fail. When Maximilian ultimately accepted Napoleon's offer in April 1864, Sanford mistakenly assured Seward that the archduke had disregarded Leopold's advice.[18]

Sanford's forecast of Maximilian's fate proved more accurate than his appraisal of Leopold's role. The king, who coveted a throne for his daughter, Charlotte, and her husband, had previously advised Maximilian to accept the Greek throne and had unsuccessfully attempted to aid him by securing a guarantee of the new Mexican monarchy from Great Britain. Once the young couple sailed for Mexico, his support was unflagging. Leopold received a Mexican minister plenipotentiary in May 1864; transferred Edouard Blondeel, Belgium's minister resident to the United States, to Mexico the following fall; directed his diplomats to assist Mexican representatives at their respective courts; and facilitated the recruitment of 1,500 Belgians for a special "Empress Guard" to fight on Maximilian's behalf. In July 1864 the Belgian minister of war ordered all his generals to aid this effort and offered a two-year leave of absence to any regular Belgian army officers who joined the guard.[19]

Sanford ably represented Seward's Mexican policy. Although refraining from threats or official protests, he articulated United States displeasure with Belgian actions. He privately informed Foreign Minister Rogier that the United States would not "protest" as a "nation" but that Americans as a "people were greatly disappointed" with Belgian connivance in this antirepublican project. He emphasized that the Belgian army's provision of furloughs for those volunteering for the Empress Guard and the boarding of these men in Belgian army barracks prior to their departure constituted direct government aid. Sanford also skillfully conveyed Seward's objection to Blondeel's returning to Washington after his mission to Mexico. Drawing on his good working relations with the Belgian court, Sanford relayed the message to Baron August Lambermont, secretary general at the Foreign Office, in a casual, unofficial visit. While expressing the American sense of displeasure, Sanford menaced neither Belgium nor Maximilian. When Maximilian's position began to deteriorate in 1866, Sanford coined a standard reply to constant queries whether the United States would move against the figurehead emperor: America had drawn the "Elephant Mexico in the lottery of 1847–8 and [was] too wise to be caught again."[20]

Confronted by subtle but increasing United States pressure, serious financial problems, stout domestic opposition, and an assertive Prussia, Napoleon III scrapped his abortive Mexican project in January 1866. As Sanford observed, "He [was] like a man with his fingers between two cogwheels in motion." Following the departure of the last French troops in March 1867 and the precipitous decline of Maximilian's fortunes, Leopold II requested Seward to intercede with the Juárez government to secure mercy for the hapless emperor.

Sanford added this appeal to similar pleas from Austria and France, but Seward's messages to Juárez were unavailing. On June 19, 1867, Maximilian died before a Mexican firing squad.[21]

Sanford's reaction to the Belgian court's official mourning period was dramatic and unorthodox. Lest he convey any impression that the United States had approved the Mexican venture, Sanford refused to adopt the appropriate mourning dress. He also boycotted a funeral service for Maximilian because the tone of the function's announcement made his "presence on this occasion impossible as implying a sort of retrospective recognition of a political status that we had ever denied." Though refusing to comply with the public display of grief, Sanford privately consoled Leopold II, and he was convinced that "we are respected none the less for holding fast to our principles."[22]

Sanford rounded out his diplomatic work by negotiating several unspectacular but nonetheless important treaties with Belgium. Secretary of State Seward placed considerable importance on securing naturalization agreements, extradition treaties, and conventions promoting trade and commerce. He found an eager and able assistant in Sanford, whose most significant negotiations involved the capitalization of the Scheldt dues. In creating Belgium in 1831, the Great Powers had authorized Holland to levy taxes on commerce on the Scheldt River as far as Antwerp, Belgium's principal port. Although these taxes were to fall proportionately on the countries using the river, Belgium promoted her commerce by temporarily assuming the entire amount. By 1861 Belgium could no longer bear this burden and had come to favor a single capital payment to Holland. This proposed capitalization was to be financed by Belgium and her trading partners, with each contributing according to its use of the river.[23]

Charles Rogier presented this proposition to Sanford in November 1861. The foreign minister noted that although the 1858 Belgian-American commercial treaty had abrogated Belgium's obligation, she had continued paying America's share of the customs. In January 1862 Belgium agreed to continue paying the dues through December 1863, but Rogier warned that without a settlement United States tonnage would become subject to both Belgian and Dutch duties.[24]

Sanford endorsed the capitalization project and repeatedly argued its merits with Seward. He contended that the United States was honor-bound to assume the payment of her Scheldt tonnage duties, and he characterized the proposal as an opportunity to cultivate the goodwill of Belgium and her influential monarch—an opportunity which could hardly be ignored given the "present condition of our affairs abroad." Seward did not share Sanford's enthusiasm for the project and emphasized that the United States could not take the lead when there was a serious doubt that the others would follow. Moreover, as the American war raged on, more pressing matters demanded Seward's attention. By December 1862 he confessed to Sanford that the question had "passed completely from my mind."[25]

After Great Britain and Belgium concluded a preliminary capitalization agreement in February 1863, Seward relented and allowed Sanford to begin negotiations with Rogier. These talks culminated in the signing on May 20 of a convention obligating the United States to contribute 2,779,200 francs ($555,811) of the 36,000,000-franc payment to Holland. Belgium agreed to pay one-third of the 36,-000,000 francs, with the remainder being divided proportionately among the other European countries. Belgium also consented to abolish all tonnage duties, to reduce pilotage duties between 20 and 30 percent, to reduce all Antwerp city duties, to allow United States vessels to transport salt on the same basis as Belgian ships, and to grant a reduction in import duties equal to those recently extended to England and France.[26]

After Belgium reached similar agreements with the remaining interested parties, a congress assembled at Brussels on July 15, 1863, to combine the individual accords into a general treaty. Although he participated actively in the deliberations, Sanford deferred to Seward's directive and the sensibilities of isolationist congressmen by refusing to sign the general treaty. Instead he concluded a second agreement with Rogier on July 20, 1863, designed to "complete the convention signed on the 20th of May 1863." This pact essentially reiterated the provisions of the prior understanding and noted the agreement of Holland and the European nations to the capitalization project.[27] Sanford's work did not elicit unanimous approval. James Shepherd Pike, United States minister to the Hague, termed the agreement a "swindle" and a device to massage Sanford's "vanity." He judged that Sanford had "sold himself and his government."[28] Although several senators agreed with Pike's assessment, both treaties were approved in February 1864.[29]

Sanford skillfully employed Belgium's desire for the Scheldt treaty to obtain a revised Belgian-American consular pact. Although he was unable to extract an understanding in 1863, he succeeded in affixing a declaration to the May 20 accord in which Belgium stated her "sincere" intention of coming to "an agreement as early as may be possible." Another five-year effort was required to gain the consular convention of December 5, 1868. Indeed, 1868 proved a productive year—as Sanford also signed a trademark convention and a naturalization treaty.[30]

The conclusion of these various negotiations in late 1868 ended Sanford's substantive activities as minister resident to Belgium. Although his Belgian duties had not been crucial to the Union's Civil War diplomacy, he had conducted America's relations with this small country in a creditable fashion. He had accurately represented Seward's views to the Brussels government while simultaneously providing the secretary with a meticulous account of Belgian political, diplomatic, and economic developments. By clearly, though unthreateningly, expressing American displeasure, he had skillfully handled the delicate Maximilian matter. Following the war, he had negotiated four very useful treaties.

The personal significance of Sanford's tenure in Belgium reached far beyond diplomatic developments. On September 21, 1864, he married Gertrude Ellen du Puy of Philadelphia in a wedding so lavish it was the talk of Paris' American community. The newlyweds were a striking couple. Now forty-three, Henry had matured into a man of solid stature, neither portly nor obese, but much stouter than the lithe bachelor who had moved so easily through European society. A mustache and full beard, chestnut like his hair, now covered his thin lips and dimpled chin; and his ever-present pince-nez sat atop his thin, rather high-bridged nose.[31]

Nearly twenty years Sanford's junior, Gertrude had, since the death of her parents, lived mostly in Europe with her aunt, Mrs. John Wurts. Blond, blue-eyed, and buxom, she was of slightly less than average height with a lovely, full face. Henry proudly described his new bride as a "blonde young lady of 23 who, to great personal attractions has all the solid ones possible, save fortune." He glowingly confided to his old friend Thurlow Weed, that she was "the very person you would have selected had I put your good taste and shrewd knowledge of human—*woman* nature, in requisition for me, the very one I have had, ideally in my mind's eye for so long!" The tributes to her beauty were legion: John Bigelow considered her "one of the most attractive women" he had ever seen; others portrayed her as the "most beautiful woman in Europe"; and a family member predicted that "many men will put on two prs. of spectacles for the benefit of Mrs. Sanford."[32]

After a brief honeymoon in Spain, during which Sanford characteristically forwarded Seward his impressions of Spanish affairs, the couple established an opulent household in Brussels. In Gertrude, Henry had found a mate who enjoyed gracious, aristocratic living as much as he, and Brussels offered a most congenial setting. Described by some contemporaries as a "Paris in miniature," Brussels offered boulevards, cafés, parks, shops, and public amusements similar to those that had so captivated Sanford's fancy in Paris. If the Park, the Allée Verte, and the Bois de Chambre were "modest" compared to the garden of the Tuileries, the Champs Elysées, and the Bois de Boulogne, so too was the relative cost of living.[33]

During the remainder of his years as minister, Henry and Gertrude maintained dual quarters at the United States legation and at "Gingelom," a rambling house in the Belgian countryside. The legation, a massive, three-story marble structure, contained several drawing rooms, a gallery, a conservatory, and a study, and was sumptuously decorated with beautiful rugs and curtains, marble statues, elegant chandeliers and paintings, and the best furniture. Surrounded by colorful gardens, Gingelom was also imposing: three stories of brick, replete with towers and spires, and similarly furnished. A staff of servants complimented these lodgings. Numbering approximately eight, it included a chef, butler, coachman, maids, gardeners, and tutors.[34]

Visitors marvelled at this elegance. Writing in the late 1860s, John A. Kasson noted:

> [I] came back by way of Brussels. Stopped for weekend with Mr. Sanford, who is my good friend. He has a beautiful wife, a beautiful house, and is a good minister, fond of the show his private fortune enables him to make.

Edwin D. Morgan resorted to even greater superlatives in arguing that Sanford had:

> ...the best house, the best furniture, the finest horses and carriage, the best servants, the best table, and perhaps I may say, the most attractive and accomplished wife of any of the United States Representatives at Foreign Courts.

Aaron Goodrich, Sanford's secretary of legation, agreed with these descriptions but drew a less optimistic and more prophetic conclusion. In commenting on a party at which Henry and Gertrude entertained over 200 guests, the old Minnesota judge warned, "It makes you Enemies, envy begets hate, and hate begets calumny, etc., etc., spend less money & you will have more friends."[35]

Amidst such finery, the remainder of the decade was a happy time for the Sanfords. Henry delighted in showering his young wife with gifts such as two "lovely black saddle horses" on their honeymoon and the replica of a cloth-top carriage Gertrude had casually admired in Paris. The newlyweds also relished the European social life. They regularly attended parties, balls, and court functions in Brussels, often traveled to fashionable resort spots, and were received by Napoleon III in Paris and Queen Victoria in London. Although their strong attachment to, and unwillingness to leave Europe would ultimately handicap Henry politically and financially, these difficulties were still in the future. As Henry admitted to his mother in 1868, "I shall probably never again spend money as I have the past few years." But he had no regrets: "I see no object in not spending half my income or the whole of it if I found pleasure in it. The position is an exceptionable one. Youth does not last forever."[36]

Material and social considerations were not the sole bases of their happiness; they were also deeply in love. Writing some years later, Henry conveyed his feelings when he assured Gertrude of his "unbounded love . . . & devotion. . . . You have all my heart . . . I am going 'full speed' . . . to get back to your arms . . ." The young bride reciprocated the sentiments of her admiring spouse: "My darling, my dashing I wonder if I fill your heart & complete your life as entirely as you do mine." Later she wrote, "But I am too hopeful & too happy to think of anything my lover but the joy & blessing it will be to feel your arms around me again & to look long into your eyes & to feel your lips everywhere!"[37]

The first product of this love, Henry Jr., arrived on July 17, 1865, gratefully welcomed, but too late to win his father's friendly wager with Charles Sumner on who would sire the first son. Six other children followed: Gertrude (1869), Frieda Delores (1871), Ethel (1873), Helen Carola Nancy (1876), Leopold C. (1880), Edwyne Wilhelmina MacKinnon (1881). A doting father, Henry delighted in slipping off early from the legation in the 1860s to play with his son in the afternoons.[38]

Sanford financed his lavish lifestyle primarily from investment income and from the proceeds of the Aves Island prosecution. Aves yielded over $140,000 in 1864, and several of his stock holdings provided consistently high dividends through the 1860s. The most profitable of Sanford's investments was in the Wheeler and Wilson sewing machine company. From 1863 through 1869, Wheeler and Wilson paid more than $15,000 annually on average dividends of over 60 percent. Together with his Uncle Edward N. Shelton he owned the largest block of stock in Scoville Manufacturing Company, which produced parts for Wheeler and Wilson and also declared 75 percent dividends in the mid-1860s. In 1863 Uncle Ed steered Henry into the Jackson Iron and Steel Works and more 70-percent dividends.[39]

Sanford augmented these resources by continuing his father's practice of speculating in western American lands. Retaining agents in Michigan, Illinois, Indiana, and Ohio, he usually purchased tracts from the United States government but occasionally worked through land companies or acquired property at tax sales. Returns from the sale of the lands averaged near $5,865 per year from 1863 through 1867, and in 1872 he extravagantly valued his remaining 4,814 acres at $60,800. When combined with his stock profits, these proceeds provided Sanford an annual income of approximately $25,000 in addition to his $7,500 yearly salary as minister and the money from the Aves settlement.[40]

Sanford's net income would have been much greater had he confined his investments to solid industrial stocks. Unfortunately, he became involved in several other decidedly less remunerative ventures. In fact, his tendency toward speculative undertakings in less developed areas of the country forecast a pattern that ultimately led to his financial downfall. From 1864 through 1869, he put at least $27,000 into various mining operations; these included $6,000 into a Minnesota coal mine, $10,350 into the Consolidation Coal Company of western Maryland, $8,000 into an Arkansas zinc company, and approximately $3,500 into a Nevada silver mine. With the possible exception of Consolidation Coal, none of these companies proved profitable.[41]

Beginning in the mid-1860s, Sanford also purchased an interest in a number of European inventions which he attempted to patent and market in the United States. The first of these was a frame for spinning wool. Working with his Uncle Philo S. Shelton, who had a long-standing interest in patent schemes, Sanford secured a trial at the Lowell Manufacturing Company. The test demonstrated that the device would spin only worsted wool and that the thread produced was "very fuzzy" and not the "smooth perfect" fiber expected. Although Shelton promoted the spinner over the next seven years, he was understandably unsuccessful.[42]

Sanford's special box for lubricating the axles of railroad cars with water yielded similar results. Sanford and his American agent, Alex Trippel, contended that the gadget operated with *"decidedly less friction* than *oil or grease,"* but a trial on the Erie Railroad in 1867–68 revealed that the boxes could not stand the pounding of America's rough roads.[43] Trippel also served as Sanford's agent for the introduction of a supplementary railroad locomotive tender. Attached to auxiliary cylinders and engines or onto the regular locomotive tender, this appliance was supposed to conserve wasted power and thereby reduce the train's operating costs. In reply to Trippel's inquiries, American railroad officials unanimously rejected the tender as unnecessary, complicated, and too expensive. When it became apparent that he would have to finance the entire $12,000 to $13,000 construction cost of a trial model, Sanford abandoned the scheme.[44]

His final patent, an "Analyseur" for removing the "injurious constituents" from "bad flavored alcoholic liquids" and redistilling inexpensive whiskey into a higher grade intoxicant, suffered a fate like that of the lubricating box and the locomotive tender. Before constructing the still in Brooklyn and commencing operations in December 1867, Trippel projected profits of $40 per day. The would-be whiskey magnates discovered how optimistic this figure was when they encountered a succession of crippling misfortunes: harassment by corrupt revenue agents, machinery malfunctions, burglaries, a fire in October 1868, and the still's failure to operate as anticipated. Altogether, the loom, analyseur, lubricating box, and locomotive tender cost Sanford at least $25,000.[45]

Western railroad investments led to still greater losses. Sanford had speculated heavily in Illinois Central stock during the late 1850s and early 1860s, losing at least $5,000. Even more devastating was his association with the Lake Superior and Mississippi and the Northern Pacific railroad companies. In 1864 he invested $24,700 in the Lake Superior and Mississippi line, for which he received $38,000 in second mortgage bonds. In order to run their 140-mile road north from St. Paul to Duluth, the Minnesota incorporators needed to deposit $20,000 with the state legislature by June 15, 1865, and grade the first 20 miles of the route by December 1865. The first step would secure a congressional land grant of alternate sections along the line, and the second would obtain a $250,000 bonus from the city of St. Paul.[46]

William L. Banning, the president of the road, made the $20,000 deposit but was unable to raise the funds to continue the grading. In June 1865 he turned to Sanford. Although fearful there was "some nigger in the woodpile [that] I don't see," Sanford felt compelled to protect his initial investment. On June 2 he offered to advance another $20,000 in government bonds on the condition that he would become president of the road and be able to name four of the seven directors.[47]

Banning accepted the $20,000 but then ignored Sanford's stipulations. When Sanford protested, Banning denied having received the letter containing Sanford's version of the contract; and David Stewart, a fellow investor through whom Sanford had sent the letter, was unable to remember the particulars. Stewart cut to the heart of the matter and forecast Sanford's subsequent frustrations with transatlantic management when he wrote, "The whole difficulty about this matter seems to be that you wanted to manage and control the road without being here to attend to it." Sanford considered legal proceedings but feared that a suit would only threaten the company's charter without yielding any monetary satisfaction.[48]

The company languished until early 1868, when a Philadelphia group led by Jay Cooke, J. Edgar Thompson, and Thomas Scott, took control. In the ensuing settlement, Sanford received $10,000 in full paid stock for his 1865 advance of $20,000 in government bonds; approximately $5,400 in interest payments; another $60,000 in stock from the settlement of debts owed him by Charles H. Oakes, one of the road's founders; and an option to purchase an additional $29,500 in bonds at $85 per bond.[49] Sanford exercised this option in June 1869 and then sold the bonds back to Cooke at $92.50 per bond for a profit of $2,212. He sold forty-five more bonds in September 1869. As late as 1870 he retained $165,000 in stock, but he sold his final $38,000 in bonds the following year. When Jay Cooke expanded his interests to the Northern Pacific, Sanford followed. He was among Cooke's original pool of investors in the latter road, subscribing for $35,000. Although it is impossible to determine precisely the size of Sanford's investment in these two roads, when the panic of 1873 drove them into receivership, he undoubtedly lost heavily.[50]

The mining ventures, patent schemes, and railroad speculations were more characteristic of Sanford's subsequent business endeavors than were his solid investments in Wheeler and Wilson or Scoville. Although Sanford had long dealt with shrewd businessmen and had been manipulating capital since the 1840s, he never acquired the systematic business training or savvy that might have come from immersing himself in the management of a single enterprise. Unlike John D. Rockefeller or Andrew Carnegie, or even his Uncle Ed, he had never served his apprenticeship. As a result, he grasped at flashy, faddish, "get-rich-quick" opportunities, became involved in too many ventures simultaneously, and failed to give sufficient personal attention to his investments.

While serving in Belgium, Sanford persistently sought to secure a more prestigious diplomatic post. His efforts were two-pronged: to have the status of the Belgian mission elevated or preferably to succeed William L. Dayton as minister to France. Harboring a profound sense of his own worth, Sanford considered his status as minister resident to Belgium both demeaning and annoying. In November 1863 he complained to Seward that this rank was "obsolete" and utilized only by "little states" to avoid the expense of a full mission. Not only was this grade inconsistent with the "dignity and position among nations of a great power like the United States," but it also forced him to follow ludicrously behind the full ministers from minor Latin American republics and German duchies and prevented his working on an equal footing with the representatives of more important nations. Even on "festive occasions the right to be in immediate proximity to a high official of the Government" was of no "trifling advantage." Moreover, he argued, both "courtesy" and "expediency" dictated elevation of the mission. Belgium's full mission in Washington invited reciprocity, and this step would encourage "cordiality" between the two countries by serving as a "token of respect" for Leopold I. To bolster his cause, Sanford requested Thurlow Weed and Senator Henry B. Anthony of Rhode Island to intercede with Seward.[51]

Anthony took Sanford's case to the powerful Charles Sumner, chairman of the Senate Committee on Foreign Relations. On March 14, 1864, the Massachusetts senator attached an amendment to the annual consular and diplomatic appropriations bill calling for the Belgian mission's elevation. Endorsed by both the Foreign Relations Committee and the State Department, Sumner's amendment would have upgraded the mission one step to envoy extraordinary and minister plenipotentiary, although retaining the $7,500 salary Sanford received as minister resident. With support from Anthony and Connecticut Senator Lafayette S. Foster, Sumner forcefully reiterated Sanford's contentions and emphasized Leopold's position in Europe.[52]

William P. Fessenden, chairman of the Committee on Finance, led the opposition. While professing a high regard for Sanford as "a gentleman, a scholar, and a diplomat," Fessenden refused to "raise a place from one grade to another merely for his accomodation. . . . I believe it is a mere matter for the gratification of the minister." He predicted that this measure would set an undesirable precedent for raising the missions to other secondary powers, such as Switzerland and Holland. John P. Hale of New Hampshire agreed and suggested that far from elevating the mission to Belgium, there was "no public want for any minister there" at all. Overcoming this opposition, Sumner steered the amendment through the Senate by a vote of twenty-one to eighteen. The measure found no champion of Sumner's stature in the House; instead, it drew the ire of Thaddeus Stevens, who defeated the amendment from his position as chairman of the House Ways and Means Committee.[53]

Sanford's abortive attempt at upgrading his mission elicited numerous vitriolic newspaper attacks. The Democratic *New York World* applauded the amendment's defeat and flailed the "carpetbag diplomat" for his trips through Europe and his returns to the United States on leaves of absence in 1862 and 1864. The earlier trip had led him through Venezuela on his continuing prosecution of the Aves claim, and the *World* speculated that his return route in 1864 might be "by way of San Francisco, Bering's Straits, Kamchatka, the Amoor, Ural Moutains, and St. Petersburg." Turning from sarcasm to serious accusations, the *World* charged him with profiteering in his purchases of arms and saltpeter for the Union.[54]

Incensed at these "malignant attacks," Sanford decided that they were "inspired" by Charles Eames and "circulated" by Adam Gurowski. He was probably correct. While prosecuting the Aves claim in the 1850s, Sanford had criticized and threatened Eames, then United States minister to Venezuela, for bungling the case and collaborating with a rival claimant. Gurowski, a Polish expatriate and one of the most caustic men in an age famed for personal invective, was a close friend of the Eames family. The Polish count had treated Sanford roughly in his recently published *Diary* and had referred specifically to the purchase of military supplies:

What a devoted patriot this Sanford in Belgium is; he has continual *itchings in his hand* to pay a *higher price* for bad blankets that they might not fall into the hands of the secesh [*sic*] agents; so with cloth, so perhaps with arms. *Oh, disinterested patriot!*

From this thinly veiled charge it was only a short distance to the *World's* explicit allegations. Gurowski also had strong ties to the radical wing of the Republican party and was a confidant of Senator Fessenden. When Sumner introduced his amendment, Gurowski called upon Fessenden to block it and to spread the "truth" about Sanford. Fessenden's emergence as the leader of the opposition was hardly coincidental.[55]

Although maligned and defeated in 1864, Sanford did not abandon his elevation scheme. He repeatedly promoted the issue with Seward and maintained his contacts with Weed, Anthony, and Sumner. His persistence promised dividends in March 1867 when Seward and Sumner renewed their campaign to upgrade the mission. Though Sumner was confident of victory, the Senate, meeting in executive session, rejected the proposal. Opposition to the measure again rested ostensibly on "public grounds"; but William Hunter, the second assistant secretary of state, informed Sanford that "many of the Senators have been crammed with objections to the measure by your personal enemies, such as Eames, Pike, and [George C.] Fogg."[56] Sanford's politics also hurt him. With a growing breach in the Republican party and hostility between Congress and the Johnson administration, Sanford's public support for the president, adovacy of leniency for the South, and hostility toward the "nigger," further undermined his position. His close association with Seward, Weed, and the conservative wing of the party was no longer the asset it had been earlier in the decade, and this defeat was only one of several rebuffs dealt Seward by the Senate in the spring of 1867.[57]

Sanford also explored other avenues for advancement. On December 1, 1864, William L. Dayton, the American minister to France, died suddenly. Sanford had long looked enviously at the Paris post and had consistently tried to upstage his older colleague, whom he considered a timid, ineffectual diplomat. In a remarkable note to Seward, he aggressively solicited the position:

It is possible that you may have thought of me to fill up the gap here [Paris] for a time. . . . Your desire to have me keep up and extend my social and political relations here since you first sent me out, has led me to this, perhaps, presumptuous opinion that you wished to be prepared for some such emergency as this one, so that no serious break should occur in the Gov't here. I am, therefore, emboldened to write to you on the subject, not however, without doing violence to my sense of delicacy, to say, that as far as concerns myself I am entirely at your orders & I think I could, at this juncture render the Gov't real service here.[58]

Sanford once more enlisted the aid of Weed, Foster, and Anthony. Weed, Seward's oldest and closest political associate, interceded with the secretary. He proposed that Seward transfer Sanford to France and replace him with John Bigelow, then serving as consul general in Paris. Though tempted to appoint Sanford, Seward opted for Bigelow, first making him chargé and later elevating him to minister. As he explained to the disappointed Sanford, "What was done in regard to the French legation was not only the easiest but the best that could be done, and it is universally satisfactory here."[59] Sanford would ruefully discover over the ensuing twenty-five years that he could no longer muster the political capital necessary to secure another diplomatic mission.

This became even more apparent with the election of Ulysses S. Grant in November 1868. Despite a liberal contribution of $500 to the Republican canvass, Sanford anxiously observed: "It has seemed to me that the time might come when my long experience abroad might be needed in a wider field, but now I am not certain that my place here may not be required of me by the winners." Although none of his friends could alleviate the anxiety by providing advance word on Grant's "attitude toward personnel," Sanford took solace in his impressive support. Both Sumner and Anthony lobbied Hamilton Fish, the new secretary of state, and Sumner went directly to President Grant. Within the state department, Bancroft Davis and William Hunter, the first and second assistant secretaries of state, respectively, were Sanford's allies. By April these supporters had converted Secretary Fish, and Anthony enthusiastically informed Sanford that it would be "one of the strangest things of this strange administration if you were disturbed."[60]

Anthony soon learned otherwise when Grant arrived in Washington determined to replace Sanford with J. Russell Jones. Characterized by Oliver P. Morton as "about the most elegant gentleman that ever presided over a livery stable," Jones was the uncle of Grant's private secretary, Orville E. Babcock, and a personal favorite of the president. When Fish took office, he found that Grant and Elihu B. Washburne, who served briefly as secretary of state before becoming minister to France, had already designated Jones as minister resident to Belgium. After seeking unsuccessfully to reverse this decision, Fish persuaded Grant to transfer Sanford to Spain.[61]

The press denounced Sanford's nomination. Disparaging him as the "poet of clothes," his old nemesis, the *New York World* declared Sanford "the worst selection that could be made for so critical a post." As minister to Belgium, he had "put his nose into Russia, his voice into England, his clothes into Italy, and his foot into it generally." Even the *New York Times,* which had been consistently friendly to Sanford, feared that "neither his abilities nor his training qualify him so well for the more serious and important services" as minister to Madrid.[62]

The Senate killed the nomination. Both Sumner and Anthony fought valiantly, but the opposition was too great. Sanford's long absence from the country and his lack of strong, geographically based political connections proved fatal. Hostile Republicans, including Cameron, Fessenden, and William A. Buckingham of Connecticut, argued that he was only "half a Republican, that his views [were] at best doubtful." Referring to the split in the Republican party, Buckingham declared Sanford's "radicalism . . . as doubtful as his militia-commission." Others ignored political or diplomatic criteria and attacked Sanford's personal behavior. He was, they asserted, a "snob." Without presidential support, conspicuous by its absence, there was no hope; on April 23, 1869, the Senate tabled Sanford's nomination by a vote of thirty to twenty.[63]

With his nomination defeated and Grant still determined to send Jones to Brussels, Sanford resigned on May 19. His bitterness was evident as he thanked Sumner for his efforts:

I have been, perhaps too careless about ingratiating myself with the public press. I felt that if I was to succeed in a career which I had undertaken, it would not be by newspaper puffings, but by *results* . . . and that the time would come when that experience and devotion to duty would find its reward in promotion.

Alas, he concluded, he had paid too little heed to the "malicious and envious!" In fact Sanford was not so oblivious to public appearances. Even as he wrote to Sumner, he was requesting Henry T. Tuckerman, a journalist, and William Hunter, second assistant secretary of state, to provide an "epitaph strewing a few flowers on my official grave."[64]

Stripped of his diplomatic post, Sanford turned most of his attention after 1869 to diverse investments stretching from Florida to the Congo basin. Although his financial well-being depended on these business ventures, he and Gertrude continued to live in Brussels, and the diplomatic service remained his first love. He desired "an opportunity to *do* something to gain a solid reputation," to leave his mark on history. Experienced, linguistically talented, and intimately acquainted with Europe, he correctly considered himself more qualified than the great majority of American representatives abroad. As he confided to Seward: "I ache—sometimes to be in harness when I see how our power and influence are wasted—or thrown away or belittled by some of the insignificant ignoramuses" to whom it is entrusted. This longing for historical reputation was reinforced by attacks on his character. After 1869 Sanford sought another ministerial appointment as a rebuttal of the newspaper "absurdities" and a "vindication" of his integrity.[65] Despite his abilities and aspirations, it was Sanford's misfortune to seek a long-term diplomatic career prior to the establishment of a professional foreign service. Through the remainder of the nineteenth century, political influence remained the key to all diplomatic appointments, and Sanford's lack of this influence denied him the major post he so doggedly sought.

CHAPTER 5

INVESTING IN THE NEW SOUTH, 1867–1879

IN APRIL 1866 Sanford's old friend William E. Curtis observed, "It is my impression that emigration & capital are moving South." Disillusioned by his experiences with the Minnesota railroad and other northern mining projects, Sanford agreed. Three years later he informed his Uncle Edward N. Shelton that he too favored "moving Southward for investments."[1] As the 1860s drew to a close, he sought to capitalize on depressed southern land values by shifting his primary investments from industrial and railroad stocks to southern real estate and plantation ventures. He joined a growing throng of Northerners who looked to the South as a new "frontier," an area ripe for burgeoning profits. To Sanford's chagrin, this reorientation ultimately led to his financial ruin.

Like most Yankees who moved south following the Civil War, Sanford faced the charge of being a "carpetbagger." By either contemporary or historical standards this epithet was undeserved. Contemporary Southerners regarded carpetbaggers as those who manipulated black voters, incited racial tensions, and profited from political office. Although Sanford eventually took an active interest in Florida politics in the early 1880s, he was guilty of none of the other offenses and had not moved south for "office sake." Since political activity was the essential contemporary criterion, it is difficult to "justify" the term " 'economic carpetbaggers' . . . on a historical basis."[2] Even if one accepts this ahistorical terminology, Sanford again fares rather well. To be sure, he invested in Louisiana and Florida for personal gain, but in so doing he became an active participant in Florida's "Era of the Developers" and ranks with Henry B. Plant and Henry M. Flagler as a major contributor to Florida's late-nineteenth-century economic growth. Neither Sanford's input nor his profits matched those of the better-known capitalists; however, his contributions to the emerging citrus industry led the pro-Southern, Dunningite historians, George Winston Smith and T. Frederick Davis, to praise his work and the closest student of Florida's citrus developments, Jerry W. Weeks, to characterize him as the "founder" of the industry.[3] The long-range Northern influence in Florida was economic rather than political,[4] and Sanford was in the vanguard.

Sanford began "*reconstruction* after [his] own manner" in January 1868 by renting Barnwell Island, a sea-island cotton plantation in Prince William Parish near Beaufort, South Carolina. The plantation belonged to William H. Trescot, a former assistant secretary of state, whom Sanford had met during the 1850s. Sanford agreed to a three-year lease obligating him to pay Trescot $1,000 per year rent, operating costs up to $10,000, and 10 percent of the net proceeds. Trescot agreed to provide "general supervision" equivalent to his former role of resident planter and to retain a "competent overseer." He promptly hired Middleton Stuart as overseer and contracted to pay him and his assistant a combined salary of $1,600 per year.[5]

This investment placed Sanford in the company of between 20,000 and 50,000 northerners who tried cotton planting between 1862 and 1876. He shared several characteristics with the "typical" northern planter. Like the majority, he had a business and professional background and was interested primarily in speculation. He also differed from his transplanted contemporaries in significant ways. At forty-five, he was twelve years older than the average, and unlike a sizeable minority, he had no interest either in aiding blacks or leading a simpler life. Finally, he came on the scene later than most northern planters, who had gone south between the fall of 1865 and the summer of 1866.[6]

Sanford chose an inauspicious time to launch his venture. Cotton prices had plummeted in 1867, and the costs of operating a plantation were double those of 1860. Specific difficulties at Barnwell compounded the impact of these general trends. A cold, wet spring, combined with the fact that the plantation had not been cultivated since 1861, impeded progress. Periodic uncertainty over the labor supply of newly-freed blacks further complicated matters. Trescot reported that, although there had been efforts in February to prevent workers from signing on at the "Yankee" plantation, "good rations" and "prompt payment" of wages had remedied the problem. In April a Freedmen's Bureau program for supplying rations to all owners of ten-acre plots threatened to draw labor away. Trescot quickly moved to block potential defections by persuading the bureau agent in Beaufort to withhold rations from those leaving Barnwell.[7]

Despite these difficulties, Trescot and Stuart planted 150 acres of cotton, 70 acres of corn, 20 acres of peanuts, and 10 acres of potatoes. Trescot pronounced the work "thoroughly well done," and on July 15 he declared that he had never seen a "more magnificent crop of cotton." Exuding optimism, he predicted the cotton would gross $21,000 and provide Sanford a $10,000 net profit. Only one thing, Trescot concluded, could prevent this handsome gain—caterpillars. When the furry creatures appeared during the fall and destroyed the crops, Sanford lost at least $11,000.[8]

Against the sage advice of his Uncle Edward, Sanford renewed his lease for 1869. Trescot assured him that the year's work would reduce expenses and that the disasters of the two preceding seasons would raise cotton prices. Trescot and a new overseer, James Patterson, planted 150 acres of cotton and 25 acres of corn, and the crop again looked promising until the caterpillars ravaged at least half of it. Patterson reported in October 1869 that he hoped to salvage forty bales; Sanford's losses were decidedly less than the previous year, but losses nevertheless.[9]

After a third year of losses in 1870, Sanford abandoned his venture in cotton planting; this brief experience had revealed patterns that would characterize his subsequent "New South" investments. First, he had undertaken a high risk investment in a tumultuous region with an uncertain labor supply. Second, he did not personally manage the plantation, but entrusted it to Trescot; and when the enterprise began to sour, he alienated this agent. In May 1868 Sanford complained about the limited acreage planted. He later chastized Trescot for keeping inadequate accounts, for failing to return a $450 personal advance, for claiming expenses for the 600-mile trips from his home to Barnwell each month, and for assigning the crop to Fraser and Dill, Charleston factors. Trescot countered that he had never before kept accounts; that since he was receiving no compensation for his managerial role he could not be expected to finance his journeys to Barnwell; and that it had been necessary to retain Fraser and Dill to ensure credit for working the 1869 crop. His most telling rejoinder concerned Sanford's tendency to manage from afar: "I will give you only one piece of advice. Select your agent but let him manage the estate here according to his judgment on the spot. You cannot safely direct it so far away."[10] Sanford's agents would repeatedly echo this refrain over the next twenty years.

Even before abandoning his cotton investment, Sanford had turned to a second, ultimately more costly experiment in sugar planting. In January 1869 he and his brother-in-law, Samuel B. Rogers, purchased Oakley Plantation in Iberville Parish, Louisiana, for $24,-000 and $1,000 in legal fees. Located ninety miles above New Orleans on the Mississippi River, Oakley contained 500 acres (125 of which were woodland,) a dwelling house, carriage house, brick sugar house, ten cabins, corn crib, stable, and sixty mules. Rogers, the president of Columbia Steam Sugar Refinery in Philadelphia, selected the property and dispatched William Harrah, a trusted acquaintance, to organize the planting.[11]

Both Sanford and Rogers envisioned spectacular profits. Oakley had allegedly yielded 350 hogsheads of sugar annually before the war, and the novice planters anticipated similar prospects. Sanford considered sugar planting especially opportune given the Cuban rebellion against Spain. With the Cuban sugar supply disrupted, he planned to run the plantation at a cost of $10,000 per year, garner "large returns," and then sell the property and "transfer the capital to Cuba." Referring to the Barnwell Island debacle, Rogers asserted that sugar, unlike cotton, was "nearly always sure," and by October 1869 he was predicting a crop of 300 hogsheads worth $50,000.[12] Naively accepting Rogers' judgments, Sanford reiterated them to William H. Seward: "I have made a 'ten strike' in my sugar plantation—could sell out today for double its cost & if all goes on as now for a couple of years will give it back twice yearly."[13]

Soon after purchasing Oakley, Sanford joined Rogers in another sugar-related endeavor. At Rogers' behest, Sanford invested $25,000 in the Keystone Sugar Refinery, a Philadelphia concern. Keystone returned small profits during the summer of 1869 but closed in September 1870, after several months of losses. Sanford and Rogers lost their capital, and Rogers was left virtually bankrupt when his Columbia Refinery burned the same month. Rogers' misfortune also dealt Sanford a grievous blow; in addition to losing $25,000 he was left to bear the operating cost of Oakley alone.[14]

Over the first half of the 1870s these costs proved quite burdensome. With Sanford's consent, Rogers purchased three adjoining tracts at a total cost of $22,000. State, parish, and local taxes averaged more than $1,000 per year; annual outlays for labor, rations, and overseers ran between $4,500 and $5,000; and factorage and other marketing fees added another $1,500 to $2,500. Maintaining the sugar house machinery further strained Sanford's resources. Rogers had originally judged this equipment to be in good condition and estimated it would require no major repairs for at least two years; however, by June 1870 he had called on Sanford for $1085 for a new boiler and $600 for other maintenance. In May 1872 Rogers bought a $2,500 vacuum pan designed to improve the quality of their refined sugar, and the following October another $425 went for replacement tanks. Other miscellaneous expenses added to the debit side of the ledger: new mules, the essential beasts of burden, cost over $100 per year, and the establishment of a saw mill and store buildings added unanticipated expenditures. All told, yearly expenses undoubtedly exceeded $10,000. By March 1875 Sanford had sunk more than $69,000 in Oakley, and Rogers owed him $27,600.[15]

Following his setbacks at the Columbia and Keystone refineries in 1870, Rogers devoted increasing attention to Oakley. Seeking not only to save himself financially but also to repay Sanford's losses and loans, he spent all of 1871, 1872, 1874 and 1875 at Oakley and went south for the grinding seasons in 1870, 1873, and 1876. Rogers had chosen an inauspicious time to learn the trade of sugar planting. The ravages of war had brought Louisiana's sugar industry to the "brink of extinction"; sugar property had declined in value from $200 million in 1861 to little more than $25 million in 1865, and the 1862 output was not equalled until 1893. Labor costs, seed cane scarcities, high interest rates, rising costs for provisions and equipment, short crops in 1872 and 1873, flooding in 1874, and steadily declining sugar prices made the early 1870s a disastrous period for Louisiana planters.

Rogers lacked both the experience and managerial ability to cope with these difficulties. This, together with wishful thinking, led him consistently to underestimate expenses and overestimate profits. His predictions were encouraging: for 1870, 300 hogsheads worth at least $50,000; for 1871, 250 hogsheads worth $25,000 in sugar and $10,-000 in molasses; for 1872, 250 to 400 hogsheads; for 1875, a crop grossing $25,000 to $30,000. The yields never matched these projections: for 1870, a gross of $11,092; for 1871, 180 hogsheads; for 1872,

75 hogsheads; for 1873, 76 hogsheads and 103 barrels of molasses; for 1874, 75 to 80 hogsheads; and for 1875, 125 to 145 hogsheads. Calculating a hogshead at roughly one thousand pounds and the average price of sugar at no more than ten cents per pound, Oakley would have grossed around $18,000 in 1871 and an average of $8,750 over the next four years. Rogers supplemented some crops by refining sugar for neighboring planters, but this added only $2,000 in 1873, $1,000 in 1874 and $2,200 in 1875. Not until 1876 did the plantation render a sizable gross return of $36,616.[16]

Ironically, this brief glimmer of hope broke off Sanford's partnership with Rogers; the prospect of the first substantial profits in five years brought veiled tensions and hostilities into the open. Sanford had previously complained about his sacrifices in financing Oakley and about Rogers' inability to estimate expenses accurately, and in 1874 Rogers had surrendered a third of his share (or one–sixth of the whole) as compensation for Sanford's $17,500 in advances. Frustrated by economic failures and anxious over his wife's poor health, Rogers grew tired of Sanford's repeated criticisms. In July 1876 he bristled at Sanford's "orders" and continued: "Not another word about those advances. I think the sacrifices I have made & work done to save, protect, & bring out your property fully compensate for them." Sanford was unmoved; he denounced Rogers' offer to purchase his share of Oakley for approximately $22,000 as rank "speculation" and unfairly charged his partner with irresponsibility and deception: "You must or ought to have known in going into it, that you had not the means to carry it on & ought not to have involved me, who trusted entirely to you & your professed ability, into carrying this heavy & unexpected load for both."[17] Working covertly through Richard Millikin, Oakley's New Orleans factor, Sanford unsuccessfully attempted to retain all the profits from the 1876 crop as partial compensation for Rogers' debt of $27,600. Rogers accused Sanford of "breach of trust" and talked bravely of his refusal to be "frightened or bullied," but he had no financial leverage. As a result, Sanford forced him out of the partnership, taking his half of the plantation in return for the "accumulated debts."[18]

Beginning in February 1877, Sanford entrusted the management of Oakley to Milo L. Williams, his long-time Michigan land agent. Knowing even less about sugar planting than Rogers, Williams fared no better. Oakley grossed more than $14,000 on 132 hogsheads of sugar and 266 barrels of molasses in 1877 but lost at least $2,000. Prospects brightened briefly in 1878 with a $7,500 profit on 209 hogsheads; however, 1879 again illustrated the uncertainties of sugar planting. A cold winter and improper drainage destroyed much of the fall planting and stubble cane, and a September storm blew down a large portion of the crop and badly damaged the sugar house. Williams harvested only 87 hogsheads, and the year's work resulted in a $5,000 deficit.[19]

Sanford made only one trip to Oakley during the period of Williams' tenure. Terming his stay in late 1878 "most dreary," he found the weather terrible and the house cold and dilapidated. In evaluating the personnel, he judged Williams "faithful and honest," the overseer "a burly reckless incompetent man," and the black workers "a wretched lot generally." After several days of "squabbles" with the blacks over wages and painful scrutiny of the payrolls, he sighed in departing, "I have done Oakley & I have no care to see it ever again."[20]

Given his dismal first decade of sugar planting, Sanford's reaction was hardly surprising. Only in 1876 and 1878 had Oakley yielded a cumulative profit of approximately $20,000. In contrast to these meager returns, Sanford had invested at least $75,000, and when combined with the Keystone debacle, he had lost close to $80,000. Although he optimistically claimed Oakley's value at more than $140,000, these assets were not liquid, and he was unable to extract his capital.[21]

The situation remained essentially unchanged during the 1880s; Oakley continued to be a financial albatross. Unpredicitable and inclement weather took its toll: rain and frost injured the stubble cane in 1881, and flooding claimed 180 acres of cane, 50 acres of corn, and 30 acres of rice the following year. Managerial problems also persisted. Plagued by poor health, limited knowledge of sugar growing, and an inability to deal with blacks, Williams was barely adequate. He left abruptly in June 1883, appointing John F. Dupuy in his stead. Dupuy stayed until February 1884, departed without cause, and sued Sanford for a full year's pay of $1,835. In desperation, Sanford turned to B. Maes, a Belgian, who had been working at Oakley as a bookkeeper and store manager. Maes was an "excellent storekeeper and good at the books," but he was incapable of managing the overall operation. Unexpected expenses further emptied Sanford's coffers. Old mortgages, which had been unpaid and undiscovered at the time of Oakley's purchase, required more than $5,000, and another $5,000 went for repairs to the sugar house in 1883.[22]

Burdened by these difficulties and a lack of capital, Sanford had no real prospect of recouping his investment. Although he experimented with rice planting after 1882 and even derived a substantial profit from that portion of the plantation in 1883, this new crop produced no ongoing reversal of his fortunes. In "good" years, such as 1880, 1883, 1885, and 1887, he broke even; in bad ones, such as 1881, 1882, and 1886, he probably lost between $5,000 and $10,000 annually. Following the 1886 season, he discontinued planting and parceled out the land to sharecroppers. He assured Gertrude that this was a much safer approach; although he might not "make much money," neither would he "lose much if any." But even this step failed to halt the drain on his resources. In 1888 he spent another $5,000 on the sugar house to fulfill his commitment to grind his tenants' cane. While he had hoped that these improvements would make the plantation more marketable, this too proved illusionary. That he owed Maes nearly $6,500 in back wages and other advances by 1889 clearly indicated Oakley's unprofitable operation during the 1880s. Desperate for income, Sanford sold Oakley in 1889 for the paltry sum of $20,000.[23]

Just as with his Barnwell venture, Sanford had chosen an inopportune time and place to try his hand at agriculture. Sugar grows best under very specific conditions: a temperature near 75° for the entire year, much sunshine, no freezes, fertile, well-drained soil, and sixty inches of rainfall annually. As evidenced by the freezes and drainage problems, Oakley (and southern Louisiana) did not consistently provide these conditions. Late-nineteenth-century sugar culture was, therefore, a marginal and unpredictable undertaking. The decade of the 1870s had been one of recovery and transition, with planters experiencing their most trying times in 1872, 1873 and 1874, the very years Sanford began cultivating Oakley. By the end of the century, technological advances, better seed cane selection, improved drainage techniques, and new implements and processing methods offered the possibility of consistent profits. But these changes came too late to benefit Sanford, who had lost roughly $100,000 on this ill-advised investment.[24]

Although Barnwell and Oakley were characteristic of Sanford's postwar southern investments, his most important activities and most lasting contributions came in Florida. In 1870 he purchased 12,547 acres of raw land in Orange County. During the next twenty years he actively promoted and publicized the state, founded the town bearing his name, and advanced the development of central Florida. Most significantly, by importing numerous varieties of citrus and experimenting extensively at his Belair grove he became the "founder" of Florida's modern citrus industry.[25] While these achievements far outstripped his work in South Carolina and Louisiana, the financial returns were similar. Once again he lost vast sums.

As had been the case with Barnwell and Oakley, the prospect of huge profits attracted Sanford to Florida. By the late 1860s Florida was becoming the "most advertised state" in the Union.[26] A wide variety of travelers' accounts and promotional literature loudly trumpeted Florida's climate, cheap land and labor, and potential for citrus culture. "Orange fever," the exaggerated expectation of citrus profits, infected Sanford and innumerable others during the last thirty years of the century. Writing in 1882, James H. Foss typified their enthusiasm: "There is not at present any pursuit, where the tilling of the soil is involved, that will yield larger returns with less fluctuation." J. O. Matthews agreed so strongly that he guaranteed prospective investors in his Florida Orange Grove Company that the value of their shares would "increase at the rate of 100 percent annually."[27]

Sanford initiated his Florida speculations in 1867 by purchasing a St. Augustine grove containing fifty trees and a small house. Two years were required to perfect the title, which was finally transferred in April 1869.[28] After his resignation as minister resident to Belgium, Henry and Gertrude traveled to Florida in February 1870 to inspect their new purchase.[29] They found a southern frontier, a "wild and new State" with fewer than 200,000 people scattered over 60,000 square miles. Florida had no colleges or universities, no public library of 10,000 volumes, and only twenty-three newspapers and periodicals. Candid travelers often complained of the scarcity of "good milk and butter," and one particularly disgruntled northerner characterized "wholesome and well-cooked food" as the "choicest and rarest of blessings in Florida." Jacksonville, the most common destination of tourists and travelers, was described as a "flourishing little city" and a "Northern City in a Southern latitude"; but it had only 6,000 inhabitants, and its eight principal sand streets wandered off into pine woods or palmetto scrub.[30]

Following the usual tourist route, the Sanfords landed at Jacksonville and set off up the St. Johns River by steamboat. Six hours and

100 miles south of Jacksonville, they arrived at Palatka. With a population of 500, two large hotels, and eight stores, Palatka offered comfortable accommodations, but it was infested with the "most wickedest" fleas. Before departing Palatka, the dividing point between the "lower" and "upper" St. Johns, Sanford undoubtedly scrutinized H. L. Hart's flourishing 500 tree orange grove.[31]

Steaming south toward Lake Monroe, another 100 miles below Jacksonville and the head of steamboat travel on the St. Johns, they entered a land of semitropical beauty and fascination. The river's low banks were covered with lush vegetation: cypress, maple, pine, water oaks, and palmetto draped with moss and wild jasmine. Complementing this engaging scene were occasional lagoons and floating islands and scores of ducks, curlews, cygnets, and herons. Like most male tourists, Henry "amused himself shooting" alligators from the deck of the steamer. The area around Lake Monroe was even wilder and more thinly inhabited than that near Palatka. On the western shore stood Mellonville, with a wharf, a small warehouse, and one humble dwelling. Enterprise, on the eastern shore, had a half-dozen more buildings and a hotel.[32] Captivated by the region's beauty and climate, Sanford was convinced that the strategic location at the southernmost point of navigation on the St. Johns and the potential for citrus growing made the land around Lake Monroe a lucrative investment.

In May 1870 Sanford purchased 12,547.15 acres from Joseph Finegan for $18,200. Embracing more than twenty square miles, the "Sanford Grant" lay on the south side of Lake Monroe. The acreage fronting on the lake, where the town of Sanford was ultimately located, was generally low, with pine, cypress, and cabbage palms. The more inland areas consisted of higher, more rolling land of light, sandy soil covered with yellow and black-jack pine and dotted with beautiful, clear water lakes.[33]

The Barnwell and Oakley experiments had demonstrated Sanford's lack of sound business judgment. The Florida experience repeated that failing and again revealed his penchant for poor, haphazard management. He originally planned to finance a slaughterhouse and sawmill and to utilize their proceeds, together with those from land sales, to support his citrus groves. These improvements acquired their own momentum. He added a store and wharf to enhance the mill's possibilities and constructed a hotel and boarding house to augment the area's attractiveness for tourists and settlers. By the close of the decade, Sanford had fulfilled his Uncle Philo Shelton's 1871 prediction:

> You are spending large sums of money for which *I am sure* you will not for years see any adequate return. . . . if you go on the way you are building Wharves and Buildings, cutting & piling up lumber until it is wanted or using it upon buildings yourself, you will use up so much of your property that now produces income *that.* . . . this drain added to your very Extravagant expense of living will use up your property so that in a few years you will be comparatively a poor man.[34]

Sanford's managerial deficiencies were devastating. He initiated far too many of these collateral undertakings simultaneously; the demands for both capital and supervision surpassed his capacity and commitment. An absentee landlord, his personal oversight was intermittent and erratic, usually totalling about a month per year. Relatives, agents, and friends repeatedly urged him to become more actively involved. In September 1870 Uncle Philo warned, "You will be *stuck* badly I fear unless you come home & go down there & see just [how] your money is being spent & how the business is done[.] If you don't I think you will lose largely." The following June Edwin G. Eastman assured him that were he to give the property "close attention. . . . for a year or two," he would recoup his money and still retain "plenty of land." In 1875 James S. Mackie reiterated these sentiments to Gertrude: "I think that if he could give one year *now* of his personal attention on the spot to his interests here it would be worth ten times as much. . . . as a great deal more time five years later."[35]

Sanford's refusal to devote his full, personal attention to the project prevented him from realistically assessing his interests. Far too dependent upon his agents' information, he invariably reached overly optimistic conclusions. Writing to Gertrude during one of his flying visits to Sanford in December 1875, he typically predicted "a good deal of money this season out of Sanford Hotel, sawmill, land and the hotel alone might make $8 or 10,000." Another three years without profits did little to change his perception. He again assured Gertrude that their holdings constituted the "basis of solid fortune," that the Belair Grove would return expenses within two years, and that the financial "corner is almost turned."[36] Ironically, Sanford derived great satisfaction from his personal visits and consistently went away convinced that he had accomplished much. But his attachment to Europe, his diverse interests, and Gertrude's refusal to move to America precluded a long-term presence.

Although Sanford's brief sojourns in Florida at least temporarily improved the management of his property, they were not uniformly beneficial. His brusque manner and thinly veiled contempt for southerners frequently offended Floridians. When compared to his own "push and go ahead," he found southerners "slow," "tardy people —not only tardy in paying their debts, but in everything else." "Man is vile enough anyway, as you go South," he informed Thurlow Weed in 1871, "but 'reconstruct' him with the negro and carpetbaggers & the result is villanous!" Southerners were, he concluded, without either "money or public spirit."[37]

His attempt in 1875 to have the county seat moved from Orlando to Sanford illustrated how these attitudes thwarted his endeavors. By making his town both the center of county government and the head of navigation on the St. Johns, Sanford hoped to stimulate land sales and his diverse businesses. Opposing his campaign was Jacob Summerlin, a prosperous cattle rancher and businessman and Orlando's most prominent citizen. Their initial meeting said much about Sanford's difficulties. Sanford strode confidently into Orlando carrying a "heavy gold-headed cane" and "dressed in the most correct styles of the day, with a high silk hat and spotless linen." Going directly to the Summerlin Hotel, he demanded of the clerk, "Where can I find this gentleman, this Mr. Jacob Summerlin, who I am informed, dares to oppose me in my efforts to locate the county seat in the town of Sanford? I, sir, am General Sanford." The clerk took him to Summerlin, who was "smoking a corncob pipe" and clad in a "blue flannel shirt, coarse trousers and heavy shoes." Sanford spoke with the astonished Summerlin, but he had no more success in convincing Florida's "Cattle King" than he did with the county commissioners the following day.[38] Incidents and postures such as these were partially responsible for Sanford's complaints of "spite & malignity & jealousy" being directed at him by Orange County residents.[39]

Sanford's failure to provide consistent, direct supervision made it critical that he secure capable employees and work well with them. His inability to do so constituted still another liability. Writing to Edward Shelton in December 1870, Edwin G. Eastman cut to the heart of Sanford's early problems: "All his agreements are *verbal* and with people of no property and I think of very doubtful reputation."[40] The roster of his associates was not impressive. John A.

Ferguson, whom Sanford initially placed in charge of the mill, was at best an inept, haphazard businessman and at worst simply dishonest. Joseph W. Tucker, Sanford's associate in the slaughterhouse, badly miscalculated the potential business, and his failure cost Sanford at least $2,500. R. N. Whitner, Jr., one of the men hired to clear and plant St. Gertrude Grove, drank excessively and managed the workers poorly. J. B. Sterling and Howard Tucker, both of whom managed St. Gertrude briefly, shared Whitner's problems. Stirling also succumbed to alcohol, and Tucker failed to control the labor force.[41]

Although Sanford's two most important agents during his first decade in Florida were improvements on this quintet, his relationship with them was not the smooth, functional one best calculated to advance his interests. From early 1871 through approximately mid-1876, Henry L. De Forest worked hard, at times even heroically, but Sanford never fully trusted him. In December 1875 he complained to Gertrude that De Forest's "shortcomings," especially his "thoughtlessness" and "arbitrary" behavior, had been very costly.[42]

Not until August 1878 did he retain a truly superior general agent, James E. Ingraham. Energetic, resourceful, and loyal, Ingraham had worked for Sanford as a clerk since 1875 and later became president of the South Florida Railroad. Sanford recognized that Ingraham was "good & true" but criticized him for being "slow & always behind hand." Desperate for funds in the late 1870s, Sanford pressed Ingraham incessantly for collections and current accounts. "When," he demanded of Ingraham on one occasion, "*will you* have done with this scatterbrain shiftlessness & send me my accounts. . . . ?" Ingraham truthfully rejoined that he was doing his best and that it was difficult to work "with any heart where my efforts are not appreciated."[43] Sanford's reluctance to delegate authority, unrealistic expectations, and discourteous communications produced troubles with even the best of his employees.

As if Sanford's problems with supervisors were not sufficiently troublesome, he encountered further impediments in securing a sufficient, reliable labor force. J. N. Whitner and Richard Marks initiated their work at St. Gertrude and Belair in 1870 with local white workers. Whitner's "ill-disguised contempt for men" of this "class" and the workers' undependability necessitated the search for an alternate work force. Marks declared the "native white. . . . not worth a dime," and Thomas Haight contended that the people around Lake Monroe "work *one* day and *play* three. . . ."[44]

When Whitner and Marks sought to relieve the labor shortage by importing blacks from north Florida, they aroused the ire of the displaced whites. In September 1870 "low white wretches" fired on and wounded several of the blacks. Guards stationed around the Negro camp deterred further attacks for two weeks; additional assaults then caused the blacks working at the slaughterhouse and sawmill to flee temporarily. After threatening to arm the laborers and call in the cavalry, Joseph Tucker reported on November 11 that the harassment had ceased and that the "colored men are now satisfied, & all goes on smoothly & safely." Although temporarily stabilized, the situation portended future trouble.[45]

Hoping to replace both blacks and local whites, Sanford utilized the contract labor law to bring thirty-three Swedes to Orange County in May 1871. Each of the twenty-six men and seven women cost Sanford approximately $75. This included both transportation and a $10 commission to Dr. William A. Henschen, the recruiting agent. Sanford agreed to provide the Swedes with rations and living quarters and to reward those who fulfilled their contracts with a parcel of land. In return, each immigrant pledged one year's labor.[46]

Although several observers described the Swedes as contented, useful workers, Joseph Tucker noted that they were mostly artisans and contended that "upon the whole. . . . they are less efficient as *field laborers* than an equal number of natives, white or colored." Henry De Forest similarly found that he could assign the Swedes only three-quarters of the tasks he had delegated to black workers at St. Gertrude.[47] Difficulties also arose over the Swedes' living and working conditions. Many arrived without adequate clothing or bedding, which Sanford had to provide. More troublesome was the Swedes' contention that Dr. Henschen had promised them they could ply their trades rather than labor in the fields. When De Forest refused, they claimed the original contract abrogated. Only the combination of De Forest's threats and persuasion and the prospect of acquiring land after a year's work kept most of the Swedes on the job. Still, they remained discontented and complained bitterly about the regime of ten-hour days Monday through Friday and half days on Saturday. These complaints culminated in action in July 1871 when three of the Swedes stowed away on the Jacksonville steamer. De Forest promptly pursued and apprehended them, but the situation remained tense.[48]

Sanford further complicated matters by contracting for an additional twenty Swedes who arrived in November 1871. The new arrivals became similarly disaffected and soon grumbled about mistreatment and poor food. During the spring of 1872, several of them fled again, this time successfully. When the original lot of Swedes fulfilled their obligation in May 1872, eight received five acres of land each, and others went to work on various Sanford projects for wages of $12 to $20 per month plus board.[49] Sanford thereafter experimented periodically with immigrant labor at both Oakley and Belair; but he, like other southerners, had discovered that immigrants were neither the answer to his labor problems nor the alternative to blacks as the principal work force. In fact, Sanford's experience paralleled that of the South generally. Despite extensive efforts by state bureaus, land companies, railroads, and businessmen's immigration societies, relatively few immigrants moved south, and planters had little success with them as laborers. They too were plagued by "problems of disertion, discontent, language barriers, and inexperience," and most ultimately opted for freedmen as the "only reliable labor force."[50]

Sanford's reversion to hired black labor in 1872 provoked reactions similar to those of the previous summer. In June a group of local whites led by the sheriff visited the thirteen black workers at their camp and warned them to leave or be shot. When De Forest threatened to call in the United States marshal, none was shot, but one black was "badly beaten by some Crackers as he was quietly passing along the road."[51] Through the remainder of the 1870s, Sanford retained a racially mixed labor force. Like his managers, it proved periodically troublesome and hampered his chances for profitable operation.

All of these factors—Sanford's neglect and managerial shortcomings, inept and untrustworthy subordinates, and labor problems—combined with the rigor and poverty of the Florida frontier to undercut his 1870s investments. His partnership with Joseph W. Tucker in a slaughterhouse was the most immediate and complete failure. Sanford loaned Tucker more than $2,500 for a steam engine, tanks, building, and cattle. He was to receive 8 percent interest on his loans, one-half of the profits, and three-fourths of the butcher wastes for five years. Tucker had projected butchering fifty head per day at a cumulative profit of $250, but when operations began in November 1870, he discovered that the Jacksonville market could consume only eight head per week at a cumulative profit of $80 to $90. On May 30, 1871,

Tucker acknowledged the business' failure with "sadness and disappointment."[52] Sanford had lost nearly $3,000 and one of his anticipated sources of operating funds.

Sanford and Tucker also built a wharf on Lake Monroe. Tucker constructed a 540-foot wharf of yellow cypress with a 30-foot by 20-foot storehouse at the end. The structure cost $2,970 and was completed in September 1870, only to be washed away a year later by high water. By working in the flooded lake twelve hours per day for three days, Henry De Forest and a group of the Swedes saved much of the lumber, and a larger wharf was reconstructed in early 1872. Assuming that most of the original materials were recyclable, Sanford would have had at least $4,500 invested in the two wharves. Sanford's assumption that a wharf was vital to the general development of his property was probably correct, but it is unlikely that he ever directly recouped his funds from its operation. During 1874 gross receipts were $521, which would have allowed for only marginal profits. For most of 1876 and 1877 profits averaged approximately $68 per month. He had once again tied up substantial capital with little cash return.[53]

Sanford's sawmill proved equally disappointing. He furnished the construction costs of more than $3,000 and retained John A. Ferguson, another manager of meager ability. Launched in July 1870, the business was soon in a shambles. When Edwin G. Eastman arrived in December 1870 to investigate Sanford's property, he found that Ferguson had squandered $1,500 of Sanford's money through graft and mismanagement. Eastman fired Ferguson and temporarily closed the mill until the following spring. Sanford did economize by drawing on the mill for the lumber needed in his diverse projects, but this produced no cash, the commodity he needed most. Although the ledgers are sketchy, they reveal much of Sanford's difficulty. For a four-month period in 1872, the mill sawed an average of 44,235 feet of lumber, sold an average of 28,863 feet worth $488, but collected only $351 per month. When this income was balanced against monthly expenses of approximately $500, a mounting deficit was inevitable. An eleven-month sample in 1876–77 shows an identical trend: expenses averaged more than $600, book sales $872, and collections $215. The general poverty of the area dictated credit sales, and by April 1877 the mill had $2,619 in accounts receivable. As the decade closed, Sanford futilely looked for a buyer for the mill; it had become still another property which he could neither profit from nor dispose of.[54]

Seeking in part to salvage the mill, Sanford established a general store in March 1871. Edwin Eastman had advised him in 1870 that only a store from which mill workers could be paid in goods would make the mill profitable. In addition, Eastman confidently projected a yearly business of $75,000, with $10,000 to $15,000 in profits. A variety of factors rendered these goals as elusive as those Sanford was simultaneously pursuing in his other projects. His lack of capital and the difficulties inherent in purchasing the inventory in Charleston or New York periodically left the store without critical items, thereby alienating the customers. The vagaries of nature in turn often left the agricultural clientele unable to convert their crops into the money necessary to buy. The August 1871 storm that destroyed Sanford's first wharf also severely damaged crops in the surrounding area, and the 1872 cotton crop fell far short of expectations. Incidents of this type only intensified the scarcity of money in this frontier area. As with the mill, significant sales could only be made by extending credit, and Sanford's agents constantly complained of the difficulty in making collections. A four-month period during 1872 provides a useful indicator; total sales averaged more than $2,000, but cash sales plus collections averaged approximately $1,250. In January 1873 delinquent customers owed the store $4,000, and by early 1879 the accounts receivable had risen to $25,000.[55]

As Sanford's financial plight worsened, the store became an increasingly marginal operation. By October 1878 James Ingraham, Sanford's manager, had run out of groceries, and Sanford could not provide the funds to replenish the supply. Ingraham estimated the store's remaining stock of hardware, shoes, clothing, and crockery, at $10,000, $1,500 of which was "unsaleable"; the remaining $8,500 had depreciated to only $6,800 because many of the goods were of inferior quality or had been purchased at inflated prices. Unable to obtain the necessary groceries, Sanford disposed of this stock and in March 1879 leased the store, wharf, and warehouse for three years at $550 per year.[56]

Sanford undertook a final, even more ambitious project—the construction of a hotel and accompanying boarding house for mechanics. The Sanford House Hotel was designed to attract tourists and serve as a temporary residence for wealthy, prospective settlers. The Lake Monroe House was to cater to laborers and less prosperous settlers. Both buildings were completed in 1876, at a combined cost of $8,000 to $10,000. The Sanford House was an impressive structure: three stories with porches on the first two, rooms for 150 guests, a large yard with flower beds and citrus trees, and a boardwalk leading down to Lake Monroe's palmetto-lined shore.[57]

These establishments shared the fate of Sanford's other Florida ventures. Although the Sanford House was often mentioned favorably in contemporary guide books, it did not attract enough travelers to operate profitably. Available figures show no net income for the 1878–79 season and profits of only $800 for the following year. Moreover, by the end of the decade, both the Sanford and Monroe Houses had come to require additional capital beyond Sanford's means. New furnishings were needed and the proprietors to whom Sanford had leased the buildings requested increased room space. In December 1879 the manager of the Monroe House absconded, owing Sanford $500. He was apprehended, and some $400 was recovered; but the boarding house was in such a dilapidated state that another $500 was needed for repairs.[58]

Contrary to Sanford's expectations, these diverse businesses had contributed to the growth of his town without adding to his fortune or stimulating land sales. In acquiring his tract on the upper St. Johns, Sanford had purchased property in Florida's most rapidly appreciating real estate region. While land in the state as a whole had depreciated in value by an average of 75 percent in the mid-1860s, that along the St. Johns had increased by one-third. Sanford sought to capitalize on the burgeoning interest in orange culture by advertising his property nationally. In 1873 he advertised in *Harper's Weekly, Hearth and Home, Rural New Yorker,* and the weekly *New York Tribune,* and periodically throughout the decade he circulated flyers describing the area. A good example of the latter was "The Sanford Grant, A Fine Chance For Investment," which he issued in January 1877, offering lots of five acres and upward for prices from $1 to $100 per acre. His efforts attracted numerous inquiries, and sales were encouraging during the mid-1870s. Sanford later claimed that he had sold $15,000 in lots during one year, but by the end of the decade his real estate income was negligible. He grossed only $3,000 in 1878, and the following year buyers were so scarce that he became convinced that the region had "lost its favor." As the decade ended, he had sold only 1,943 of the tract's 12,547 acres.[59]

Although designed to support his orange groves, Sanford's Florida businesses had instead diverted capital from his pioneering citrus activities. Commercial orange growing had begun with British rule in Florida in the late eighteenth century and had peaked with the export of several million oranges in the two seasons prior to 1835. Thereafter, the cumulative impact of a "killing frost" in February 1835, devastating attacks by an insect known as the "scale," and the dislocation of the Civil War and Reconstruction periods produced a precipitous decline in orange culture. This trend was reversed with the founding and first great expansion of Florida's modern citrus industry in the twenty-five years after 1870. By 1895 Florida counted 100,000 acres in citrus, and oranges had become Florida's leading crop, representing 28 percent of the state's agricultural production. Henry Sanford was the leading figure in this revolutionary takeoff; by importing and testing more than 140 varieties of citrus he provided indispensable contributions to the body of knowledge underpinning the new industry.[60]

Postwar investments in citrus, like those in cotton and sugar, were highly speculative. Sanford was plunging into an area in which there was little accumulated knowledge and no consensus on preferred varieties or methods of culture. Endless debates raged during this period over budding trees versus planting seedlings, over methods of pruning, plowing, and fertilizing, and over the use of insecticides and irrigation. As was true for other areas of late-nineteenth-century agriculture, transportation and marketing problems also plagued the citrus industry.[61] Sanford's experimentation and experience at his St. Gertrude and Belair groves did much to settle many of these disputes, but the solutions often came too late for his personal financial gain.

St. Gertrude, Sanford's first grove, furnishes a telling example of the difficulties and uncertainties that pioneer orange growers encountered. It also provides further commentary on his problems as an absentee owner. In May 1870 he engaged J. N. Whitner and Richard N. Marks of Mellonville to clear and plant a 120-acre tract west of what would become the town of Sanford. Though contending with the labor problems noted above and the steaming heat of the Florida summer, they had by late September cleared 100 acres and planted over 4,300 orange and 700 banana trees.[62]

These early months heralded Sanford's lasting contributions to the industry. He was already importing numerous foreign plants. From Thomas Rivers and Sons Nursery in Sawbridgeworth, England, he purchased twenty-four varieties of oranges, four of lemons, two of limes, and one of tangerines.[63] Unfortunately, these early months also presaged many of Sanford's subsequent difficulties. Whitner and

Marks failed to fence St. Gertrude, and cattle damaged the orange trees. The two managers also neglected to follow the initial planting with proper cultivation. Even more fundamental was their selection of a grove site located over a substratum of hardpan clay. Although he did not understand the significance, Howard Tucker had discovered this clay as early as June 1870, and he and others noted the primary consequence of this soil construction—improper drainage. The over-accumulation of water fatally injured the root systems of the young citrus trees and forced Sanford to abandon the grove by the mid-1870s.[64]

But the realization that this soil would not support the grove came only after the expenditure of thousands of dollars and several years' work. At the behest of Edwin Eastman, Orlando George, the most knowledgeable citrus expert in the region, traveled from Jacksonville to evaluate the status of the grove in December 1870. George noted the drainage difficulties but believed that extensive ditching was the remedy. He advised that salvaging the grove would require immediate action and a $30,000 investment in labor and materials over the next five years. For a yearly salary of $1,500 he offered to oversee the work.[65]

Unprepared either to commit himself to these outlays or to abandon the grove, Sanford opted for a middle course and continued to cultivate St. Gertrude for three more years. The Swedish contract laborers spent much time there, and as late as February 1873 Sanford's overseer was conscientiously trying to replace all the dead trees. Although the grove's appearance periodically improved, the crucial soil and drainage problems were insurmountable.[66]

In 1873 Sanford shifted his emphasis to Belair, his second and ultimately much more significant grove. Located three miles southwest of Sanford in rolling sandy pine lands, Belair possessed soil better suited to successful orange culture. It was at Belair and the adjoining 10-acre nursery that Sanford made his great contribution to the citrus industry. By 1889 he had expanded Belair to 145 acres: 95 acres in oranges and 50 in lemons. Over these sixteen years, he visited and studied European groves and imported and sponsored the testing of some 140 varieties of citrus. Among his most important introductions were the Jaffa, Majorca, Maltese Blood, Ruby, Valencia, Sanford Blood, and St. Michael oranges and the Villa Franca lemon. Since Belair served as a source of nursery stock for many of the surrounding groves, these strains were rapidly distributed. In addition to citrus, he also tested a wide range of other plants including olives, figs, bananas, pineapples, grapes, almonds, coffee, and tea.[67]

Both contemporaries and subsequent historians recognized Sanford's importance. As early as 1876 *The Semi-Tropical* characterized Belair as "the experiment station" of central Florida; and as Sanford wrote the secretary of agriculture the following year, he was doing on a "small scale what Congress should provide to have done extensively and under the auspices of your department." In 1893 Walter Swingle told the Florida State Horticultural Society that it was "no exaggeration to state that two-thirds of our desirable varieties [of citrus] and a goodly share of those grown in California were brought here and first tested by General Sanford." More recently, Branch Cabell and A. J. Hanna termed his "nursery gardens the most impressive laboratory of its kind to be found in the Western Hemisphere." T. Frederick Davis concurred, judging that Belair boasted "by far the greatest variety of citrus ever privately assembled in America" and was the "outstanding grove of this period, and in some respects in the whole history of the orange in Florida."[68]

While Belair played a crucial role in the emergence of Florida's citrus industry, it yielded Sanford no profits during the 1870s. In fact, the grove failed even to pay expenses. This resulted in part from the normal, five-year "hungry-gap" between the planting of a grove and its maturation. But Sanford's experience with Belair also repeated his recurrent difficulty in securing capable, subordinate managers. John B. Stirling, who directed Belair after mid-1876, caused much of the difficulty. Fond of drink, Stirling was, according to F. G. Sampson, the owner of a neighboring grove, "always behind hand." When Sanford fired him in December 1878, the grove was badly under-fertilized and imperiled by insects. Only the timely efforts of James Ingraham, Sanford's general agent, and F. G. Lindberg, Stirling's successor, saved the grove. They removed the insects by washing and restored the trees to health with thorough fertilization. By June 1879 Ingraham reported that Belair looked "magnificently" and was the "handsomest *grove in the* County and I think in the state." Belair lemons and limes won premiums at the county fairs in 1879, and both Ingraham and Lindberg predicted that the grove would pay expenses for the first time in 1880.[69]

Sanford welcomed this news, but he was less pleased with Lindberg's estimate that it would require a minimum of $5,000 per year to care for Belair properly. Since at least 1875, Sanford had funneled

approximately $5,000 yearly into Belair only to be consistently dis-
appointed with the results. Still, he was determined to continue the
sacrifice; he remained optimistic that Belair "some day ought to yield
a large income." The grove would, he promised Gertrude, be "the
most important source of income to our family in the future."[70]

As the 1870s ended, Sanford looked with pride upon the town and
grove he had founded. In January 1879 he proclaimed that his efforts
had provided something "in which those who come after me will
have some pride & which will perpetuate my name honorably & with
the praise & respect of future generations." Moreover, he was confident that the town and grove would provide Gertrude and the children "a competence that will abide in all probability for their
lives."[71]

Sanford's contribution to Florida was substantial, but when added
to his South Carolina and Louisiana debacles, the Florida investments were financially devastating. By the end of the decade he was
heavily in debt and pressed for funds on all sides. The prolonged
financial strain and his continuing inability to secure a diplomatic
post took their toll on Sanford's health, disposition, and marriage.

After eight years as minister resident to Belgium, Sanford found
the transition to life outside the diplomatic corps difficult. Gertrude
scolded him for being so "dissatisfied and restless" and for failing to
enjoy the children. Henry admitted his discontent and longed for his
former, more-ordered regime. "I sometimes think," he replied, "you
would find me better, brighter, & more loveable if forced into action
& continuous employment. . . . My temperament requires occupation & is fretted and galled by helpless idleness—by the feeling that
I am not prospering nay more losing ground while time & precious
years slip away."[72]

Nagging health problems aggravated his dissatisfaction. His old
eye ailments periodically recurred, and the uncertainties and difficulties of meeting his obligations led to fits of depression and insomnia.
Distressed at both her husband's irritability and his sickness, Gertrude felt that when "bilious," his temper "amount[ed] to almost
madness." Writing in February 1879, Sanford succinctly summarized the decade's impact: "I feel the lines of my face deeper, my hair
whiter since these few months past & feel in my whole system the
effect of this strain & pressure."[73]

Sanford endured these ordeals tenaciously. To be sure, he suffered discouragement, frustration, and doubt: "In my lonely moments I get heart sick." He asked himself, "Why strive?—enjoy what remains of life, float with the current"; but his pride and ambition would not permit this. He took "a certain pleasure in . . . meeting . . . and fighting the various stumbling blocks laid in my way." Characteristically, he resolved, "I will fight it out, I will not give up—life was meant for struggle not for sloth and idleness & material ease." "Perhaps," he reflected, "the trials were needed to teach us humility & to lead our minds to higher things."[74]

Several of Henry's less philosophical reactions to the problems of the 1870s produced serious friction with Gertrude. As the decade progressed, he became increasingly disillusioned at living abroad. He correctly concluded that his prolonged absence from the United States had been fatal to both his political and financial aspirations. "We are reaping," he lectured Gertrude, "the fruits of a wrong commencement—the logical results of trying to live in two hemispheres!" With the family's future at stake in Louisiana and Florida, he found "peace of mind . . . impossible" in Europe. He was also becoming disaffected from the aristocratic circles he and Gertrude had so enjoyed in the 1860s: "I do not find the life in Brussels satisfying to my taste or temperament—the lack of men with ideas common, of contact with sympathizing spirits among those gentle dullards who form the best society, I feel I am rusting under it." In terms that echoed fears expressed by his mother and Uncle Edward thirty years before, he worried that the children would be distracted and hampered by growing up in Europe. He feared that "life abroad" led one to forget the important "things of life" and "to turn to trivialities." Finally, when confronted by a worsening financial plight, he saw return to America as a means of economizing.[75] Short of a move, Sanford urged Gertrude to pursue all possible household savings. He was convinced that Oakley and Belair would soon pay substantial dividends and that in the interim the family would have to sacrifice to support these investments.

Despite Henry's rhetoric, the Sanfords actually persisted in a way of life that was increasingly beyond their means. They continued to live at Gingelom at a cost of $1,000 per year in rent and taxes. Other expenses included over $1,000 per year in wages for seven servants, $2,000 per year for food, $480 for washing, $300 for lights and fuel, $500 for carriage hire, $300 for piano and other tutoring for the girls, and $1,000 for Henry, Jr.'s schooling at Eton. Henry's idea of sacrifice was to deny Gertrude a chef, to veto new furniture, to curtail entertainment, and to avoid costly appearances at court functions and other Belgian social events.[76] Meanwhile, he continued to spend lavishly in Florida.

Gertrude was unreceptive either to a move to the United States or to Henry's suggestions for economizing. Like Henry, she too had difficulty adjusting to the family's declining fortunes. Their early married years had been idyllic, and the young bride had expected that "we *could* have everything—houses & horses & jewels & finery & year after year." This was not to be; "ignorant of all housewifely detail" at the time of their marriage, she soon found herself a mother of seven with the uncongenial task of managing the household during Henry's frequent and prolonged absences. Gertrude felt neglected and occasionally wondered about the depth of Henry's love. "It is a strange destiny," she complained, "that has fated that *all* the supreme moments of my life should be endured *alone*"; and later, "I do often feel so little importance in your life compared to the external things that absorb & interest it."[77]

She was adamantly opposed to returning permanently to the United States. Although pleased that they had gone to Florida to inspect their property in 1870, Gertrude departed with the vow that she did "not intend going again for a long time." When she and Henry spent the first half of 1872 in Jacksonville, her reaction conveyed only boredom and irritation. "I really have nothing to tell you," she wrote her mother-in-law. "No one comes to see [us] & I go nowhere. It is too hot to stir & I don't believe one *would* were it not for the fleas & mosquitos roaches & spiders the size of yr hand!!" Subsequent trips to other more agreeable American spots, such as Newport, failed to mollify her. In 1876 she concluded, "I detest Florida in particular & America has offered to me on my different visits a cup of mingled disagreeabilites [*sic*]."[78]

Determined to remain in Brussels, Gertrude mounted arguments concerning life style, health, and the children's development. When Henry suggested a northern Virginia farm, she responded that "*we* have outgrown farmhouses & rough American food & I tremble to expose our children to malaria & rough American doctors . . ." The environment would be especially detrimental to the girls who might ape their peers and become "fast & ill mannered & talk thro their noses."[79]

She was equally annoyed at Henry's pleas for curtailing their social life. Although she periodically attempted to meet his demands for household accounts, her efforts were neither consistent nor effective. More fundamentally, she disagreed with Henry's priorities. "I cannot understand," she protested, "the necessity of making the daily life joyless for the sake of some future good we may never attain." Nor could she resist reminding Henry of how ill-advised his investments had been: "year after year good money going after bad. . . . you saying that what I give up & do without is of no consequence compared to what *you* think important—tho it means for me humiliations of all sorts and the position and influence that makes [*sic*] one's life pleasurable or not."⁸⁰

Gertrude's grumbling frustrated Henry. He chided her for failing to "comprehend . . . the situation" and minimized her "little cares & annoyances" when compared to his efforts to ward off "poverty, ruin, [and] distress." Her lack of support was also disconcerting; he lamented that "I need in this time of worry & distress of mind . . . words of cheer—not of complaint. We have to deal with the situation as it is & with the best possible spirit."⁸¹

Despite their bickering, Henry and Gertrude remained deeply committed to one another. Even as they were exchanging their most pointed barbs, Henry assured his "dear little wifey" of his love and lauded her as a good wife and mother. Gertrude responded in kind and perceptively observed that, "I do not doubt that you love me—indeed ours must be a strong affection or it would not have supported such a long & incessant strain."⁸²

In fact, the 1870s had been a long and incessant strain. Seeking to capitalize on depressed real estate prices and ostensible opportunities in a reviving southern agriculture, Sanford had jumped headlong into many high-risk speculations. His poor judgment, managerial deficiencies, and absentee status poved disastrous. Oakley and his Florida projects consumed all of his available funds, and by the end of the decade he was paying nearly $1,000 per month in interest on his mounting debts. He had sunk his capital into investments which neither produced appreciable cash flow nor generated resale demand. As he confided to Gertrude in August 1879, "If I could, I would get out of Florida, & never put foot in it again. . . . but I am in it—the future fortunes of you & the little ones depend on it."⁸³

CHAPTER 6

STRUGGLING FOR SURVIVAL IN FLORIDA, 1880-1891

WITH HIS FORTUNE inextricably mired in Florida, Sanford had no choice but to continue his efforts at developing the property. He did so throughout the 1880s, but his second decade of southern investment proved as frustrating as the first. Although he organized the Florida Land and Colonization Company (FLCC) in 1880 to stimulate land sales and poured thousands of additional dollars into Belair, profits remained maddeningly elusive. Financial failures were matched by political ones. In 1880 and 1884 he mounted futile campaigns to influence Florida politics and to secure a domestic or diplomatic office.

Sanford had considered organizing a joint-stock company to support his projects in 1876 but had been unable to attract investors. He would have had similar luck four years later had not Sir William Mackinnon come to his aid. Mackinnon, a wealthy Scottish industrialist whom Sanford had met through his work with the African International Association, took a one-quarter interest in the company and recruited the other principal investors from his circle of British friends and business associates.[1]

Officially chartered in London on June 1, 1880, the company was to have a capital of £250,000, divided into 12,500 shares of £20 each. Sanford received £60,000: £10,000 in cash, on which he was to pay 5 percent interest for five years, and £50,000 in stock, of which £20,000 was to be held in escrow. As the largest single stockholder, Sanford became president of the company and a member of the board of directors but was allowed to vote only 100 shares of his stock. In return, he was to transfer titles, "free from any encumbrances," to all his Florida properties except Belair by January 6, 1881. Only 1,000 additional shares, carrying a £5 obligation at the time of allotment were taken in the initial stock subscription. After paying Sanford his £10,000, there remained a working capital of only £40,000. Although the FLCC held more than 80,000 acres scattered over nine counties by the mid-1880s, scarcity of operating funds proved chronic and caused serious internal friction.[2]

The company's cash payment of roughly $50,000 was opportune. Together with his mother's estate, it provided Sanford a brief but welcome financial respite. "The relief," he wrote Gertrude, "from the hard pressures of these years past by comparative ease in money matters is very great & gives my mind freedom to act in other matters than the struggle 'to finance.' " His comparative ease was short-lived, as he quickly became embroiled in a prolonged struggle with the London directors over the company's operation. He saw the FLCC as a personal vehicle to develop his town and to facilitate land sales. While his British partners agreed with this general goal, they questioned most of his specific recommendations and were critical of his haphazard, impulsive business methods. Edwyn S. Dawes, another of the directors, explained to Sanford that Englishmen "move slowly and with more caution than you are accustomed to in America." The company's continuing want of capital aggravated these differences in managerial style. Sanford repeatedly advocated actions that his London counterparts deemed too "bold." He further alienated the Britishers when he was unable to substantiate several of his land titles and when his negotiations for additional lands occasioned troublesome and costly lawsuits.[3]

The discord between Sanford and the board began almost immediately upon the company's formation. In October 1880 Sanford complained about delays in town improvements, such as waterworks, and about the board's "distrust and want of confidence" in refusing to make him a special land agent. Speaking for the board, George A. Thomson and Gerald Waller explained that the company's capital would support the management of its present holding but would not sustain extensive improvement projects. Before initiating the waterworks project, the board required a detailed estimate of the costs and a working financial commitment from the town. Moreover, the general lack of specific information, such as annual tax bills, exact land acreage, and clear titles, precluded the board's issuing a prospectus

and soliciting additional capital. Thomson and Waller criticized Sanford and James E. Ingraham, the FLCC's local Florida agent, for
failing to provide these needed materials: "There is no way," Thomson lectured, "of getting more capital until we have sufficient data
to go upon to show prospects of satisfactory returns."[4]

While Ingraham compiled information, Sanford negotiated for
additional land with the board of trustees of Florida's Internal Improvement Fund. He and Thomson agreed that more extensive holdings should provide the basis for attracting new capital. During
February 1881 the Internal Improvement Board accepted two Sanford propositions. The first allowed Sanford to purchase one million
acres of land at forty cents per acre. Two hundred and fifty thousand
acres were to be selected and paid for within ninety days, and the
remainder within a year. The second proposal authorized Sanford's
company to build a canal from Moss Bluff to the vicinity of Lake
Harris or Lake Eustis. As compensation, the FLCC would gain title
to the swamp and overflow lands it was able to reclaim in the area
of these lakes and the Ocklawha River.[5]

The FLCC's failure to act on either of these offers epitomized the
growing rift between Sanford and the board. Sanford had not even
mentioned the canal project to his London associates, and upon
receiving the details, Thomson quickly vetoed the scheme as beyond
the company's purview. But to Sanford's dismay, Thomson reversed
himself and also rejected the more conventional million acres purchase. In July he informed Sanford that such large acquisitions were
"somewhat bold." Instead, he advised and the company adopted the
policy of selecting smaller, more manageable parcels.[6]

This episode also caused one of the several legal squabbles that
harassed Sanford and the FLCC. When the FLCC failed to complete
the million-acre deal, Alexander St. Clair Abrams, the attorney Sanford had retained to negotiate with the Internal Improvement Board,
demanded compensation for his services. In March 1882 the company supplied $2,000, which Sanford passed on to Abrams as pay-
ment. Abrams accepted the money but then successfully sued
Sanford for another $20,000 in 1884. When Sanford again turned to
the FLCC for help, Thomson informed him that it was a personal
rather than a company problem. Already strapped for funds, Sanford
was forced to begin a protracted legal battle, which remained unsettled at his death.[7]

Sanford's quarrel with his London colleagues grew even more
bitter following this fiasco. While visiting Florida in November 1881,

Sanford unilaterally initiated some of the action he had considered sadly lacking over the previous year. He directed the planting of fruit trees and vegetables around Orange Lake, sold the Monroe House for $5,000, moved the Fort Reid Town Hall to Sanford for use as a boarding house, and arranged for improvements at the mill. In reporting these measures, he signed himself as "Managing Director." His presumption drew the ire of the London board. Thomson objected to Sanford's use of this title and informed him that the board had "in no way granted you authority to take general and sole direction of the Company's affairs." Thereafter, he continued, all such decisions were to be cleared through the London office.[8]

Sanford was incensed. He immediately fired off a letter threatening to withdraw his name and counsel from the FLCC operations. He would stay only if entrusted with current business operations and if the London office ceased "unnecessary interference" in matters it knew "little or nothing" about. The board, he charged indignantly, treated him with the "distrust" worthy of "an enemy rather than a friend." As he explained with some exaggeration to William Mackinnon, "Now I do know about this business in which I have been hitherto most successful & among a people who esteem and respect me." Money lost through procrastination and inactivity was rankling, but this "attempt to crowd me out of all direction in Florida is the last straw & my self-respect will not permit my accepting this false position." Sanford's threats, however, were hollow; he had neither the voting power nor the financial resources to displace the British directors. Edwyn Dawes accurately analyzed Sanford's situation: he should either secure new capital to buy out the original investors or cooperate. Unfortunately he could do neither.[9]

Although the FLCC paid a 3.5 percent dividend for fiscal year 1880 and 3 percent for 1881, Sanford remained dissatisfied. This resulted in part from the board's continued caution. It reluctantly agreed to the waterworks construction and hotel and mill renovation in 1883 but rejected his plan for development of an extensive lemon grove. Even more important was Sanford's desire, even compulsion, to exercise a decisive role. He railed at all restraints, and his strident criticism of E. R. Trafford, Ingraham's successor as the FLCC's local agent, illustrated this yearning for power. Unlike Ingraham, Trafford paid first loyalty to the board and provided Sanford little information. Frustrated at being deprived of first-hand intelligence, Sanford sought to have Trafford replaced; however, the board was pleased by the same behavior that distressed Sanford. It pronounced Trafford a "competent trustworthy manager" and blocked all efforts for his removal.[10]

Against this backdrop Sanford initiated his second major confrontation with the board in the fall of 1883. He demanded full managerial authority in Florida for one year at a salary of £2,500, which was one-half the previous year's expenses. In return he guaranteed a 5 percent dividend. Mounting a two-pronged attack designed to pressure the board into accepting this proposal, he appealed to the powerful Mackinnon for aid and threatened to transfer a portion of his stock to his wife, Gertrude. By this second device he hoped to circumvent the charter's limitation of his personal voting power and to gain a majority voice in a general meeting.[11]

Sanford's plea for aid left Mackinnon in a delicate situation between two sets of friends. The canny old businessman avoided the November board meetings, withheld his proxy from both factions, and appealed for "harmony." Sanford's scheme for increasing his voting power also went awry when the board refused to sanction the stock transfer without Sanford's agreement that no voting rights were to be conveyed. Although these specific pressure tactics failed, Sanford's general threat of returning to Florida and interfering in local FLCC operations convinced the board to make several concessions. In return for his pledge not to go to Florida, his British rivals agreed to a dividend for the previous fiscal year and to release his £20,000 in stock from escrow. They also purchased from him a tract known as the Powell Grant for £3,000 of the company's debenture bonds.[12]

This compromise proved only temporary. By early 1884 Sanford had renewed both his attacks upon Trafford and his attempt to control the company through stock manipulation. The directors countered by delaying the release of his stock from escrow and by threatening liquidation if he persisted in the maneuver for additional voting rights. In warning him not to force the voting matter, Edwyn Dawes graphically portrayed Sanford's impotence. Dawes noted the FLCC owed £6,600 to his own banking house and a like sum to Mackinnon. Should Sanford break up the company, the trustees would retain all the property and satisfy these debts. Sanford's majority shareholder status would be worth little if the company failed. Dawes concluded that, short of destroying the FLCC, Sanford's only hope for control was to secure the capital necessary to buy out the original investors.[13]

This defeat marked Sanford's final serious effort to wrest control of the FLCC from the British board. Though he did not attempt another coup over the final six years of the decade, the pattern of his behavior remained unchanged. He continued to criticize Trafford's performance in Florida (until his replacement by Frederick Rand in 1887) and to hurl barbs at the London office. Sanford also repeatedly promoted measures, such as additional land purchases and new stock issues, which the board deemed too rash.

The year 1884 not only marked Sanford's defeat, it also signified the high point of the company's fortunes. For the year ending June 30, 1884, the FLCC garnered £14,778 from land sales, earned a £5,269 profit, and declared a 5 percent dividend. Thereafter, the trend was steadily downward: for fiscal year 1884, land sales of £9,200, profits of £3,332, and a 4 percent dividend; and for fiscal year 1885, land sales of £7,530, profits of £2,939, and another 4 percent dividend. Sales rebounded to £9,418 the following year, but debenture and interest costs and repairs to the waterworks, precluded a dividend. Jacksonville's yellow-fever epidemic decimated real estate and tourist activity during much of 1888, and the company's sales plunged to £4,333, resulting in a £5,983 loss. By 1890 the FLCC was a static enterprise seeking only to avoid further losses and debts.[14]

The FLCC had repeated in the 1880s many of the same mistakes Sanford had committed in the 1870s. At Sanford's urging, the company had duplicated his error of attempting to support extensive collateral projects aimed at stimulating the primary objective of real estate sales. None of these projects produced revenues commensurate with investments of capital or time. The mill consistently lost money and by September 1887 had accumulated $4,160 in uncollectable bills. The hotel limped along much as it had since 1875. The FLCC may have recouped the £1,440 in repairs, but the purchase price from Sanford of more the £3,000 was lost. In 1887 the hotel was generating so little income and had deteriorated into such a "miserable condition" that the FLCC considered moving the structure in order to free the valuable midtown lots for sale. With the company unable to provide the £3,498 needed for renovations, the hotel joined the mill as an unsalable liability. The waterworks drained company resources even more severly. Construction and maintenance costs for the decade ran near £9,259, and while profits averaged £384 in the mid-1880s, the waterworks was operating in the red by 1890.[15]

Land sales also ran closer to Sanford's disillusioning experience of the 1870s than to his optimistic projections for the 1880s. Lots within or near the town sold readily and commanded good prices, but as Trafford reported in June 1884, "The lands on the Grant as a whole" were "not particularly attractive." The bulk of the outlying acreage was "low" and required extensive drainage before being marketable. The FLCC also found that almost all its clients required credit, which subsequently proved difficult to collect. By early 1887 the company had amassed nearly $61,000 in virtually nonnegotiable notes.[16] As the company's fortunes darkened after 1885, business was further depressed by a series of unforeseen events—a devastating freeze in January 1886, a major fire that destroyed three city blocks of Sanford in 1887, and a yellow fever epidemic in 1888.

Although the company had failed financially, it had assumed Sanford's role by promoting the growth of his town and central Florida. The FLCC budgeted $1,000 for advertising in 1883 alone, and its numerous circulars and broadsides publicized Florida in both the United States and Great Britain. This advertising not only aided the growth of the town of Sanford but also contributed to neighboring communities such as Orlando, Titusville, and Rockledge.[17] The FLCC's support of Sanford's development also went far beyond publicity. The waterworks provided an indispensable service and dispelled the notion that the area was "unhealthful." The FLCC's drainage work and street construction were crucial to the town's steady expansion. The company also continued Henry Sanford's practice of providing cash and land subsidies to railroads and prospective business. To insure that the South Florida Railroad would run through the grant in 1880, Sanford had financed the grading of the first three miles of road bed and donated three acres of land on Lake Monroe. In 1885 the FLCC similarly contributed $10,000 worth of land to the Indian River Railroad to forestall the adoption of an alternate route through Longwood.[18]

Benefitting from the FLCC support, Sanford grew into a thriving little town during the 1880s. Its population increased from approximately 200 in 1880 to more than 2,500 in 1886. By the mid-1880s it had become the point of intersection for five railroads and included among its several businesses a wagon factory, fertilizer factory, steam shingle mill, and machine shops. The community also boasted gas-lighted streets, three newspapers, four hotels, one bank, and four churches. With the aid of the FLCC, Sanford's vision of a town had materialized.[19]

He took justifiable pride in the town which he referred to as "my baby, my pet child." Although he periodically complained about its "malignant" and "malicious" people, he was genuinely flattered by the reception given to him in December 1886. The mayor and a citizens' committee met him at the train station and escorted him to the opera house, where he was honored as the town's founder and primary benefactor. After the mayor had praised his "foresight," "inventive genius," and "boundless liberality," Sanford doggedly reiterated his estimation of the locality: lying at the head of navigation on the St. Johns and "below the line of injurious frost," the town would become "the commercial emporium of South Florida." He closed with sincere thanks for the town's "cordial and unexpected manifestation of friendship and regard."[20]

Sanford derived more than psychological benefits from the FLCC's work. While the company never provided the profits he had envisioned, his stock and debentures did furnish the basis for badly needed credit. William Mackinnon, whom Sanford aptly characterized as a "true, good friend," was the source of most of these loans. The kindly Scot repeatedly came to Sanford's financial rescue after 1885. He personally loaned the FLCC the funds needed to meet debenture payments in July 1888 out of a "desire to protect [Sanford's] interests." Without this aid the company would have failed. He also extended Sanford large personal loans; by September 1890 Sanford had borrowed more than $75,000 (£15,000) from Mackinnon and from Edwyn Dawes' banking house, with FLCC stock as his principal collateral. A significant portion of these funds went toward the support of Belair, the only Florida property that Sanford had not deeded to the FLCC in 1880.[21]

By the early 1880s Belair was attracting widespread attention and seemed on the verge of yielding the great returns Sanford so desperately needed. The editor of the *Dayton Journal* (Ohio) referred to it in 1883 as the "gem of the continent" and "the rarest grove in the state." That same year the Jacksonville *Daily Florida Union* noted that Belair contained 8,000 young trees that would soon produce 3 million oranges annually. The United States Department of Agriculture had also come to view Belair as a model worthy of study. James H. Foss visited the grove in 1882 while collecting material for his pamphlet on Florida's agricultural prospects, and William Saunders lauded Sanford's efforts in his report to the secretary of agriculture the following year. Similar references continued through the remainder of the decade. The *Southern Sun* referred to the grove as "The Renowned Sanford Farm and Experimental Garden," and the Department of Agriculture's "Report on the Condition of Tropical and Semi-Tropical Fruits in the United States in 1887" carefully catalogued Sanford's extensive orange and lemon imports.[22]

Despite recurrent setbacks, Sanford held tenaciously to this optimistic image and to his conviction that Belair would ultimately pay huge dividends. Following his alienation from the English members of the FLCC board, he increasingly looked to Belair as the key to his economic salvation. His June 1885 projection was typical: "If I can keep it [Belair] on for four or five years . . . it alone should then suffice amply for all our wants." Three years and one devastating freeze later, he still stubbornly contended that the grove should yield 75,000 boxes of fruit annually.[23]

A variety of factors placed returns of this magnitude beyond his grasp. Most fundamentally, Belair's location was far from ideal. By establishing his second grove on high pine lands with "light sandy soil," Sanford had avoided St. Gertrude's ruinous drainage problems. In fact, if anything, the drainage was too good. The grove was frequently damaged during the critical spring months by irregular rainfall and temporarily arid conditions. Sanford concluded in 1884 that only an irrigation system would remedy this problem, but he was financially unable to begin installing the system until 1888, and then only on a limited basis. Belair's soil was also distinctly inferior to the preferred hammock lands and required extensive fertilization to support citrus culture. Finally, despite Sanford's protests to the contrary, Belair was located north of the frost line. In 1886 and again in 1894-95, Belair fell victim to freezing temperatures. Only after Sanford's death did area residents learn that the region was best suited to the growth of vegetables, particularly celery.[24]

Sanford's decisions regarding the grove's composition and size compounded these difficulties. By planting 50 of Belair's 145 acres in lemons, he committed 34 percent of the grove to a crop even more speculative than oranges. Although his Belair premium and Villa Franca varieties were recognized as Florida's best in the 1880s, he was unable to raise them profitably. Lemons are especially vulnerable to cold, and the climate at Belair was even harder on them than on oranges. Following the 1886 freeze, Sanford's agent, T. F. Huggins, advised that he had "faith in lemon raising, but it must be done further South from here." In 1890, after a much less severe frost and four years before the destruction of 1894-95, David Houston, the foreman at Belair, believed the lemon grove was essentially destroyed. It was "badly frozen" and would take years before it could be gotten "into a fruiting condition." Even during those years when the lemon crop escaped the cold, Sanford received discouraging returns. Belair's lemons were often rough, knotty, and marred by rust mites; and the crop consistently matured in August, too late to take advantage of the best prices.[25]

Sanford also erred in attempting to cultivate such a large grove. With 145 acres he violated the maxim of implementing an "intensive" rather than an "extensive plan." Contemporary manuals wisely warned against planting more citrus than could be maintained in the "highest state of cultivation,"[26] and Sanford's financial problems precluded this kind of attention. He was continually pressed to provide the funding necessary to sustain the grove. Monthly labor payrolls averaged $260 to $300 through most of the decade and reached figures of $350 and $400 after 1888. Meat and groceries for this labor force averaged $90 to $100 per month, and overseers' salaries demanded another $50 monthly. For 1886 to 1888, fertilizer costs ran nearly $2,700 per year, and annual taxes ranged between $300 and $350. He expended another $1,400 in a futile attempt to drill an artesian well and put $2,000 into an irrigation system. Packing paper and boxes, work horses, cultivating equipment, and wagons added additional burdens. Total annual costs approached at least $7,500, and Sanford's claim in January 1888 that he had spent $120,000 on Belair seems reasonably accurate.[27]

Transportation and marketing problems further dimmed Sanford's prospects. Throughout the decade Sanford employed the consignment system to market his crop. Under this arrangement commission houses sold the fruit and deducted freight, cartage, and a 10 percent commission. His experience substantiates the conclusion that this system profitted merchants and transportation lines while impoverishing the growers. Railroad rates from Florida to New York City were twice those from California, and Sanford regularly paid between 30 and 50 percent of his gross receipts for shipping. When these costs were added to merchant fees and cartage, Sanford often netted less than 60 percent of the gross sale price of his fruit. Sanford also had to contend with a highly unstable national market. Florida citrus was competing both with other domestic fruits and with Mexican and Mediterranean imports. Production periodically surpassed the capacity of the marketing system and resulted in drastically depressed prices. This occurred during both the 1884–85 and 1886–87 seasons.[28]

Sanford's chronic shortage of funds and his disagreement with the marketing decisions of his agents produced debilitating conflicts like those that had soured his relationship with subordinates in the 1870s. Lyman Phelps, Belair's chief overseer from January 1881 through February 1885, frequently felt the sting of Sanford's criticism. He responded by elaborating on the difficulties of managing the grove without adequate finances. In 1884 he complained that while he had personally advanced more than $1,000 to keep Belair going, Sanford had not only been slow to repay him but was also months behind with his salary.[29]

Phelps' successor, T. F. Huggins, also complained of having to employ personal funds at Belair, but he and Sanford clashed most bitterly over marketing practices. In October 1888 Huggins secured an offer of $1.60 per box for Belair's orange crop on the trees. While this contract would have avoided the administrative problems and financial uncertainty associated with the consignment system, Sanford declined the offer. Huggins angrily replied, "I am sorry you did not leave the matter to my judgment which should be worth something, or what am I hear [sic] for [?]" "I also," he continued, "can see things better than you can in Belgium." Sanford ignored Huggins and instructed him to prepare the crop for export to Europe. Huggins grudgingly followed these directions, which included the purchase of special-size boxes for the European market, only to have Sanford cancel the order and direct him to work exclusively through a St. Louis company. Huggins again obeyed, but he protested that the St. Louis firm did not handle fruit and bluntly stated that Sanford had "no idea about handling an orange crop."[30] While Sanford ultimately acquiesced in shipments through several other commission houses, the episode is painfully reminiscent of his clash with William H. Trescot over the marketing of sea-island cotton twenty years before. Sanford had learned little in the interim. Unwilling to devote adequate first-hand attention to his interests, he continued to criticize and countermand the day-to-day decisions of his agents.

Finally, as Thomas Haight had written Sanford in 1871, it appeared that the "fates" were against him. Just as the grove had come into relatively full production in the mid-1880s, the severe "glut" of citrus in northeastern markets depressed prices. Even more devastating was the freeze in January 1886. On January 9 the temperature fell to 19°, and two days later a "blizzard" destroyed the crop and severely damaged the trees. Huggins reported that Belair looked like "a fire had gone through it," and Sanford estimated that the freeze had set the grove "back two years" and cost him $35,000 in actual losses. Misfortune struck again in the late summer of 1888 when a yellow fever epidemic and scare gripped Jacksonville and many of the settlements along the St. Johns. Resulting quarantines disrupted citrus shipments and cost Sanford and other growers dearly.[31]

These cumulative difficulties prevented Sanford from realizing the great profits he had envisioned. He ended his second decade of orange growing still awaiting the fabulous 75,000-box crop about which he often talked. Returns had been so erratic that he was forced to borrow against Belair in 1888, and at his death Gertrude inherited a $19,440 (£4,000) mortgage along with the grove. Following the great freeze of 1894–95, Gertrude sold the grove to John Sanford, who sold it in turn to S. O. Chase in 1902 for a mere $2,000.[32]

In addition to his business activities, Sanford periodically dabbled in the "muddy pool of Florida politics," an arena even more chaotic and unsettled than late-nineteenth-century agriculture and land speculation.[33] By 1879 Sanford was sure that he had "done more for" Florida "than any man in it," and that "if I wished it & made this my real basis, I could be anything I chose in the State & wield very great power and influence."[34] His political endeavors closely resembled his Florida business career. Potentially important and successful, he was again unwilling to establish the permanent presence and do the grassroots work necessary to achieve power. Instead, he preferred working with Washington and Florida politicos and sought to gain office through manipulation rather than by cultivating support among the rank and file. Without a constituency, he found domestic office-hunting as fruitless as his post-1870 quest for diplomatic appointment.

Sanford's purchase of land on the St. Johns had coincided with an especially complex period in Florida politics. In the wake of the Civil War, two Republican factions struggled with the Conservative-Democrats for control of the state. Radical Republicans, such as Liberty Billings, Daniel Richards, and William U. Saunders, were most immediately concerned about Negro equality and punishment of ex-Confederates. Moderate Republicans, led by Harrison Reed and Ossian B. Hart, promoted economic development through an alliance between government and private business and opposed racial equality and policies benefitting blacks at the expense of southern whites. In philosophical terms, these latter Republicans closely resembled their Democratic opponents. Headed by David Walker and David L. Yulee, the Conservative-Democrats constituted a vocal and effective minority who sought to end Negro suffrage and Republican control.[35]

By cooperating with the Democrats against the radicals, the moderate Republicans had gained a tenuous ascendancy in 1868. The marriage of convenience secured the moderates' draft of the new state constitution, which discriminated against blacks in apportioning representation and failed to proscribe ex-Confederates. In May 1868 Florida voters ratified this constitution and elected Harrison Reed governor. With Reed's inauguration in June, the situation grew more chaotic. Moderate Republicans promptly began attacking one another with a ferocity formerly reserved for the Democrats; radicals continued their opposition; and Democrats rejected Reed's overtures for an ongoing partnership and instead used his constitutional and political concessions as the vehicles for a frontal assult.[36]

It was this fluid and confusing political landscape that Sanford surveyed in 1870. Although his political, philosophical, and racial views accorded most closely with the moderate Republicans, the Democrats first made overtures for his services. In March 1871 John P. Sanderson and Edward M. L'Engle, Jacksonville law partners and railroad investors, confided to Edwin G. Eastman that they would back Sanford for United States senator. The next year moderate Republicans led by Jonathan C. Greely, also a Jacksonville lawyer and railroad investor, and E. K. Foster, Sanford's St. Augustine attorney, approached him regarding a coalition with the Conservative-Democrats. They consulted former Governor David Walker and other prominent Democrats, but the scheme collapsed when Sanford refused to go over to the Democratic party.[37]

Sanford's name also surfaced briefly in both 1873 and 1875 as the legislature wrangled over the choice of a United States senator. Hoping to emerge as a compromise candidate, Sanford traveled to Tallahassee in January 1873 and issued a public letter calling for the removal of the sand bar blocking navigation on the upper St. Johns River, the construction of a customs house at Jacksonville, all "proper assistance" for black education, and a share of the patronage to qualified Negroes. At least one observer belittled his position as "Too Thin!"; he was never a serious contender, as former State Treasurer Simon B. Conover won the election. Still, Alva A. Knight, fourth circuit judge and a fellow moderate Republican, assured Sanford that he had not wasted his time: "I find you gained many friendships . . . & though you did not win the prize you have laid the foundation for success if you desire to enter the race two years hence." Sanford was among those prominently mentioned in January 1875, but after two weeks of balloting, the legislators chose Charles W. Jones, a dark horse Democrat from Pensacola in Escambia County.[38]

As the 1876 elections approached, the position of Florida's Republicans grew increasingly precarious. Torn by their usual dissension and confronted by the resurgent and united Democrats, they could be assured neither of reelecting Governor Marcellus Stearns nor of carrying the state's four electoral votes for Rutherford B. Hayes. Writing to Thurlow Weed in a public letter ultimately published as a pamphlet, Sanford condescendingly attempted to "save" southerners "from themselves and the inevitable and pernicious consequences of Democratic rule upon the prosperity of the South." He warned that a Democratic victory would return to power the "same class of old Bourbon extremists, violent able and reckless . . . who forced secession on an unwilling majority." Their renewed control would inflame racial antagonisms, bring further repudiation of Southern war debts, increase national taxes by recognizing southern claims, lead to national currency inflation, and curtail the flow of capital and immigration to the South. By contrast, a Republican victory would bring "peace and prosperity to the South and protection to its best interests, and rapid progress in population and wealth." Sanford decried much that had been "done in the Southern States by the federal administration through mistaken policy or bad advice," but assured southerners that the Republican party was "reforming out of office" those "army bummers" and "irresponsible adventurers" who had been primarily responsible. So cleansed, the Republicans were best able to "carry the South" through its political and social revolution with minimal disruption.[39]

Neither Sanford's writings nor extensive post-election maneuvering could salvage Republican fortunes on the state level. George F. Drew, the Democratic gubernatorial candidate, earned a clear majority and promptly dealt a death blow to moderate Republican hopes of cooperation by channeling appointments to former secessionists. This patronage policy, together with the newly established Democratic control of the election machinery, forecast the demise of Florida's struggling Republican party. In 1878 the Democrats carried both houses of the state legislature, easily elected one congressman, and captured a second congressional seat through blatant fraud. Two years later, the Democrats again swept the governorship and both congressional seats, as well as all the southern states in the presidential election. The solid South had become and would long remain a political reality.[40]

Through the latter 1870s, important Republicans, such as Malachi Martin and William J. Purman, periodically suggested that Sanford run for governor.[41] Although he was too busy with business matters to pursue these overtures seriously, Sanford had by the end of the decade formulated very definite, if outmoded, opinions on the needs of Florida's troubled Republican party. The party required a fundamental change in leadership and direction. He criticized "some of the so-called 'leaders' of the party" whom he considered "the very worst specimens of the carpetbag politician." These "professionals," such as Dennis Eagan, Simon B. Conover, Leonard G. Dennis, and Horatio Bisbee, were simply "place hunters who represent nothing but themselves." "They have arrayed the two races against each other," he wrote President Chester A. Arthur in November 1881, "and by persistent antagonizing, made the democratic party a compact union of nearly all the Southern Whites."[42]

Sanford hoped to replace these "men of the old system" with a leadership representing "property and intelligence," with a "better element who pay taxes and have influence *among white men.*" To attract *"more white men,"* Sanford advocated the de-emphasis of race and an end to the " 'color line.' " By concentrating on economics, the Republicans could attract the "old-Whig & anti-secession element" and split the Democratic party. He envisioned a much less important role for Florida's black Republicans and had "no fear" of alienating "any considerable portion of those of African descent. They will be always our friends naturally, and look to our party for support."[43]

Sanford's plan for reducing the influence of the old "Carpetbagger" and black elements in the Republican party and conciliating conservative southern whites ostensibly resembled President Rutherford B. Hayes' southern strategy. Much to Sanford's dismay, Hayes refused to cooperate in his first important attempt to implement this policy. In January 1881 Sanford, John G. Long, and Sherman Conant concocted an involved scheme aimed at making Sanford a United States senator. Long and Conant struck a bargain with Florida Democrats to put Sanford forward as a compromise candidate to replace the incumbent Democrat, Charles W. Jones. Jones was to be compensated by being made chief justice of the Florida Supreme Court, and the sitting chief justice, Edwin M. Randall, was to be promoted to judge of the United States district court for northern Florida.[44]

The key to this office shuffling was Hayes' willingness to appoint Randall to the district judgeship. The president, who had shown little enthusiasm for Sanford in his 1877 diplomatic appointments, again dragged his feet. On January 14 Sanford decided that Hayes' "backwardness in making [the] essential appt." required that he "go on & see him & have it out with him face to face." When his personal interview did not have the desired effect, he lamented his failure to Thurlow Weed: Had Hayes made "two merited promotions, *I would* have succeeded and we would have had a Republican majority" in the next senate. On January 16 Sanford confessed defeat: "I have accomplished nothing here—the Presdt . . . dislikes me." While the viability of Sanford's scheme was questionable, Hayes' response symbolized his inept handling of southern patronage. His policy of "appointing many southern Democrats to federal positions even at the expense of able, honest southern Republicans; of choosing unsuitable Republicans and passing up qualified ones; [and] of preferring native white southerners to northern residents in the South," helped destroy the Republican party's "fragile" southern organization.[45]

Finding consolation in the fact that Hayes' tenure would last "only six weeks more," Sanford anticipated much greater influence with the incoming Garfield administration. He had for many years been friends with both the president-elect and James G. Blaine, the new secretary of state. He had solicited funds for the 1880 canvass in Florida, had unsuccessfully attempted to have Simon Conover removed as the Republican gubernatorial nominee, and following the election had pressed his views of the state's Republican party on Garfield.[46] These Washington connections were reinforced by growing recognition among certain Florida Republicans, especially those opposed to Bisbee, Conover, and Eagan. Florida's Republican Executive Committee and the Republican members of the state senate and assembly signed letters in January 1881 placing Sanford "at the head of the party as its leader, in the strongest and most complimentary terms." To retain this following he needed to control the new administration's Florida patronage distribution. As one follower advised with some exaggeration, "You have a constituency of 26,000 earnest Republican voters in Florida who now look to *you* for such assistance, under the new administration, as will build up & strengthen the party."[47]

Sanford was optimistic about parlaying this influence into either a domestic or diplomatic office. He boasted to Gertrude, "I have now at last put under my control the federal patronage of this State," which "puts me . . . in the van as the standard bearer of the Party in Florida." Moreover, he continued, "I can see & *feel* that I am strengthening daily for a recognition by Garfield. . . . I would not be surprised if a place in the Cabinet might be in the cards." In an early test case, he successfully lobbied for the appointment of Hamilton Jay as Jacksonville postmaster over Bisbee's candidate, William Ledwith; and while visions of the Cabinet were unrealistic, Garfield and Blaine were leaning toward his appointment as United States minister to Italy.[48] Both his embryonic political leverage and potential appointment perished with Garfield's assassination.

Undeterred by this twist of fate, Sanford continued lobbying with the Arthur administration. Although he ultimately played a decisive role in Arthur's African diplomacy, he was unable to affect the New Yorker's Florida policies. In a November 1881 letter to the president, he reiterated his fundamental strategy: a shift of the patronage away from the office holding clique led by Bisbee, Conover, and Eagan; deemphasis of black influence in the party; and the conciliation of southern whites. He predicted that these steps would prepare Florida Republicans to take advantage of the imminent "disintegration of the democratic party."[49]

When the anticipated rift in Democratic ranks materialized in 1884, Sanford waged his last major campaign to influence Florida politics. Disgruntled by a lack of recognition and nominations from the older Bourbon leaders, Frank W. Pope and Daniel L. McKennan had led the defection of younger Democrats to an independent ticket. Problems with party solidarity were not, however, confined to the Democrats; Republican disunity was even more far-reaching. Black Republican leaders had become dissatisfied with the party's white leadership, and after a February meeting in Gainesville they called openly for collaboration with the independent Democrats. Preferring to lose the state to the regular Democrats rather than share federal patronage with the independents, Horatio Bisbee and white Republican officeholders refused to join the growing independent alliance. Other white Republicans had no such reservations. A third Republican faction, a "reform" group led by Sanford and ex-Governor Harrison Reed, perceived this fluid situation as an opportunity to combine with maverick Democrats to control the state government and simultaneously wrest federal patronage from the office-holding "ring" in their own party.[50]

Sanford and Reed recognized the necessity of an expedient "understanding" with the independent Democrats, but their ultimate goal was to absorb these dissidents into a Republican party restructured around Florida's "anti-Bourbon, anti-secession, anti-free trade element."[51] In short, Sanford was once more attempting to resurrect a white-dominated, old-Whig party. Sanford and Reed agreed that realization of this ambitious objective hinged on several factors. They needed patronage help from the Arthur administration; they needed financial support from the Republican National Committee and wealthy businessmen such as Hamilton Disston and Henry B. Plant; they needed to launch a vigorous Republican newspaper; and they needed to overthrow Horatio Bisbee's leadership of Florida's Republican party.[52] Overestimating both Sanford's wealth and influence, Reed and the other "reform" Republicans looked to him as the one in their midst able to secure the necessary patronage and funds.

Sanford sought unsuccessfully to fulfill these expectations. While he spent most of the spring of 1884 seeking United States recognition of the Congo Free State, he also approached the Arthur administration on the patronage issue. Speaking through Senator Joseph R. Hawley, a Connecticut Republican, he implored President Arthur to unseat Bisbee as the dispenser of Florida's federal patronage. Arthur refused; and Hawley explained, "I confess I don't see how he can ostracise [sic] any leading republicans in Florida." Sanford was no more successful in procuring funds. Hamilton Disston would take no stock in the proposed newspaper, and appeals to Hawley and William Astor also went unheeded.[53]

Despite these failures, Sanford and Reed proceeded with their plans for a Republican paper. Reed emphasized its political indispensability: "A paper here properly conducted can compel a 'full vote & fair count' by intimidating treacherous allies and dividing & entangling elements of the opposition." He also assured Sanford that it would be a profitable financial investment and that its value would double within a year. Sanford probably considered the second consideration decisive. Reed and his associates were looking to Sanford for backing, but he was in such serious financial straits that he could hardly consider shouldering the costs of a paper. Only after nearly two months of effort was Reed able in April to gather the $1,000 required for a down payment on the *Putnam County Journal.* Confiding to Sanford that he would have to trust to "providence" for the remaining $3,500 of the purchase price, Reed moved the *Journal* from Palatka to Jacksonville. He assumed the editorship and made Solon A. Adams, the paper's former publisher, his business manager.[54]

Reed published the first issue of his *Jacksonville Florida Journal* the following month. He appealed to the business community, opposed Bisbee's renomination for Congress, and encouraged the cooperation of reform Republicans and independent Democrats. The veteran politician pointedly warned that the *Florida Journal* would support only those candidates who favored the tariff and resisted direct taxes. The economics of reform Republicanism translated into "home labor and American industry." Following the Independent state convention in June, Reed endorsed the ticket of former Democrat Frank W. Pope for governor and former Republican Jonathan C. Greeley for lieutenant governor.[55]

From the outset the paper experienced financial difficulty. Anticipated aid from the Jacksonville business community failed to materialize, and "jealousies" and "divisions . . . among what remain[ed] of the Republican party" aggravated the situation. Sherman Conant refused to contribute because Reed and Greeley were interested, and Greeley later withdrew aid because he objected to one of the paper's writers. Bisbee and his followers effectively forestalled all access to Republican office-holders, and in mid-June Solon Adams informed Sanford that a minimum of $2,000 was needed to maintain the paper's biweekly publication. Another $5,000 would be necessary to begin daily circulation.[56]

The *Florida Journal*'s impending demise placed Sanford in an embarrassing situation. As John Long wrote him in June, the paper's failure "would be a very grave & serious political misfortune to you, as it has been announced that you were at the bottom of it and that it rested upon a solid financial basis." Sanford's affiliation with the *Journal* had elicited public attacks by both Bisbee and the *Jacksonville Times Union,* and Bisbee privately stated that he would use every opportunity to "hit [Sanford] on the head."[57] Still, Sanford simply did not have the financial resources to sustain the paper and his political credibility.

In a final attempt to escape this dilemma, he attended the Republican national convention in Chicago in June. He sought to land Florida's seat on the Republican National Committee and thereby become "the organ of the State in Republican politics & a real power." This would also have enabled him to secure funding for the paper and be "a commencement at the right end for political preferment." On the eve of his departure for Chicago, he confessed to Gertrude that he was pessimistic. "I wish now," he added, "I had attempted nothing—Life is too short—to say nothing of over limited means." He would make this one final attempt; "If I don't succeed, I think I shall cease further effort, save to try at" Washington for a diplomatic post.[58]

His forebodings of failure were well-founded. He was unable to gain the national committee seat, and he again failed to wrest patronage and funding from the officeholders' ring. Despite scrupulous efforts to remain neutral, his presence provided "Bisbee and the 'Ring' representatives" material to convince the Arthur administration he had been working for Blaine. Soon after this fruitless trek to Chicago, the final proof of his failure to restructure Florida's Republican party came to hand. On July 9, 1884, Bisbee easily secured the Second District Republican nomination for Congress.[59]

Exhausted physically, emotionally, and financially, Sanford sailed for Brussels in July, leaving the tattered Republican reform movement in his wake. Although Reed continued the *Florida Journal*'s publication through the election and many Republicans voted for Pope and the Independents, the Democrats swept the state. Sanford's inability to influence events had contributed to the debacle, but there were other, more crucial determinants. Arthur had failed to aid Florida Independents, in sharp contrast to similar movements in other southern states. The Independents had been unable to locate a sufficiently attractive gubernatorial candidate and to convince Floridians of Democratic corruption. In the last analysis, the great majority of white Floridians detested both Republicans and blacks, two of the key groups in the Independent coalition. Still, the Independents had frightened the Democrats. The next year's Democratic-sponsored constitutional revision included a poll tax which disfranchised blacks and sealed the doom of Florida's Republican party.[60]

Both Sanford and Florida's late-nineteenth-century Republican party had mounted their final, unsuccessful campaign in 1884. Although significant party leaders, such as Rutherford B. Hayes, had shared Sanford's strategy of constructing a conservative, white coalition under the Republican banner, the plan was unworkable. It ignored critical realities of post-Civil War southern politics: the irretrievable death of the Whig party a generation before, the Reconstruction legacy of white hatred for Republicans and fear of black supremacy, the tendency of southern Republicans to eschew unity and party welfare for factionalism and personal gain, and the Democrats' capacity to nullify Republican votes through fraud and violence.[61] Not only was Sanford's grand scheme flawed, but he was unable to control events. Thurlow Weed, always the consummate political analyst, had succinctly appraised his friend's situation in 1880: "I have always believed that if other claims upon your time did not keep you so much away from Florida all would be well."[62] Sanford had neither the time nor the inclination for fundamental politics. He never recognized that maneuvering such as he employed in legislative lobbying or diplomatic negotiations was of no avail without a supporting constituency. The two closest students of Florida's 1884 elections have concluded that had Sanford acted more decisively he might have wielded real power, but this would have required a commitment to grassroots work that he was temperamentally and economically unable to make. In the final analysis, his Florida political activities were strikingly similar to his business ventures—unsystematic, even haphazard, and lacking in on-the-spot, personal involvement and supervision.

CHAPTER 7

SANFORD AND THE CONGO, 1877–1888

FOLLOWING THE Senate's rejection of his nomination to Madrid in 1869, Sanford repeatedly sought other diplomatic appointments. When he was unable to obtain either a diplomatic post or domestic political office, his craving for public life and a solid, enduring reputation led him into the service of Leopold II. From the late 1870s through the late 1880s, he labored faithfully and effectively on behalf of the Belgian monarch's African ventures. In so doing, he became the most influential person in the formation of American policy toward the Congo. His activities demonstrated both the central role which private individuals played in late-nineteenth-century American foreign policy and the country's economic expansionism.

Sanford, like many of his contemporaries,[1] fell victim to Leopold's charm and personality. The two men had much in common. Energetic, ambitious, and visionary, both consistently sought to expand their horizons, to engage ever-larger areas of responsibility. Leopold's powers of personal persuasion intensified the initial attraction wrought by these similarities. Described as a "delightful conversationalist" who "always knew what ailment to ask about and the names of wives and children," he recognized Sanford's usefulness and carefully cultivated the relationship. Following the Senate's rejection of Sanford's nomination to Belgium in 1877, the monarch displayed characteristic solicitude. Leopold's personal secretary expressed regret at Sanford's misfortune and continued, "The King is pleased that you will continue to reside among us where all the world loves and appreciates you."[2] Always vain, Sanford found this royal attention extremely flattering, especially in contrast to his repeated political and economic disappointments in the United States. His inability to discern Leopold's true motives demonstrates the same poor judgment that characterized his business pursuits.

Although Sanford eventually sought employment and other economic concessions from the Congo Free State, these were not his initial objectives. Rather, as Gideon Welles had observed many years before, he sought to be "consequential . . . to figure and to do." Accepting Leopold's assurances of free trade and humanitarian concern for the natives at face value, Sanford sincerely believed that he was promoting programs that would benefit not only his friend the king but also the United States and Africa. He clung doggedly to the outmoded concept of colonization as a solution to America's race problems and fastened on Central Africa as an ideal area for the resettlement of American blacks. Leopold's oft-repeated aim of opening the Congo region to free trade was even more influential. Sanford had "great faith" in American enterprise and was confident the United States would not be "out-distanced" in any equitable "commercial race." To be involved in a project of such great promise could, he concluded, only serve others and redound to his credit. In sum, his actions derived variously from naiveté, ambition, and idealism.[3]

Sanford's post-1869 pursuit of a diplomatic position had proved extremely frustrating. Over the balance of Grant's term, he had written often to Secretary of State Fish concerning diplomatic and political developments and had even attempted to convert Grant with a personal visit. By the mid-1870s he was sure that Fish favored his cause, and he had enlisted Postmaster General Marshall Jewell in the effort; but the president still withheld the coveted appointment.[4]

With the election of 1876 and the conclusion of Grant's presidency, Sanford intensified his efforts. During the spring of 1877, he established a temporary residence in Washington and launched a lavish round of entertainment similar to that preceding his nomination to Belgium in 1861. Included among the influential politicians attending his dinner parties were James A. Garfield; William Dennison, former governor of Ohio; and William M. Evarts, soon to become secretary of state under Rutherford B. Hayes. The press delighted in assailing these activities. Referring to him as the "peripatetic patriot," the *New York Sun* charged that Sanford had "set up a house where the friends of the Fraudulent President are dined and wined freely, as a short cut to a foreign mission." When he separated one of his gatherings from the remainder of the hotel dining room with a blue ribbon, he immediately became known as "Blue Ribbon" Sanford. Even more damaging were the old allegations of war-time profiteering. The *Sun* and other papers reiterated these rumors, with one journal cuttingly referring to him as his "Excellency Belgian Musket Garibaldi Sanfwar."[5]

Troubled by these public accusations, Evarts demanded an explanation. Sanford answered on May 29, 1877, with a long letter categorically denying all charges of wrongdoing. This rebuttal, combined with the influence of Thurlow Weed and Henry B. Anthony, convinced Evarts of Sanford's innocence. In July Weed reassured Sanford that the newspaper attacks "annoy but do not alarm me. Evarts when here, some three weeks ago re-assured me so frankly that I cannot entertain a doubt." Encouraged by Weed's news, Sanford concluded his campaign by writing Evarts several long letters describing the European diplomatic scene. He hoped both to keep his name before the secretary and to demonstrate his expertise as an interpreter of European events.[6]

Weed's confidence was rewarded when Hayes nominated Sanford as his minister resident to Belgium on November 8, 1877. Again, as in 1869, Sanford's nomination provoked fierce opposition, with the newspaper barrage resuming immediately. George P. Smith, the quartermaster agent with whom Sanford had clashed over a Confederate cloth contract in 1861, had previously denounced Sanford's alleged profiteering to President Hayes. He now aired his charges in the *New York World* and the *New York Tribune.* The *New York Times* and *New York Evening Telegraph* responded with favorable reviews of Sanford's career, and Sanford hurried off a second letter to Evarts explaining his dealings with Smith. He argued that Smith had been the would-be profiteer, and he enclosed a letter from the French agent in the contract negotiations corroborating his version of the episode.[7]

Sanford's efforts went for naught when the Senate Committee on Foreign Relations reported unfavorably on his nomination in late November. Fearful that a Senate vote would also be negative, Anthony and Evarts let the nomination lie until the regular session of Congress began in December. Anthony hoped that the "powerful influence" of James G. Blaine, who had been ill during the special session, might turn the tide. When Congress reassembled, Anthony and Blaine canvassed the Senate and were convinced that they had secured the necessary votes. Evarts simultaneously prodded Hayes to resubmit the nomination; but the president, who had never shared Evarts' commitment to Sanford, stubbornly refused. Instead, on February 15, 1878, he shattered Sanford's hopes by selecting the less controversial Cassius Goodloe of Kentucky.[8]

Sanford's subsequent relations with the Hayes administration followed a pattern very similar to those of the Grant years. Although he maintained a good rapport with Secretary of State Evarts, who admitted in 1878 that he "wish[ed]" he had Sanford "abroad," Sanford again found the "hitch . . . at the White House." In fact, the impediments to Sanford's nomination reached far beyond presidential hostility. Sanford himself acknowledged that his long residence abroad, which by 1878 amounted to nearly twenty years, was "fatal." It had bred prejudices against him and deprived him of a domestic political base. Moreover, Seward and Weed, the men most responsible for his nomination in 1861, no longer exercised a decisive influence in Republican counsels. Seward had died in 1872, and as Weed lamented, "Once I could have vindicated you. Now I am powerless"[9]

Despite these repeated disappointments, James A. Garfield's election in 1880 rekindled Sanford's optimism. Both Garfield and Blaine, the incoming secretary of state, were old friends from whom he expected kinder treatment. Sanford remained conspicuous by corresponding regularly with Garfield concerning campaign and patronage matters; by making a trip to Washington in January 1881; and by receiving endorsements from Hamilton Fish, Senator Anthony, and Truman Smith. These efforts bore fruit in the late spring of 1881 when Garfield advised Blaine that he intended to nominate Sanford as minister to Italy. Before the president could fulfill this commitment, both he and Sanford's nomination fell before Charles Guiteau's bullet.[10]

Refusing to concede, Sanford continued the campaign with Chester A. Arthur and the new secretary of state, Frederick T. Frelinghuysen. Weed, Anthony, Bancroft Davis, Edwin Morgan, William B. Allison, and Eugene Hale all lent their support, and Sanford helped arrange Arthur's visit to Florida in 1883. Even the vivacious Gertrude attempted to charm the chief executive. In March 1884 she assured the "very kind and very sensitive" Arthur that he could compensate for the "treacherous conduct" of President Hayes and carry "out the last wishes of the Departed" Garfield by sending

Henry abroad. Despite his assurances to the aging Weed, Arthur did not proffer a European mission.[11]

Although eminently qualified in terms of ability and experience, Sanford's lack of a strong political base precluded a second appointment. Those most responsible for ongoing diplomatic activities, such as Secretaries of State Seward, Fish, and Evarts, and Assistant Secretaries Davis and Hunter, consistently recognized his value and endorsed his candidacy. However, those more politically motivated, such as Presidents Grant, Hayes, and Arthur, and diverse United States senators, frustrated his efforts. Spurned by American politicians, Sanford offered his talents to Leopold II.

Leopold II had ascended to the throne in 1865 determined to make Belgium a colonial power. After a decade of unsuccessful attempts to buy or lease an existing colony in the Far East, he shifted his attention to Africa. Unable to count on the support of the Belgian assembly and without military forces, Leopold turned to international collaboration. In September 1876 he hosted a conference of distinguished European geographers and explorers. At Leopold's direction, the conference established the *Association Internationale Africaine* (AIA), with the ostensibly philanthropic objectives of scientific exploration, repression of the slave trade, and construction of a series of stations for hospitable and scientific purposes. The king's plans had not yet crystallized, but he hoped that the AIA would provide him badly needed information about Africa and possibly furnish an institutional guise for a "private enterprise" or commercial company. The conference closed with a call for the formation of national AIA committees in Western Europe and the United States.[12]

With an eye toward American philanthropists, Leopold wrote a flattering letter urging Judge Charles P. Daly, president of the American Geographical Society, to organize a United States AIA committee. Daly's society had long served as a meeting place in New York City for businessmen, scientists, and explorers interested in Africa. The judge also drew on a generalized American fascination with the "Dark Continent." At this time, economic expansionists increasingly looked upon Africa as a potentially lucrative market; missionaries eagerly contemplated millions of native converts; and the remnants of the American Colonization Society clung tenaciously to the hope of returning American blacks to Africa. In addition, Americans of all classes and occupations had thrilled at Henry M. Stanley's location of Dr. David Livingstone in 1871 and had subsequently followed the exploits of Stanley and the prominent European explorers.[13]

On May 8, 1877, Judge Daly culminated six months of work with the formation of the American Auxiliary Society of the AIA. The auxiliary society chose John H. B. Latrobe, long-time chairman of the American Colonization Society, as president and selected Henry Sanford and Henry M. Schieffelin, an American residing in Paris, as delegates to the upcoming AIA meeting in Brussels. Sanford was about to return to Belgium after spending the spring in Washington lobbying for a foreign mission. Although he knew little about Africa and had no prior involvement with the AIA, he was undoubtedly familiar with Leopold's 1876 conference, due both to the proximity of his home in Brussels and his personal acquaintance with the king and his ministers. This familiarity, combined with his residence near the conference site, made him a natural choice for the American delegation.[14]

On June 20 and 21, 1877, delegates from nine European countries and the United States gathered in Brussels for what proved to be the AIA's only plenary session. Since England had withdrawn and Sir Bartle Frere of London had resigned his seat on the executive committee, the conference chose Sanford as the representative of the English-speaking nations. Pleased by this recognition, Sanford was especially flattered by Leopold's compliments at the time of his selection. After adopting a blue flag with a gold star as the AIA's emblem and planning the organization's initial expeditions into East Africa, the delegates concluded by renominating Leopold as chairman of the executive committee.[15]

In reporting the conference's work to the American society, Sanford enthusiastically predicted that a "great work of civilization and humanity" had begun. Since "nearly 5,000,000 of our people are of African race—descendants of slaves," the United States had a special interest in the expeditions. Contact with the white race had, Sanford argued, rendered American blacks "by far the superiors" of their forefathers, and Leopold's undertaking provided them the opportunity of "returning to civilize and regenerate the parent country."[16]

As the AIA prepared for its initial expeditions in the fall of 1877, news of Henry Stanley's most recent discoveries reached Europe. Following his location of Livingstone in 1871, the intrepid Welshman had led a second expedition. He traced the course of the Congo from the heart of Central Africa to the Atlantic, where he emerged on August 10, 1877. Leopold had been contemplating the establishment of trading stations in the Cameroons, but he immediately recognized that the Congo offered an avenue to the middle of the continent and that Stanley might be the man to spearhead his commercial company.[17]

Leopold deputized Sanford to confirm Stanley's usefulness. Sanford immediately inquired whether James Gordon Bennett, owner of the *New York Herald* and sponsor of Stanley's two journeys, had been satisfied with the explorer's "economy, prudence, reliability, character, etc." Gratified by Bennett's reply, Leopold dispatched Sanford, whom he termed "perfectly suited" for the mission, and Baron Jules Greindl, secretary-general of the AIA and the king's personal secretary, to recruit Stanley.[18]

Sanford and Greindl met Stanley in Marseille on January 13, 1878. That evening Sanford had a "long talk" with Stanley at a banquet given in the latter's honor by the Marseille Geographical Society but was unable to extract a commitment from the exhausted explorer. While Stanley protested that illness and fatigue precluded consideration of Leopold's offer to develop the Congo, he actually hoped to enlist Britain as his sponsor. Leopold was not deterred by this initial refusal, and Sanford continued to serve as an important intermediary. On March 8, as Sanford prepared to go to America, the king directed him to "pressure" Stanley as he passed through London. Sanford also maintained his contacts with Bennett. He lauded the publisher's "enterprise and liberality" and stressed that the AIA would make a concrete offer only after Stanley had amiably terminated his contract with the *New York Herald.* Sanford reinforced his letters with a personal visit to Bennett in March.[19]

Sanford's efforts were important but not decisive. Only after failing to arouse English interest did Stanley seriously entertain Leopold's overtures. Following several months of intermittent negotiation, including another "formal interview" with Sanford, Stanley agreed in November 1878 to serve Leopold's latest organization, the *Comité d'Etudes du Haut Congo* (CEHC). The CEHC, which Sanford loosely characterized as a "sub-organization of the Association," was to underwrite a study of the Congo region's trading prospects and to assess the possibilities for a railroad around the river's cataracts. Although organizationally distinct from the International Association, the CEHC adopted the AIA's flag; and when

Leopold dissolved the CEHC in 1879, he continued to use the name to mask his true intentions in the Congo. Toward the end of 1882, the king adopted still a third label, the *Association Africaine Internationale du Congo* (AIC), to designate his African venture. A masterful propagandist, Leopold encouraged and played upon the public confusion between the original philanthropic and international *Association Internationale Africaine* and the imperialistic and personal *Association Internationale du Congo.*[20]

Sanford was among those deceived by the monarch's philanthropic pose. He revealed his naiveté in June 1879, when the Afrikaanche Handelsvereeniging, a Dutch commercial house holding stock in the CEHC, failed. In a letter and subsequent interview, Sanford urged Leopold to use this opportunity for bringing the enterprise under his exclusive authority. He argued that the expedition could be cleansed of all speculative stigma and restored to a "purely philanthropic" basis by placing it under the "sole name & control of the King."[21]

Sanford's increasingly important liaison role between Leopold and strategically placed Americans demonstrated this same trust. On his visit to New York in the spring of 1878, Sanford had prodded America's AIA committee to become more active and had searched unsuccessfully for an American explorer to participate in the projected expeditions. In early 1879 he warned Secretary of State William M. Evarts that Portuguese substantiation of their claim to the Congo's mouth could block the free entry of United States vessels and goods into central Africa. At Sanford's suggestion, Commodore Robert Shufeldt, commander of the U.S.S. *Ticonderoga,* visited the area in June 1879 but expressed little enthusiasm for the prospects of American commerce there.[22]

Sanford continued his correspondence with Judge Daly and the American Geographical Society and extended his contacts in March 1879 by addressing the influential New York Chamber of Commerce. He assured New York's business elite that Leopold's AIA offered the most "practical plan" for opening the Congo's huge population and vast resources to both "civilization" and "commerce." Warming to his subject, he painted an enticing picture of throngs of unclothed natives hungering for American cotton goods. In return, the Africans offered products seemingly "endless in richness and variety: ivory, gold, copper, palmoil, oil nuts, grain, cotton, gums, dates, coffee, sugar, ebony, dyes, aromatic woods, feathers, etc., etc." To insure a "share of a trade destined to be of the greatest importance to commercial nations," American businessmen had only to support the king of the Belgians.[23] Over the ensuing five years, Sanford would repeatedly return to the theme that Leopold rather than his European competitors offered the United States the best trading opportunity in central Africa.

While Sanford promoted Leopold's projects in the United States, Henry Stanley laid the basis for the monarch's African state. Stanley began his expedition up the Congo in August 1879. During the next four and one-half years, he negotiated hundreds of treaties by which the native chiefs formally transferred sovereignty over their lands to the CEHC. Stanley's work elicited both French and Portuguese challenges to Leopold's enterprise. In September 1880 Count Pierre Savorgna de Brazza and Chief Makako, a native king, concluded a treaty giving France title to strategic areas on the north bank of Stanley Pool. In ratifying this treaty two years later, the French Parliament not only threatened Leopold's access to the navigable Congo basin but also spurred the Portuguese and British into action. Although Portugal had claimed sovereignty over the mouth of the Congo since its discovery in 1843 by Diego Cam, she had done little to legitimize this claim through actual occupation. Desirous of maintaining free trade in the Congo region, Britain feared an extension of France's protectionist fiscal system. This mutual fear of France produced the Anglo-Portuguese Treaty of February 1884, in which Great Britain recognized Portuguese sovereignty over the mouth of the Congo and Portugal guaranteed Britain free trade and navigation on the Congo and most-favored-nation status in Portuguese territories.[24]

Confronted by these challenges, Leopold moved to establish the sovereign status of the *Association Internationale du Congo*. As a "semi-private enterprise" the AIC had not received formal recognition from any European state and had no official standing in the international community. To overcome this international impotence, the king turned to the United States for diplomatic recognition of his Association. Several factors influenced this decision. Considerable American interest in Africa and the Congo region already existed, and the Liberian experience presented a precedent for an initially private association acquiring the rights of sovereignty.[25] Most importantly, Henry Sanford was willing and eminently qualified to direct the recognition campaign.

During the early 1880s, Sanford had maintained his association with Americans interested in the Congo, and he actively lobbied the key figures in the Garfield and Arthur administrations. In June 1881 he wrote his old friend, Secretary of State James G. Blaine, recounting the work of Leopold's "International African Association . . . the greatest and most liberal individual philanthropic enterprise of modern times." He predicted that Brazza's activities would provide a pretext for British intervention and urged Blaine to endorse freedom of commerce on the Congo. Following Garfield's assassination, he lectured Arthur's secretary of state, Frederick T. Frelinghuysen, on the threatening aspects of the Brazza-Makako Treaty. Declaring that the Congo, "more than any hitherto unoccupied part of the globe," offered a market for America's manufacturing surpluses, Sanford warned that the United States could not allow the French to "secure exclusive privileges" there. Beginning in January 1883, he repeatedly urged Secretary of the Navy William E. Chandler to grant two or three United States naval officers leave and to allow them to command the stations Stanley was establishing. He suggested that these officers could be paid by the Association but still be designated United States "consuls" or "agents." In the absence of American action, he feared that British citizens would fill these positions and enhance the influence of another commercial competitor. "The Pear is ripe," he advised Chandler, "and I hope we may pluck it!" Finally, in June 1883 he edited and transmitted a letter from Leopold to President Arthur. In an accompanying note Sanford reiterated his proposal that a United States consul to the Congo could be "employed at a suitable salary by the Association." By August Sanford's persistent efforts had begun to yield results; after still another letter, Frelinghuysen confidentially assured him that he favored "recognition of the neutrality of the stations along the Congo" and would call the matter to Arthur's attention.[26]

Thus, as Sanford and Leopold planned the final recognition campaign in November 1883, the groundwork was well laid. Before leaving Brussels, Sanford helped Leopold draft a second letter to Arthur. The king claimed that the "African International Association" was directing the rapid and peaceful division of the Congo region into indepenaent states and solicited United States recognition of the AIA's banner as a friendly flag. The AIA promised freedom from customs duties, full liberty for United States citizens to acquire and occupy land, and most-favored-nation status. Sanford reached New York on November 27 and hurried on to Washington that evening. The next day he personally delivered Leopold's letter to the president and presented Frelinghuysen with a draft recognition agreement. Unprepared for a definite commitment, Frelinghuysen cautiously questioned whether the association's position warranted recognition.[27]

Still, Frelinghuysen was essentially receptive and requested that Sanford draft a paragraph for inclusion in Arthur's annual message to Congress. Sanford readily agreed and scored his first lobbying coup on December 4, 1883, when the president naively propagated Leopold's Congo position:

> The rich and populous valley of the Kongo is being opened to commerce by a society called the African International Association, of which the King of the Belgians is the president and a citizen of the United States [Stanley] the chief executive officer. Large tracts of territory have been ceded to the Association by native chiefs, roads have been opened, steamboats placed on the river, and the nuclei of states established at twenty-two stations under one flag which offers freedom of commerce and prohibits the slave trade. The objects of the society are philanthropic. It does not aim at permanent political control, but seeks the neutrality of the valley. The United States cannot be indifferent to this work. . . . It may become advisable for us to cooperate with other commercial powers in promoting the rights of free trade and residence in the Kongo Valley free from the interference or political control of any one nation.[28]

Convinced that the administration's "spirit" was "good," Sanford skillfully brought a broader spectrum of "influence to bear." Drawing on his experience as minister to Belgium, he marshalled support from powerful segments of the press. Both the *New York Times* and *New York Herald* lavishly endorsed Arthur's comments, emphasized the limitless prospects for American commerce in the Congo, and denounced the French and Portuguese claims. The *Herald* characterized Brazza's treaty negotiations with Makako as "quixotic proceedings" and dismissed any Portuguese claim based solely on prior discovery. Both papers criticized the negotiations then in progress for the Anglo-Portuguese Treaty and portrayed all such European maneuvers as threats to freedom of trade and American profits on the Congo.[29]

Ostensibly, only Leopold's association confronted these greedy European states. "The association," asserted the *Times*, "engages in no money-making enterprise directly or indirectly, acts in the interest of no Government, uses no force, but makes its way peacefully and honorably, and devotes itself faithfully to the task of an unselfish pioneer of civilization." The *Herald* agreed and added that each of the association's twenty-two republics constituted a union of states open to the commerce of all nations. The *Times* concluded by urging the nation's commercial bodies, particularly the New York Chamber of Commerce, to exert their influence for free trade in the Congo Basin. The *Herald* went one step further and advocated recognition of the association's flag as the appropriate means for protecting potential American interests.

With Sanford's guidance, the New York Chamber of Commerce soon responded to the *Times'* appeal. Early in December Sanford had contacted two old friends, Abiel A. and Seth Low, both prominent, highly respected members of the New York Chamber. Sanford had known A. A. Low, a prosperous China merchant, and Seth, the Mayor of Brooklyn, for many years, and both men responded to his appeal. Working with Judge Daly, Sanford drafted a series of pro-recognition resolutions, which A. A. Low introduced at the chamber's January 10, 1884, meeting. These resolutions denied the legitimacy of the Portuguese claims on the Congo, advocated "recognition . . . of the flag of the African International Association," and recommended that the president dispatch an accredited agent to confer with the AIA and secure "free commercial intercourse" for American citizens along the Congo. The Chamber unanimously adopted the resolutions and forwarded them to President Arthur.[30]

By recruiting Frelinghuysen, the Lows, and Daly, Sanford had enlisted persons strategically placed in the nation's diplomatic, commercial, and geographic-scientific establishments. He soon added two more crucial persons and in so doing forged inroads into their respective institutions: John H. B. Latrobe, president of the American Colonization Society, and John Tyler Morgan, a prominent member of the Senate Committee on Foreign Relations. Latrobe, an old Sanford acquaintance and the original chairman of the AIA's American committee, proselytized his friends in government, mobilized the American Colonization Society, and tendered Sanford the use of the society's Washington offices.[31]

Morgan's role proved far more important. The former Confederate brigadier was a fervent economic expansionist and unbending white supremacist, who viewed the Congo as a potential dumping ground for both America's manufacturing surpluses and her unwanted blacks. Once Morgan began "reading up" on the Congo situation, Sanford was delighted to furnish him appropriately pro-

AIA source materials. Sanford added personal support through numerous private conversations and by entertaining the Alabama senator at several lavish dinner parties. Aided by the radiant and charming Gertrude, Sanford hosted a number of these parties for Morgan and other congressmen. Suave and facile, Sanford was especially effective and persuasive at these unofficial gatherings. After one such affair, Morgan thanked him for the "most agreeable entertainment and for the great pleasure of the acquaintance of Mrs. Sanford." At another "charming dinner," Latrobe carefully compared the Liberian experience to that of the AIA, for the edification of several senators and representatives. William H. Trescot's reply to a Sanford invitation was revealing; he agreed to dine *"with"* Sanford, "but," he continued, "don't betray me with a formal dinner party or I will head an anti-Congo party at once." Activities such as these, the circulation of the New York Chamber of Commerce's resolutions among members of Congress, and his own living expenses cost Sanford nearly $7,500 between November 1883 and May 1884.[32]

By enlisting Morgan, Sanford made himself the primary source of information on Congo affairs for the two groups responsible for United States treaty-making: the State Department and the Senate Committee on Foreign Relations. Early in January 1884, Morgan set the congressional "Congo Ball in motion" by writing to Frelinghuysen and requesting all relevant State Department information. Frelinghuysen's January 18 reply bore the clear stamp of Sanford's influence. The secretary denigrated Portugal's claims, echoed the Brussels version of the AIA's philanthropic work, and depicted the Association's ultimate objective as the establishment of a powerful, self-sustaining native state. Based on this misleading material, Morgan introduced a resolution in the Senate on January 21, 1884, directing the Foreign Relations Committee to inquire into Congo affairs and return recommendations for the promotion of American commerce in that region.[33]

With the Congo question officially before his committee, Morgan asked Frelinghuysen on February 6 to outline the administration's position on the Anglo-Portuguese Treaty. Frelinghuysen in turn solicited Sanford's views, and the latter responded with a lengthy letter on February 9. He conceded Portugal's claims of prior discovery but countered that her failure to establish effective occupation of the Congo's mouth voided all sovereign rights. He observed correctly that Great Britain was seeking "to arrange a sort of protectorate through Portugal, by a partial recognition of claims always heretofore denied." To permit the area to fall under Portuguese influence would, Sanford argued, be a crime against humanity and a threat to future United States commercial prospects. Portugal was both an "active abettor of the slave trade" and a proponent of protectionist fiscal policies. In sum, it would be a mistake "to admit . . . these claims of Portugal, still less under the protection of Great Britain."[34]

Frelinghuysen's belated March 13 reply to Morgan's inquiry again mirrored his dependence on Sanford. He fully subscribed to the Brussels contention that a private philanthropic organization could found a state and offered the American experience in Liberia as a noteworthy precedent. In a statement virtually identical in phrasing to one first used by Jules Devaux in Brussels, and later by Sanford, Frelinghuysen noted: "The International Association exists only for its stations. It has no commerce; it gives no dividends. It is part of their life until it dissolves into them, the future Free States of the Congo." Discarding his caution of the previous November, Frelinghuysen officially advocated recognition of the AIA flag.[35]

While Morgan awaited Frelinghuysen's reply, he also had undertaken actions that revealed Sanford's guiding hand. On February 24 the senator sent Sanford a "rough draft" of a resolution he planned to submit to the Senate the next day. Apologizing for rousing Sanford from bed, Morgan encouraged his confidant's "free criticism" of the draft. The final version, which Morgan introduced on February 25 termed the AIA's treaties with the natives legitimate and contended that the agreements entitled the association's flag to "the recognition and respect of other countries as the flag of the Free States of Congo." The following day Morgan introduced a second resolution recommending that President Arthur take immediate action to secure unrestricted commercial access to the Congo Basin. Though unstated, Morgan's implication and Sanford's oft-repeated claim were that this could be most readily obtained through diplomatic recognition of the AIA. The Senate referred both resolutions to its Foreign Relations Committee.[36]

Bolstered by Sanford's materials and information, Morgan presented the committee's report on March 26. Over fifty pages in length, the document faithfully reiterated Sanford's familiar arguments and advocated recognition of the AIA. Significantly, Morgan substantiated these contentions by citing and appending the same legal and historical sources that Sanford had carried with him from Belgium the previous November. Sanford's congressional lobbying efforts came to fruition on April 10 when the Senate adopted Morgan's recommendations.[37]

Assured of Senate approval, Frelinghuysen promptly exchanged declarations with Sanford, who acted on behalf of the *"International Association of the Congo. "* The Association agreed to levy no import duties on American goods; guaranteed foreigners the right to purchase, sell, or lease real estate; and extended most-favored-nation status to the United States. Washington reciprocated by recognizing *"the flag of the International African Association as the flag of a friendly Government. "*[38]

In securing this recognition, Sanford had scored a diplomatic and lobbying coup. In April 1884 the French minister to Washington had offered a vivid contemporary appraisal of Sanford's effectiveness: "His activity at the State Department, the Senate and his contacts with the American press, had put more drive than is customary into the Parliamentary procedure which here determines all questions of external policy." Sanford had unknowingly represented what Jean Stengers later termed "a fictitious entity . . . a name and nothing more." While Stanley had negotiated 400 treaties and established twenty-two stations, the Association was not exercising control over the region equivalent to effective sovereignty. When America's first representative to the "Free States of the Congo" reached Europe in the fall of 1884, he found himself "accredited to a country which did not in reality exist."[39] Both the creation of a viable state and the atrocities that shocked the world would come later.

Ernest R. May has described a group of late-nineteenth-century "foreign policy opinion leaders" who parlayed business or professional prominence, a "special knowledge" of foreign developments, and acquaintance with foreign and domestic statesmen into a disproportionate influence on American policy.[40] Sanford was certainly a member of this group. He had recruited prominent, strategically placed persons, and his success demonstrated the ability of individuals to influence the course of American foreign policy in the Gilded Age.

Personal charm and persuasiveness partially explain Sanford's facility for attracting this support; but even more significant was his ostensible expertise in Congo matters and the promise of AIA-guaranteed opportunity for American trade and commerce. Economic depression had plagued the United States since 1882 and would continue into 1886. Amidst widespread business failures, Frelinghuysen proved very "assertive" in "matters appearing to offer sizable economic advantage to the United States." Although it would become apparent, much to Sanford's personal chagrin, that he had greatly overestimated the immediate commercial potential of the

Congo, the Senate and the Arthur administration had proven receptive. Both Sanford's arguments and the administration's decision for
recognition demonstrated the important role of economic considerations in late-nineteenth-century diplomacy.[41]

Sanford, like Leopold, had played upon the public confusion over
the truly international and humanitarian *Association Internationale
Africaine* and the Belgian-dominated, imperialistic *Association Internationale du Congo*. Sanford's exchange of declarations with Frelinghuysen was symptomatic: Sanford signed on behalf of the AIC,
and Frelinghuysen recognized the long-defunct AIA. Together with
many contemporaries, Sanford was far too willing to accept Leopold's professions as sincere. In so doing, he failed to discriminate
among the varying names and activities of the monarch's organiza-
tions.

American reaction to Sanford's coup was mixed. The *New York
Herald* believed the Arthur administration had made a wise decision, but the *New York Tribune* charged that the State Department
had been "duped and placed in a false position." The *Tribune* feared
that the United States had compromised its isolationist tradition, and
subsequent students have agreed, observing that AIA recognition
constituted blatant interference in European affairs. Control of the
mouth of the Congo was still in dispute, and the Anglo-Portuguese
Treaty was simultaneously under consideration in the British Parliament. This latter consideration lead the London *Times* to characterize the United States action as a "piece of very sharp practice—an
act of immorality, in fact." By contrast, Leopold and his lieutenants
paid "hommage to the skill" with which Sanford had "conducted
this delicate and difficult negotiation." Gertrude, who had originally
disparaged Leopold's African aspirations as "*wild cat* schemes" and
had warned Henry not to get involved, wrote describing her break-
fast with the royal family: "I cannot begin to tell you of all the
flattering things the King said about you[.] He really is delighted &
I never have seen him so gay & so good humored. . . . My dear
nothing could have been more flattering to you or tender to me than
were both the King & Queen."[42]

While Sanford waged his recognition campaign, Leopold had skillfully exploited European colonial rivalries. On April 23, one day
after Sanford exchanged declarations with Frelinghuysen, Leopold
extracted a similar recognition from France. Fearful that the pending

Anglo-Portuguese Treaty would enable Britain to dominate the area, the French had recognized the AIC flag in return for first refusal on any future sale of Association holdings. Although Leopold had aimed this right of preemption at Portugal, it helped maneuver France, Great Britain, and Germany into positions of grudging support for the AIC. France thereafter perceived herself as the inevitable heir to Leopold's financially troubled organization, while the British and Germans paradoxically felt constrained to aid Leopold lest the Congo fall under French control. Although the Germans took Leopold's promises of free trade more seriously than did the British Foreign Office, both states were also influenced by the enticing prospect of unrestricted access to an area developed at Leopold's expense.[43]

American and French recognition had enhanced the AIC's international standing; however, territorial disputes with Portugal and France still blocked the path to full-fledged statehood. Prospects for settling these disputes arose when Germany and France jointly sponsored the Berlin West African Conference in November 1884. Bismarck had encountered a muddled, but exasperating, British opposition when he led Germany into the African colonial scramble in 1883. Britain had also alienated France in 1882 by unilaterally occupying Egypt and ending dual Anglo-French control. Capitalizing on this common enmity, Bismarck pledged his support for French demands in Egypt and suggested a Franco-German agreement to secure freedom of trade and commerce in the unannexed portions of Africa. French Prime Minister Jules Ferry considered this project too ambitious but agreed to a conference with an agenda confined to three principles: freedom of commerce on the Congo, free navigation of the Niger and Congo Rivers, and establishment of regular procedures for subsequent European colonial occupations on African coasts.[44]

In October Germany officially invited the United States to the Berlin Conference. After some hesitation, Frelinghuysen accepted with the understanding that the conference would limit discussion to the proposed agenda and that the United States incurred no obligation to accept the conference's conclusions. The secretary of state then designated John A. Kasson, America's minister to Germany, as the United States representative to the conference.[45]

Kasson's first conference-related action was to secure Frelinghuysen's agreement to add Sanford and Henry Stanley to the American delegation. A former Iowa congressman and minister to

Austria-Hungary under Hayes, Kasson was an old friend of Sanford. He had frequently visited the Sanfords at Gingelom during the 1860s and had stopped to see Gertrude and the children on his way to Berlin in September 1884. He and Sanford had seen each other often in Washington during the summer of 1884. And Sanford had lobbied the Association's cause in letters congratulating Kasson on his appointments as minister and conference delegate. Sanford's notes emphasized his principal theme of the previous spring: AIC control of the Congo offered the greatest opportunity for free trade and American commercial access.[46]

A resolute economic expansionist, Kasson proved enthusiastically receptive to Sanford's message. On October 21 Kasson solicited Sanford's services; as one "thoroughly acquainted with the views as well as the history of the African International Association," he would be of invaluable aid. Leopold and his entourage joined Kasson in urging Sanford to accept. They hoped that Sanford might help protect the interests of the AIC, which had not been invited to the conference, and control Stanley, whom they suspected of retaining earlier visions of a British protectorate on the Congo and whose lack of discretion could prove troublesome.[47]

Sanford accepted Kasson's offer on October 23. Since his American investments offered bleak prospects for recapturing the family's affluence, Sanford had already begun to look to the Congo for possible salvation. In August 1884 he had written Gertrude speculating on his prospects with Leopold's emerging state: "If I can get a good hold there, it will fix me with regard to the future. There is just the sort of work I would like, with both reputation & money to gain & the satisfaction of doing good. I think I will have it out with H[is] M[ajesty] . . . and propose a plan of operations, and offer my services." He had also mentioned a potential "commercial organization," but Kasson's invitation arrived before Sanford could approach the king. Given his Congo-related aspirations and a continuing desire for diplomatic service, he promptly accepted. It was, Sanford observed, a "chance to come to the surface again—& may lead to more."[48]

Delegates from thirteen European nations and the United States gathered at Bismarck's palace on November 15 for the conference's opening session. Acting officially as a "second plenipotentiary," Sanford exercised considerable influence with Kasson. While complaining privately that Kasson was "obstinate," "selfish," and "hard as flint," Sanford also recognized that "to get on with him, I have got to follow him." Assuming a deferential stance, Sanford subtly managed the American delegation's major positions. After visiting Berlin in early November, Willard P. Tisdel, the recently appointed American representative to the Congo Free State, pronounced Sanford the "master of the situation. Of course always yielding the first place to Mr. Kasson—as he [Sanford] knew all about the Congo, and he was looked upon as a very *important person* . . . *Which in fact he was.* "[49]

Kasson readily agreed with Sanford's belief that support of the AIC constituted the most effective strategy for furthering American economic and philanthropic interests. Operating from this assumption and with information supplied by Sanford and Stanley, Kasson consistently advocated positions favorable to the Association. At the second session of the conference, on November 19, Kasson explained the American reasons for recognizing the AIC in terms virtually identical to those Sanford had been arguing for the previous four years. Neutralization and equal commercial access to the Congo would best serve American economic interests; Leopold's promises to provide these conditions and to extinguish the slave trade logically dictated recognition. Since the AIC was pursuing such laudable objectives, Kasson announced that the United States favored extending the Association's benign rule over the largest area consistent with the "just territorial rights" of the other contending parties.[50] The United States, to be sure, was unprepared to go beyond verbal support for the AIC; but Kasson's lecture to Europe's colonial powers on proper African boundaries was itself a bold act—one hardly consistent with the accepted tenor of late-nineteenth-century American foreign policy.

With Sanford's close collaboration, Kasson also helped to enlarge the conference's definition of a central African free trade zone. Kasson's amendment doubled the area by defining the zone as the Congo's "commercial" rather than "geographical" basin, and he strongly implied that the AIC should be the "Trustee Government" appointed to administer the territory for the "common interest." With the backing of both Bismarck, the conference's guiding force, and the British delegation, Kasson's measure and its potential for an open door in central Africa gained acceptance.[51]

Kasson followed this victory by proposing that the broadly defined commercial basin be permanently neutralized. Again his recommendation benefitted the AIC; neutralization would protect the relatively defenseless Association from its more powerful colonial rivals,

France and Portugal. It was, as Leopold's secretary confided to Sanford, a "way of guaranteeing and establishing" the AIC's "frontiers." Kasson once more acted with Bismarck's approval. Having recognized the AIC on the eve of the conference, Germany, like the United States, judged it expedient to support the organization and its promises of commercial concessions. Only after the settlement of all territorial disputes did France and Portugal grudgingly consent to this neutralization project.[52]

In addition to guiding Kasson, Sanford personally introduced a proposal for the construction of a railroad around the cataracts of the lower Congo between Stanley Pool and the sea. Leopold and his associates considered this railroad essential to the commercial development of the upper Congo. Emile Banning, the influential journalist assigned to the Belgian delegation, had drafted the original proposition; but Count Vander Straten-Ponthoz, the head of the delegation, refused to introduce it. Leopold then turned to Sanford. On November 27 Sanford formally proposed that the state ultimately owning the greatest expanse of territory between Vivi and Stanley Pool be granted the "sole right" to construct the badly needed railroad. Lesser landowners would be obligated to grant the road's passage through their possessions. Since Sanford and the Belgian representatives expected the AIC to become the region's largest landowner, this measure would have helped guarantee the Association's transportation link to the sea. Recognizing this, France and Portugal adamantly resisted. Neither Sanford's second speech nor British and German support could overcome the unyielding Franco-Portuguese opposition. The issue soon merged into the critical territorial negotiations being conducted outside the conference, and in mid-February 1885 a bilateral AIC-Portuguese Treaty rendered the "proposition Sanford" superfluous by guaranteeing the Association's coveted right-of-way.[53]

It was in the settlement of these territorial disputes between the AIC and its principal rivals, France and Portugal, that Sanford played his final important role. In complaining to Ferry about the "multiple intrigues" of the "agents of the Association," the French delegate to the conference was undoubtedly referring to Sanford. Although absent from the official agenda and unmentioned in the conference's General Act, these successful territorial negotiations were the indispensable component of the Berlin West African Conference. Again, as with the free trade and neutrality issues, Germany supported the AIC's desperate quest for territorial integrity. After recognizing the Association on November 8, 1884, Bismarck persuaded Great Britain to follow suit. He then violated a preconference pledge to France by calling for a territorial settlement prior to the conference's conclusion.[54]

At Sanford's suggestion, talks between the AIC and France had begun in Berlin soon after the first session. Although she had recognized the AIC flag in April 1884, France had continued to challenge the Association's claim to the Niari-Kwilu region north of the Congo. Wishing to incorporate these two river valleys into their neighboring colony of Gabon, the French offered to waive their claim to the south bank of Stanley Pool in return for Leopold's surrender of the Niari-Kwilu. The king agreed to the territorial terms but demanded that France pay a 5-million-franc indemnity to offset AIC expenses in the Niari-Kwilu. Convinced that the AIC's financial woes would soon force its demise, Prime Minister Ferry vetoed the indemnity, and the negotiations remained deadlocked when the delegates adjourned for Christmas on December 22.[55]

When the talks resumed after Christmas, Sanford urged moderation upon Leopold and the AIC. Recognizing that the AIC faced a dire "crisis," he advocated compromise; it would be disastrous, he argued, "to have the conference and all its work come practically to naught because of the unsettled French claims." Surrendering the Niari-Kwilu region would reopen the talks and ease the Association's financial troubles. As compensation, Sanford suggested that the king demand "both banks of the Congo," the railroad right-of-way, French agreement to the neutralization of the Congo Basin, reimbursement for actual outlays on the Niari-Kwilu, and the "alienation of France from Portugal."[56]

After conferring with Leopold on December 26, Sanford hurried to Paris to supplement the work of Eudore Permez and Emile Banning, Leopold's formal delegates to the territorial talks. Sanford sought unsuccessfully to use United States influence to break the deadlock. Through Levi S. Morton, the American minister in Paris, he sent a telegram to Secretary Frelinghuysen. After outlining the contending claims, he warned that, without the resolution of these disputes, the conference was doomed to failure. Sanford prodded Frelinghuysen to inform the French that the United States desired an "equitable and just" settlement, but his appeal fell on deaf ears. Faced with growing domestic protests against American participation at Berlin, Frelinghuysen studiously ignored the telegram.[57]

On January 2, 1885, Jules Ferry seemingly broke the stalemate by proposing a French-sponsored lottery as satisfaction for Leopold's indemnity demands. In a tentative agreement, the AIC consented to the cession of the Niari-Kwilu region; and France agreed to recognize the Association's sovereign status, to relinquish claim to the south bank of Stanley Pool, to sponsor a 6-million-franc lottery in the AIC's name, and to facilitate an AIC-Portuguese settlement. The final point proved troublesome. Ferry, who had also pledged his support for Portugal's claims, now found himself in an untenable position. Leopold was demanding the right bank of the Congo and a stretch of the left bank sufficient to provide a deep-water terminus for his projected railroad. Portugal's call for the entire left bank and the right bank to Boma appeared irreconcilable. When Ferry endorsed the Portuguese position, the AIC broke off negotiations.[58]

As the negotiations in Paris languished, Sanford exhorted Leopold not to squander the Association's opportunity for securing general recognition of its territorial claims. Only after resolution of the disputes with France and Portugal could the general conference confer this vital recognition. Again serving as the voice of moderation, Sanford urged the king to adopt a conciliatory, pragmatic approach of *"immediately accepting what it enables one to obtain."*[59]

Fearful that Ferry was playing on the AIC's financial vulnerability, Leopold followed Sanford's advice. He agreed to Ferry's request that Portugal receive the Congo's left bank to Nokki, and on February 5 France and the AIC signed a treaty embodying the agreements tentatively reached in January. France granted the AIC full recognition and again promised to aid in the Portuguese negotiations. Bowing to the cumulative pressure from France, Britain, and Germany, Portugal recognized the Association on February 15 and agreed to the construction of the projected railroad through her territories. Although forced to reduce its inflated territorial claims, the Association had gained its most indispensable objectives—recognition by the European powers and access to the sea.[60]

Sanford had contributed significantly to Leopold's success. Within the conference he had controlled the American delegation, had directed its pro-AIC stance, and had presented the Association's railroad project. In the parallel negotiations with France and Portugal, he had consistently advocated pragmatic compromise, and the king's policies ultimately conformed closely to Sanford's suggestions. One historian has concluded that, "Next to Bismarck, he was perhaps the most effective participant." Two of Sanford's contemporaries concurred. William Mackinnon, the Scottish industrialist who had also promoted Leopold's projects, judged that Sanford had "done wonders"—had rendered "Yeoman service." Years later, Henry Stanley wrote Gertrude Sanford: "At the Berlin Conference the General's aid was most valuable. If any cash value was to be placed on any part of General Sanford's connection with King Leopold, I should say that the period spent at Berlin . . . deserved most consideration."[61]

The territorial wrangles resolved, the conferees concluded their work on February 23, 1885. Confident that they were ensuring unrestricted American commerce in Central Africa, Sanford and Kasson proudly signed the General Act, which ostensibly guaranteed free trade and neutrality within the Congo Basin and prohibited import duties on goods entering the area. Significant groups within the United States failed to share their enthusiasm. The *New York Times* warned of entangling alliances and characterized Sanford and Kasson as "irresponsible individuals"; the *New York Herald* considered American participation in this European conference a blow to the Monroe Doctrine; and a third paper dredged up the old charges of Civil War profiteering and contended that Sanford's appointment had tainted the American delegation. Hamilton Fish agreed with this final attack and remarked to Kasson, "I cannot divest myself of the idea that it was a mistake to have the *second* plenipotentiary at the conference." According to Fish, suspicions abounded of a "secret speculative commercial interest" between Leopold and Sanford, "the diplomatic flea . . . the peripatetic vendor of sewing machines."[62]

Democratic congressmen also dissented. On January 5, 1885, Perry Belmont of New York and Hilary A. Herbert of Alabama offered separate resolutions in the House calling on President Arthur to provide Congress with information on American participation at Berlin. Belmont feared that provisions for free trade on African rivers might be extended to streams in North or South America and that neutralizing the area might establish precedent for international control of the United States' projected interoceanic canal in Central America. Led by Congressman Belmont, the House Committee on Foreign Affairs reported on February 28 that American participation constituted a "new departure in the foreign policy of the United States."[63] The committee was correct. Not since Monroe had the nation become involved in matters so peculiarly European. Prodded by Sanford and Kasson, who sought to enlarge the nation's authority, prestige, and economic sway, the United States had intervened in the "power politics of Europe—pure and simple."[64] Grover Cleveland, the new Democratic president, agreed with the House committee. Soon after his inauguration he withdrew the General Act of the Berlin Conference from Senate consideration.

Convinced that he and Kasson had helped secure lucrative trading privileges for the United States, Sanford was disgusted at Cleveland's decision: "We are suffering from overproduction, and we are seeking new markets. This region produces what we need and will take much that we can supply." He referred disparagingly to "cavaliers against entangling alliances," and contended that in view of United States recognition of the AIA and Stanley's work in Africa, our participation in Berlin had been "eminently proper." Although many Americans had begun to question both United States presence at Berlin and the Congo's commercial potential, Sanford retained his confidence in the area's economic value. He was convinced that the Congo was "another & greater California," and might well "become the granary of the world." "Fully 50,000,000 people are there thirsty for trade and with the means to pay high prices for the goods they may buy."[65] That he was already contemplating a Congo trading company demonstrated the sincerity of his professions.

In the wake of the Berlin Conference, it was rumored that Sanford would become chief administrator of the Congo Free State. This would have fulfilled his aspirations nicely. In February 1885 he had speculated that his work at Berlin might lead to "important things," and in March he boldly solicited a key managerial post. In a memorandum to the king, he advocated an organization headed by a four- or five-member committee under Leopold's direction. Among this committee:

> [One] member should be a practical man, both in affairs and politics, capable of managing and representing its [the state's] financial and political interest under the direction of the King and His council, whether in securing means to build the railway, to secure good results from the lottery or in negotiations with or representations to other States. Such a trust I would be willing myself to accept.[66]

Sanford's hopes were soon dashed, for he did not figure in Leopold's plans for governing the Congo. The king was already discarding all pretenses of international control, and after officially becoming the sovereign of the African state in July 1885, he installed trusted Belgians in all the state's key administrative positions. Although spurning his application for office, Leopold did recognize Sanford's contributions by granting him permission to establish a commercial company on the Upper Congo. With his American projects in ruins, Sanford turned to Africa to recoup his lost fortune.

His expectations of huge profits seemed warranted. The Congo's drainage basin covered 1.4 million square miles, and both Stanley and Lieutenant Emory H. Taunt, who had made the 2,800-mile round trip between Banana Point and Stanley Falls during the summer of 1885, loudly proclaimed the area's natural wealth. The natives were reportedly eager to exchange valuable stores of ivory, rubber, gum copal, and minerals for infinitely less costly trinkets, beads, cap pistols, copper rings, and rum. Great returns seemed assured to the company that could systematically exploit these riches.[67]

After nearly six months of effort, Sanford completed the organization of his company, the Sanford Exploring Expedition (SEE), on July 1, 1886. The only American investor, Sanford was joined in the venture by Jules Levita, an old friend and French attorney, and a galaxy of prominent Belgian businessmen and politicians. The SEE's original capital of $60,000 was divided into fifty-nine shares, twenty-four of which were preferred shares allotted at the rate of one per $2,500 invested. Sanford effectively controlled six of these preferred shares and also received twenty common shares as compensation for securing the concession from Leopold. As the largest stockholder, Sanford was given four votes in all board meetings, while the other members were awarded two each. Just as he had done with the Florida Land and Colonization Company, Sanford insisted upon exercising a prominent managerial role. He joined Baron Louis Weber de Treunfels, head of the Antwerp commercial house conducting the company's business affairs, as one of the SEE's principal European administrators.[68]

Much of Sanford's optimism derived from Leopold's pledge to aid the SEE. The king agreed to rent state stations at Matadi, South Manyanga, Kinshasa, Luebo, and Equator to the SEE and to sell the SEE surplus goods. The state was also to aid in the critical area of transportation by providing, if possible, 400 porters per month at cost plus 25 percent; by transporting the company's goods on the lower river at cost; and by allowing company agents to trade from state steamers. This access to the "state plant" would, Sanford contended, provide the SEE with an insurmountable advantage over all competitors.[69]

Sanford chose Lieutenant Taunt to lead the African expedition and aided him in securing a leave of absence from the U.S. Navy. Taunt's primary subordinates were Antoine Swinburne, who had served under Stanley; William H. Parminter, a former employee of the Congo State who was to handle accounting and clerical work;

and E. J. Glave, another veteran Congo hand who spoke several African dialects. To minimize cash allocations and to tie their ultimate compensation to the SEE's profitable operation, Sanford paid these men in company stock.[70]

Arriving at Banana on July 28, 1886, Taunt ruefully discovered that Leopold's promises of aid were hollow. The state's failure to provide native porters proved the most devastating of the broken pledges. In an area devoid of railroads, serviceable highways, and beasts of burden, a viable transportation system depended upon the combination of water travel and an adequate number of human carriers. Sanford had counted on the stipulated 400 porters per month and had even hoped that the state might provide up to 1,000 men for the crucial beginning period of September through November 1886. Struggling to operate its own undermanned system, the Congo government had no surplus personnel for private companies. Over the first six months of the SEE's existence, the state furnished transportation for only sixty-nine loads of material, and when Taunt and Swinburne resorted to independent recruitment, the state impressed many of their men.[71]

L. Valcke, the official in charge of the state's transport system, compounded this difficulty by discriminating against the SEE in favor of a competing French company. Valcke lived at the headquarters of the French company, kept it informed of SEE operations, and supplied it with porters despite obligations to the SEE. According to Taunt, Valcke also charged exorbitant prices for transporting SEE goods on state steamers from the ocean to Matadi.[72]

The state's transfer of the designated river stations proved equally unsatisfactory. When the state refused to relinquish the pivotal station at Kinshasa, on Stanley Pool, the overburdened little company had to accept a less desirable location and erect buildings at a considerable and unexpected expense. The terms on which the government offered the other concessions were also troublesome. While other commercial houses were engaging property along the Congo at fixed rates and in perpetuity, the SEE was forced to rent its stations for five-year periods at an undefined rate. The state refused to honor even this five-year agreement, and in February 1887 it summarily seized the station at Manyanga.[73]

Sanford and his company also encountered the first stages of the state competition that subsequently eliminated all private endeavor on the Congo. Even though the all-encompassing state monopolies were not imposed until the 1890s, state agents were already actively pursuing the lucrative ivory trade. Given the state's superior resources, the SEE found itself at a serious competitive disadvantage.[74]

Taunt, Parminter, and Swinburne repeatedly pressed Sanford to intercede with state officials in Brussels for more equitable treatment. Sanford could exercise no leverage; his persistent inquiries elicited only bland assurances—not the substantive action so badly needed. Despite these disappointments, Sanford naively assured Taunt that the "spirit here [Brussels] from the King down is all that we could wish;" and he warned his agent to do nothing that might alienate the state, "our warm and powerful friend."[75]

These problems with the Congo Free State were complicated by the SEE's difficulty in securing and retaining capable men to direct the Congo work. As M. Montifiore-Levi, a fellow investor, wrote Sanford, "It is quite evident that if energetic and able direction from a distance is sufficient we have (in yourself) all that is necessary—but in an enterprise of this nature the value of the men in charge out there is the great point and there lies the real difficulty to my mind."[76] It was Sanford's old problem of management from afar. Parminter, Swinburne, and Taunt were the SEE's most important employees. Parminter received the SEE's shipments at Boma, routed ivory and rubber goods back to Europe, and maintained the company's financial records. Aptly described by Swinburne as the "all necessary centre" of SEE operations, Parminter was chronically dissatisfied with his compensation and, beginning in the fall of 1886, repeatedly demanded additional stock. Sanford was appalled at Parminter's "blackmailing" threats to quit but acquiesced in Baron Weber's decision to grant the agent another full share in 1887.[77] By contrast, it was Swinburne's lack of aggressive *"go ahead"* that disturbed Sanford and Weber. As the SEE representative at Stanley Pool and, after the spring of 1887, as chief of the expedition, Swinburne demonstrated a lack of managerial ability and a proclivity for dissipation. While denying Sanford's charge that he had used SEE funds to support his "African family," Swinburne acknowledged having fathered at least one illegitimate child. He lamely explained that "Africa is not my home but wherever I am, I try to be comfortable."[78]

If the conduct of Parminter and Swinburne was disconcerting, Taunt's was devastating. The young naval officer had accepted the position of chief administrator *"solely and entirely* to make money." The SEE's declining prospects, the prolonged separation from his family, and the debilitating African climate gradually took their toll. After taking temporary solace in rum, he abruptly deserted the expedition in March 1887. Weber pronounced him a "lost man," and after Taunt suffered a drinking relapse in June, Sanford discarded notions of returning him to Africa.[79]

The SEE's experience in launching the *Florida,* a twenty-ton, stern-wheel steamer, on Stanley Pool vividly illustrated the company's difficulties. Since the *Florida* was necessary for successful trading operations on the vast expanses of the upper Congo, its expeditious delivery and assembly were critical to the SEE's success. Dismantled and packed into cartons, the *Florida* was to be carried by boat from Banana Point to Matadi and by native porters around the Congo's cataracts to Stanley Pool. This twelve-day trek through the steaming jungle from Matadi to the Pool was the crucial portion of the journey.

The original plan to have the *Florida* operational by December 1886 proved hopelessly optimistic. The individual cartons, which began arriving from Europe in September, were far too heavy for the African porters to carry. The shaft alone weighed nearly 1,300 pounds and required more than fifty men to drag it along the treacherous Congo trails. Rather than dismantle the shaft into several lighter pieces, Taunt decided to carry it on a "truck" which could theoretically be manipulated by eight to ten men. Frustrated by the scarcity of porters, the Congo weather, and the machinery's bulk, the subordinate in charge of the project abandoned the shaft and boilers on the trail between Matadi and Stanley Pool in February 1887. SEE personnel recovered the equipment, but only after it had suffered several weeks of exposure to the elements.[80]

After another month's effort, the *Florida*'s body was transported to the Pool and fitted together. In April, as Swinburne awaited the arrival of the shaft and boilers, Henry M. Stanley led an expedition through the area to rescue Emin Pasha, the embattled governor of Equatoria. Stanley dragged the half-constructed craft from its building blocks and towed her away on a two-month journey up the Congo River. When she was returned in July, the *Florida* was in a "filthy condition," had numerous missing parts, a broken gangway, and a badly damaged bottom. Not until September 1887, some nine crucial months behind schedule, did the *Florida* begin operation on the Congo.[81]

Sanford characteristically seized on this incident as a means of recouping SEE losses. He immediately filed a £6,000 claim for damages with the London-based Emin Pasha Relief Committee. His strategy resembled that employed in the Aves case. He held the committee liable for both actual damages to the *Florida* and for delaying the SEE's progress. He also set the claim at an "exorbitant" figure, with the intention of settling for a lesser but not inconsiderable sum. William Mackinnon, the committee's chairman and Sanford's old friend, dismissed this sum as "absurd," and the committee ultimately offered £100. Sanford declined, and the matter remained unsettled at his death.[82]

Confronted with these myriad difficulties, Sanford searched in vain for ways to reverse the SEE's fortunes. By the spring of 1888, the SEE had placed a second steamer on the upper Congo; the *New York*, a craft of only eight tons, was designed to expand trade into the Congo's tributaries. In October 1887 Sanford instructed Swinburne to extend operations to Stanley Falls and join forces with Tippo Tib, an infamous Arab slave trader. This plan, like the one of hiring two professional elephant hunters, did not significantly increase the amount of ivory procured. Sanford estimated in mid-1888 that the SEE had purchased between twelve and fifteen tons of ivory and two and one-half tons of India rubber; but since the bulk of this material was not sold in Europe until 1889, it failed to prevent the SEE's liquidation. One of Sanford's fellow stockholders succinctly summarized the situation: "It is quite clear that we embarked with too small a capital for the successful carrying out of the undertaking."[83]

The SEE's precarious financial posture led to fundamental disagreements between Sanford and Baron Weber. From his position as head of the Antwerp firm entrusted with the SEE's financial operations, Weber exercised important influence over all decisions. When the Congo Free State failed to fulfill its promises, Weber demanded that Sanford remedy the situation. He contended that Sanford had received extra shares because of his alleged influence with Leopold, and it was therefore his "obligation" to obtain "the terms promised." Although Sanford found Weber's peremptory tone annoying, he was more troubled by the Belgian merchant's call for an increase in the SEE's share capital. Weber initially suggested this at a stockholders' meeting in November 1886 and reiterated his proposal in an official report the following February. During the summer of 1887, Weber further advocated the early liquidation of the SEE and the formation of a larger concern.[84]

Sanford stubbornly opposed any enlargement of the SEE's share capital. Demonstrating his compulsion for controlling all things in which he became involved, Sanford feared any "watering" of the stock would weaken his position as majority stockholder. He maintained that Weber should advance the necessary funds and was miffed by the merchant's refusal to extend credit. Though Sanford temporarily eased the SEE's straitened financial position by persuading the original stockholders to provide an additional $30,000, Weber was again pressing for liquidation early in 1888. Their relationship had become so strained by April of that year that Sanford complained of Weber's refusal to furnish him company intelligence and suspected that his adversary had forbidden the SEE's Congo agents to send him information.[85]

Convinced that Weber, whom he described as a "horrid Jew," was seeking "to gobble . . . up" his company, Sanford attempted to refinance the SEE in the spring of 1888. He drew up a "Confidential Memorandum" listing the SEE's operations, assets, and potential prospects and circulated it among capitalists in the United States and Great Britain. He proposed that an Anglo-American Company with a capital base of $500,000 purchase the SEE and thereby eliminate Weber and the other Belgian investors. Sanford planned to reap substantial profits from the transaction and to continue his managerial role with the new company.[86]

He spent the months of April through June in the United States presenting his scheme to American businessmen. Although some expressed interest, all politely refused. His most encouraging response came from A. H. Alden, George A. Alden, and Charles B. Flint of the New York Commerical Company, but they also declined to invest when Sanford vetoed an examination of the SEE's accounts in Brussels. Sanford's attempts to see John D. Rockefeller starkly revealed the social and financial depths to which he had fallen. In hopes of cultivating Rockefeller or his chief lieutenant, Henry M. Flagler, Sanford made a special trip to St. Augustine and stayed in Rockefeller's Ponce de Leon Hotel. Although he managed to make Flagler's "acquaintance," he complained nervously of the hotel's "collossal [sic]" prices. The man who had once spent money so freely and circulated among Europe's and America's financial elite could no longer afford a first-class hotel. After Sanford had gone to much expense and spent nearly two weeks in St. Augustine, Rockefeller refused to see him.[87]

Sanford's efforts elicited similar responses in England from his old friend, William Mackinnon, and from James F. Hutton, another associate in the African International Association. Mackinnon had previously come to Sanford's financial rescue in Florida, but he rejected the assumption that he "was the only one who could assist in a matter of this kind." Given his other obligations, he believed it would be "utter folly" to become involved. Hutton also demurred; and while both approached several friends on Sanford's behalf, no new capital was forthcoming.[88]

Having failed to locate alternative investors, Sanford faced intensified pressure from Baron Weber for disbanding the firm. Jules Levita called for a *"plan de bataille"* designed to forestall liquidation and extend the SEE's life beyond the designated termination date of December 31, 1888. But even the faithful Levita conceded that only "financial strength" could carry the day—financial strength that Sanford could not muster. In December 1888 the *Société Anonyme Belge pour l'Industrie et Commerce du Haut Congo,* a Belgian-based association founded by Albert Thys, absorbed the SEE. The society was organized with a capital of 1,200,000 francs represented by 2,400 privileged shares and 4,800 ordinary shares.[89]

Sanford's pioneering expedition had been the first commercial company on the Upper Congo, but the profits he envisioned never materialized. The "Congo market" proved as elusive as the more celebrated "China market," and the SEE's fate reemphasized Sanford's inability to avoid unwise, speculative undertakings. The absence of viable transportation facilities, a widely scattered and impoverished population, and native hostility toward foreigners virtually precluded profitable commerce in the Congo. With the SEE further plagued by insufficient capital, Leopold's failure to fulfill his promises, and a crucial series of mishaps and leadership problems, Sanford's last grasp at solvency fell short. Though he received 100 privileged shares, 430 ordinary shares, and an administratorship in the *Société*, Sanford exercised little influence in the new concern. His fears were fully realized; both profits and power were beyond his reach. Over the final two and one-half years of his life, Sanford gradually disposed of many of his shares for badly needed cash; at his death in 1891, the remainder went to his creditors.[90]

CHAPTER 8

THE FINAL YEARS, 1888–1891

THE DISMAL FATE of the Sanford Exploring Expedition was all too characteristic of Sanford's final years. When added to the failure of his "New South" business ventures, the SEE's demise left him in dreadful financial straits. His frustrations were not just financial. His twenty-year quest for another foreign mission culminated in only a minor appointment as "Additional Delegate" to the Brussels Antislavery Conference of 1889–90. Even this trifling recognition soured when he clashed with Leopold II over the Congo Free State's right to impose import duties. Nor did Sanford's family provide much solace during this trying period. He and Gertrude continued to disagree over financial matters and the location of their home; both of them were bitterly disappointed by the behavior of Henry, Jr., their oldest son; and Leopold Curtis, their second son, died at the age of five in December 1885.

Sanford's last, albeit minor, contribution to nineteenth-century American diplomacy was as a representative to the Brussels Antislavery Conference of 1889–90. Although he had greeted the Benjamin Harrison administration with his customary quadrennial appeal for a diplomatic position, his efforts lacked the old vigor. Habit and financial need compelled Sanford to go through the motions of application, but he had no real chance for a regular appointment. This became apparent when he encountered trouble even gaining an audience with James G. Blaine, the new secretary of state. On March 9, 1889, Sanford wrote to Gertrude, "I think the Blaines shun me. I can't find them so tomorrow I am determined to see him & explain my position."[1] When this halfhearted campaign, consisting of several letters to Harrison, Blaine, and E. M. Halford, the president's personal secretary, failed to land a mission, Sanford returned to Belgium disappointed but not surprised.[2]

His hopes revived in September 1889 when Leopold II included the United States among the eighteen nations invited to the Brussels Antislavery Conference. Upon learning of the conference, Sanford wrote again to Halford and also requested that John H. B. Latrobe, president of the American Colonization Society, contact Blaine. On November 22 Blaine rewarded Sanford's persistence with the position of "Additional Delegate" carrying a $1,000 expense allowance. Sanford accepted on November 27, after Blaine had assured him that he would be a "full member of the conference" serving equally with Edwin H. Terrell, America's minister to Belgium.[3]

Cardinal Charles M. A. Lavigerie's emotional campaign had crystallized European demands for action against the slave trade. In 1888 his efforts had elicited a strong response from French and Belgian Catholics and had stimulated the founding of Germany's first antislavery society. The reactions of the European governments were less humanely motivated, however, than those of the general public. By the late 1880s the European powers had encountered growing Arab and African resistance to their occupation of interior Africa, and the antislavery movement offered a timely vehicle for subduing this opposition and fostering the common imperial interest. The primary European states also pursued individual objectives: the British hoped to maintain their leadership in the anti-slave-trade movement; Bismarck sought to cultivate Germany's Catholic Center party; France desired to protect her commerce from British demands for the right of search; and Leopold II wanted to secure additional sources of revenue and forestall European objections to the Congo Free State's most extreme territorial claims.[4]

Against this background, it was hardly surprising that the conference "degenerated" from a "Christian crusade against the slave trade" into a "commercial and territorial" wrangle among the European powers.[5] From November 1889 through February 1890, Sanford and Terrell found no American interests at stake and spent much of their time as interested observers partaking freely of " 'all the dinners, receptions, and balls.' " They watched silently as the British and French compromised on a plan to suppress the maritime slave trade along the east coast of Africa. They also abstained from the debate over Belgian proposals concerning the slave trade and arms traffic in the interior of the continent. Neither objected when Britain and Germany refused a definite commitment to Leopold's plans for constructing roads, railways, and fortified posts in order to replace native porters and intercept slave caravans. Nor did they protest when the British set the ban on precision arms at twelve years (rather than the twenty-five suggested by Leopold) and restricted the "slave trade zone" to twenty degrees north and south of the equator (rather than the entire continent, as favored by France and Portugal.)[6]

Sanford ended this uncharacteristic reserve in mid-March 1890 when Lord Vivian, the British representative, called for action against the African liquor trade. Vivian sought the exclusion of liquor from those areas as yet "uncontaminated" by the traffic in spirits and the imposition of a duty of fifty francs per hectolitre in the coastal areas where the trade was already well established. Although lacking specific instructions on this issue, Sanford expressed American support for Vivian's proposals. France, Portugal, and Belgium added their ostensible backing; but Germany and Holland rejected the fifty-franc duty on coastal imports and only grudgingly agreed to ban liquor from the interior "slave trade zone."[7]

Sanford played an active role in the committee appointed to consider the liquor duty by successfully resisting a Dutch effort to reduce the proposed duty to six and one-half francs per hectolitre. To substantiate his argument for a higher figure, Sanford located several Congo merchants and inquired whether a tariff of fifteen francs per hectolitre would be onerous. When all replied in the negative, he reported the comments to the committee and suggested that fifteen francs be made the minimum figure for future negotiations. He also amended the original British proposal to require that all liquors imported into Africa meet minimum purity standards or be subject to confiscation.[8]

During an Easter recess in April 1890, Sanford sailed to the United States to attend to business matters and confer with Blaine. The secretary endorsed his actions on the liquor question and urged him to push for a duty in excess of fifteen francs. Before Sanford could return to Brussels, the committee reconvened and hammered out a compromise banning liquor from the "uncontaminated" areas of the slave trade zone but allowing the interested countries to define these regions independently. The committee also settled on a duty of fifteen francs for the first three years, twenty-five francs for the succeeding three, and a general revision at the end of six years. The conferees postponed action on Sanford's amendment until his arrival.[9]

On May 24 he presented his revised amendment, which specified that the purity of all alcoholic imports be certified by a chemist. Spirits without this written sanction would be confiscated. The proposal elicited little enthusiasm; anxious to conclude the six-month conference, the other delegates refused to reopen the liquor question. Even the British, who expressed sympathy for the measure's intent, feared that further discussion might jeopardize the principle of excluding liquor from the interior. After a heated session on the twenty-fourth, the amendment was tabled; on June 6 the matter was reconsidered, and a *pro forma* recommendation urging the signatory nations to take the necessary precautions to prevent the export of adulterated spirits from their ports was included in the protocols.[10]

Sanford was piqued by the outcome of the liquor deliberations. His pique turned to indignation when Leopold II demanded a revision of the Berlin Treaty of 1885 to enable his Congo Free State to charge import duties within the conventional basin of the Congo. Arguing that the additional revenues were necessary to implement the agreements of the Brussels Conference, Leopold refused to sign the conclave's final act unless the powers consented to the import duty. Led by Britain and Germany, all the European states except Holland quickly assented.[11]

Although Sanford was not surprised at the monarch's ploy, having warned Harrison and Blaine of its likelihood in January, he believed that Leopold had shown bad faith by failing to give the United States advance notice of his proposal. That the king had carefully cultivated the important European states was clear from their prompt endorsement of his request. Sanford viewed these developments as distressingly conspiratorial. Why, he asked the Belgian representative, had the United States not been "frankly approached," rather than "surrounded here at the conference by an outside pressure . . .?" Sanford also deplored Leopold's timing; by making his demands on the eve of the conference's adjournment, the king seemed determined to prevent serious debate.[12]

Sanford found these procedural matters objectionable, but his growing estrangement from Leopold derived from a more substantive issue. Sanford had been immensely proud of both the free trade agreement he had negotiated between the United States and the

Congo Free State in April 1884 and the similar provisions included
in the Berlin Treaty. He claimed that United States recognition of
the AIC had been responsible for "breaking down the Anglo-Portuguese treaty" and that "King Leopold, at my insistence" had given
the "United States many advantages, such as free trade."[13] Despite
the SEE's poor showing, he remained confident that he had guaranteed American access to a lucrative market in central Africa. Leopold's request for import duties was therefore both a breach of faith
and a personal affront. Sanford feared that Americans would question the wisdom and sincerity of his former association with the
monarch and his promotion of the Congo.

Leopold's true character and motivation were becoming all too
apparent. Sanford had previously judged the king guilty of ingrati-
tude in his treatment of Henry Stanley and William Mackinnon,[14]
and he was coming to realize that Leopold had defaulted on most
of the aid promised to the SEE. Sanford also discerned the hollow-
ness of Leopold's claims of humanitarian concern for the Congo
natives. During the conference, Sanford received several startling
letters from George Grenfell, a Baptist missionary in the Congo.
Grenfell reported that Congo Free State officials were participating
in the slave trade and were allowing slave caravans to pass unchal-
lenged through their stations. In short, Sanford was confronted by
mounting evidence that he had been deceitfully used by the cunning
monarch. As one of Leopold's former ministers had observed, the
king treated "men as we use lemons, when he has squeezed them dry
he throws away the peel."[15] For Sanford, who saw himself as a
worldly, canny diplomat, this proved an especially disillusioning
revelation.

Therefore, both personal and policy considerations prompted Sanford to oppose the king's request for import duties. He joined Terrell
in protesting that the conference's invitation had said nothing about
revising the Berlin Treaty. Moreover, the United States had not
ratified the Berlin agreement and could not sign the General Act of
the Brussels Conference if it included the import authorization.
Working from Blaine's instructions, Terrell suggested that the matter be made a separate act, distinct from the general treaty, and
indicated that the United States would undertake independent negotiations with the Congo State.[16]

The American position infuriated Leopold and his associates. William Mackinnon, who had not yet discerned the monarch's true
nature, chided Sanford. He expressed sympathy for Leopold's posi-

tion and remarked, "I wish it had been possible for you to have helped the king rather than hindered. From other sources I hear that some personal feeling has been . . . imported into the discussion." After a futile attempt to divide the two Americans, Leopold reluctantly consented to the separate act treating the import duties. On July 2 Sanford and Terrell signed the General Act of the Brussels Conference. All the participating nations except the United States and Holland also signed a second agreement granting the Congo Free State and the other countries in the Congo basin the right to establish a 10 percent import duty. The United States agreed to negotiate an independent commercial pact with the Congo State, which together with the General Act, was ratified by the Senate in January 1892.[17]

Sanford, President Harrison, and Secretary Blaine interpreted Leopold's acceptance of the separate tariff agreement as an American victory. Sanford concluded that without the imports amendment the General Act had become "solely a philanthropic document for the protection of the African races."[18] Although satisfied with this aspect of the conference, he was appalled by Leopold's hypocrisy. Apprehensive that his well-intentioned but naive promotion of the king's projects had been tainted, he continued until his death in 1891 to oppose any treaty that revoked America's free trade privileges in the Congo.

Sanford's indecisive role at the Brussels Conference contrasted markedly with his participation at the Berlin West African Conference in 1884–85. At Berlin he had controlled the American delegation, pressed hard for free trade on the Congo, and helped negotiate the territorial agreements that produced general European recognition of the Congo Free State. Five years later he was unable to secure his amendments concerning the purity of liquor imported into Africa or to prevent Leopold from closing the formerly "open door" to the Congo. Once a key figure in Congo developments and United States African policy, Sanford had become ineffectual and peripheral.

Sanford's accumulating disappointments further aggravated the physical and psychological maladies which had plagued him in the 1870s. By the mid-1880s his bouts of insomnia had resumed. He complained that "blue devils" consistently awakened him before dawn, and in August 1887 he noted that the previous night had been "the best sleep since months—7 hours!" When a period of serious discomfort in 1885 led him to fear a tumor, he was elated to get a Berlin doctor's diagnosis of back and lumbago disorder. He promptly informed Gertrude, "I gave him 20 marks gladly, & came away feeling better—and that's the History of my Tumor!" This proved to be one of his few light moments during these years. Every August found him taking the waters at Hamburg to rejuvenate his declining health, and during the fall of 1890 he was troubled with gout and narrowly escaped an operation for a liver ailment.[19]

Sanford's health problems were in part psychosomatic. Constant tension and disappointment stretched his nerves taut and often left him depressed and preoccupied. Gertrude urged him to "cultivate a cheerful spirit & not be *always* so stern and *absorbed.*" Living with him was "like living in a room with windows hopelessly turned to the North!" She also worried about his frantic pace and inability to relax. Writing in the mid-1880s, she observed: "Naturally nervous as you are you have *no idea* how painfully *exaggerated* your condition has become." Sanford's "mania for work and a wearing out of those near [him]—with *nervous haste* and *anxiety*" was becoming more than she could bear.[20]

Henry also recognized how injurious his situation had become, but he was unable to change it. In 1887 he admitted, "I sometimes think I shall go wild with anxiety & worry—while I have to keep a good face to the entire world." Each succeeding year brought added debts, higher interest payments, and further devaluation of his stock portfolio. His interest payments remained at or above the 1879 level of $1,000 per month, and his 1884 income failed even to meet interest and tax obligations. The following year he noted with great consternation that the family was even "living on borrowed money for . . . current expenses." By the end of the decade, mounting obligations and diminishing resources forced them to sell much of their furniture and many paintings; and in 1888 they sadly moved from Gingelom to Maillard, a lesser but still rather large château. At his death, Henry would leave Gertrude with debts and mortgages of more than $150,000.[21]

While Sanford's disastrous investments were the primary cause of his financial woes, the family's sumptuous lifestyle aggravated the problem. Although they no longer lived on the level which Gertrude deemed appropriate, the Sanfords continued to live well beyond their "income." As late as July 1888 they retained a chef, house and kitchen maids, and at least three other servants. Sanford estimated that the family's expenses for the years 1885 through 1887 had averaged 30,000 francs per year.[22]

When Henry turned to Gertrude, he found neither sympathy nor solace. Their exchanges echoed those of the 1870s but in tones even more strident and embittered. He reiterated his pleas for household economies, urging her not to "spend a franc or incur an obligation without need for it!" When she purchased furniture unnecessarily, failed to forward important business papers, or neglected to keep an accurate record of her expenditures, he chided her sternly. His account of their plight implicitly blamed Gertrude's refusal to move back to the United States. Their "senseless, useless life of expatriation" had yielded "some half educated girls, a cranky son, & an exhausted exchequer for . . . our advancing years." "We are out of the swim here" in Belgium, he concluded, and "have wasted our time, money and opportunities for naught."[23]

Gertrude responded in kind. She remained intransigent on the matter of moving to America. Deploring the "Derby standard," she asked how Henry could accept "corn bread after having plum cake"? In response to his calls for domestic saving, she argued that their social position should take precedence. She bemoaned their declining "social power": "we are . . . losing our hold here & not doing anything to increase it elsewhere. We have dropped our relations in Paris & England—made no effort . . . to continue acquaintances that would have been most useful to the children. . . . until one or two of the girls are married—we must keep *'in the swim.'* " Gertrude also refused to accept responsibility for their problems; Henry's poor judgment, not her desire for life abroad, was the culprit. She pointedly reminded him that even "in the best days of these affairs, you know I was opposed to them & submitted with as good a grace as I knew for yr. gratification." Florida had been "a vampire that . . . sucked the *repose* & the beauty & the *dignity* & cheerfulness out of our lives."[24]

She concluded her rejoinders with a scathing attack on his performance as a husband and father. Henry's travels had become "a sore point" with her and a matter for "ridicule" among their friends. "It does not seem *respectable,* " she criticized, "for a man of your age—supposed fortune & large young family to be rushing about at such a pace." "Only in America," she concluded, "where men are Fathers as animals are—with not much more feeling for their wives & children than the instinct of feeding them demands . . . are such repeated absences . . . accepted." She felt neglected and isolated and bewailed the "obligation of hearing, doing, *thinking* everything *alone* without a sympathetic mind to lean on." If Henry only understood the *"cruelty"* of this neglect, he "would not, could not repeat it so often."[25]

In the midst of this bickering and recrimination, Henry and Gertrude could agree on one matter—the shortcomings of their oldest son, Henry, Jr. (Harry). His failure to meet their expectations was still another blow to Sanford in his final, distressing years. The admiring parents had packed their eleven-year-old "Lambie" off to Cheam, a broading school in Surrey, England, in 1876; and three years later he progressed to Eton. As befitted the son of American gentlefolk, Harry followed these preparatory schools with matriculation at Harvard in 1884. His first year was uneventful, but during the second he began to miss numerous classes and to overdraw his allowance of $100 per month. Henry, Sr., feared in June 1885 that his son was not "leading the frugal, studious life he should, but getting in spend thrift habits." By the middle of his junior year, Harry's irregular attendance had led to academic probation and his extravagance to $600 in debts. Although he assured Sanford that he would be back in good academic standing by April 1887 and that he would curtail his spending, he followed through on neither pledge. Already pressed on all sides for funds, Sanford was perplexed by his son's lack of progress. I am, he concluded, "at a loss what to do with him—his obliviousness or inattention to promises—his squandering his time & money & opportunities make my heart sore."[26]

Sanford's relationship with his son continued to deteriorate during Harry's senior year. Harry served as editor of the *Harvard Monthly* and began seriously to develop his penchant for literary pursuits. He submitted prose pieces to *Century, North American Review,* and *Scribners* and received flattering comments on his writing from John Hay. But his academic and financial difficulties persisted. He amassed another $1,400 in debts and was expelled from his club in April 1888 for failing to pay his fees. Even more serious was the continued neglect of his studies, which kept him from graduating with his class in June 1888.[27]

Sanford lamented to Gertrude that they had an "impracticable crank for a Son with a good deal of talent," but "without stability of character" and "so weak as even I fear to sacrifice principle." "The great problem" of "what to do with" his son puzzled Sanford, as he was sure Harry was "quite unfitted for the battle of life." He soon decided that law school would provide Harry with both needed discipline and a marketable skill.[28]

Harry refused to accede to his father's wishes. Uninterested in law school, he desired instead to pursue a literary career. He appealed for one final year of schooling at the Bussey Institute, where he could take courses in applied sciences and hone his writing skills. Sanford denied this request and sent his son to Florida to help manage Belair. The young man was shattered. He complained to his mother that neither she nor his father understood him and that "paternal government when arbitrary [was] serfdom." His forced exile in Florida further alienated him from his parents. After two years in Sanford, Harry had become so embittered that he was certain his parents had purposely forced him into debt so as to control his behavior. Although he appears to have mended the breach with Gertrude, Harry and his father remained unreconciled at the latter's death.[29]

Sanford's disappointment with his son was the last in a long line of disillusioning experiences stretching back to the late 1860s. Together with his service at the Brussels Conference, his friction with Gertrude, and his continuing financial losses, it stripped the happiness and fulfillment from his final years. His chestnut hair had grown white, and his long beard was flecked with grey; his once taut body had become portly, and he stooped when walking.[30] His troubles claimed their due during the winter of 1890–91, when he spent much of his time confined to the lodge at Belair. When this failed to revive his health, he travelled to Healing Springs, Virginia, where he died on May 21, 1891.

Henry Shelton Sanford died with most of his goals unachieved, but to concede that he never quite attained either the fame or fortune he pursued is not to say that his life was without significance. During his forty-year career, he played a leading role in some of the most fundamental developments in nineteenth-century American diplomacy. His service in Paris and his Latin American business activities in the 1850s personified the heady, aggressive nationalism and budding economic expansion of the prewar decade. His tenure in Belgium was central to the Union's continental diplomacy. Acting as Secretary of State Seward's personal envoy, he laid the groundwork for the North's surveillance of Confederate agents, coordinated the purchase of valuable war material, directed the Northern propaganda efforts, and carried the offer of a Union command to Giuseppe Garibaldi. These activities made Sanford the equal of John Bigelow in Paris and second only to Charles Francis Adams in England as the North's most important Civil War diplomat.

In the two decades after the war, he became the central figure in the evolution of United States policies in the Congo. He persuaded Congress and the Arthur administration to recognize Leopold II's International African Association in 1884 and guided American policy at the Berlin Conference the following year. Although he subsequently discovered that he had been deceived by Leopold II, Sanford had acted in good faith. He sincerely believed that his actions had aided the African natives and promoted the expansion of American commerce. His aggressive calls for an "open door" in the Congo constitute one of the most telling examples of this theme in American diplomacy between 1865 and 1890, and his influence in Washington dramatizes the diplomatic role of private individuals during the period. He had conceived of the United States as a great power as early as the 1860s, and his desire for a more aggressive, purposeful policy befitting such status foreshadowed the transformation already underway at the time of his death.

Finally, like others of his generation, such as Thomas Randolph Clay, John W. Foster, John A. Kasson, and Andrew D. White, he was in many respects a professional diplomat long before the United States officially established a professional diplomatic corps. Over his four decades of diplomatic work, he served at all levels, as attaché, secretary of legation, chargé d'affaires, minister resident, and associate delegate to two major international conferences.

While these activities certainly qualify Sanford as an important figure in nineteenth-century American diplomacy, his significance was not confined to foreign affairs. He was also the most important single contributor to the development of Florida's late-nineteenth-century citrus industry. Both his importation of foreign varieties of fruit and the research conducted at Belair were critical to the period's citrus boom. Although this was his primary achievement in Florida, his personal promotion of the town of Sanford and his work through the Florida Land and Colonization Company were also important to the state's growth.

Unfortunately, these domestic speculations, together with those in South Carolina and Louisiana, also revealed his glaring deficiencies as a businessman. He was a terrible judge of character and had a penchant for rash actions, invariably committed without the benefit of prior research. Like many of his Gilded Age contemporaries, he was inordinately optimistic about the nation's economic future and all too inclined to grasp at each new "main chance." After thirty years of disastrous speculations, Sanford was still promoting an electrical patent and the development of Florida phosphate lands on the eve of his death.[31] Once involved in an undertaking, he refused to devote the necessary personal attention to it, and was unable to attract and cooperate with capable subordinates.

These shortcomings led him to the verge of bankruptcy by the late 1880s, and his ever-worsening financial plight in turn contributed to debilitating health problems and distressing marital tensions. A proud, vain, and stubborn man, Sanford was acutely embarrassed by his business failures and chronic debts. The succession of political and financial disappointments after 1870 aggravated his naturally nervous disposition. He was unable either to admit or to reconcile himself to the fact that he would never reach the first rank—that true greatness was beyond his grasp. The gloom, disillusionment, and sobriety of his final twenty years contrasted markedly with the gaiety, indulgence, and carefree existence of his first fifty. His legacy was a mixed one: an embittered marriage, an alienated son, heavily mortgaged properties, and a squandered fortune, together with clear contributions to American diplomacy and the Florida citrus industry.

NOTES

Persons:
HSS   Henry Shelton Sanford
Places:
PKY   P. K. Yonge Library of Florida History
Manuscript Collections:
SP   Henry Shelton Sanford Papers
SeP   William Henry Seward Papers
WP   Thurlow Weed Papers
Government Documents:
DB, DF, DG, DGrB,   Despatches from U.S. Ministers to
DI, DV   Belgium, France, Germany, Great Britain, Italy, and Venezuela
CDA   Despatches from U.S. Consuls to Antwerp
IB, IF, IG, IGrB, IV   Instructions from U.S. Dept. of State to Ministers to Belgium, France, Germany, Great Britain, and Venezuela
HED, SED, SR   House *Executive Document,* Senate *Executive Document,* Senate *Report*
WOR   *War of the Rebellion: A Compilation of the Official Records of the Union and Confederate Armies*

Preface

1. Leo T. Molloy's *Henry Shelton Sanford, 1823–1891: A Biography* (Derby, Conn., 1952), does not contradict my contention. Commissioned by Sanford's daughter, this fifty-one page pamphlet is devoid of both documentation and critical analysis.
2. Robert L. Beisner, *From the Old Diplomacy to the New, 1865–1900* (New York, 1975).

Chapter 1

1. Sarah A. Wallace and Frances E. Gillespie, eds., *The Journal of Benjamin Moran* (2 vols., Chicago, 1948), II, 860, 894.

2. Adam Gurowski, *Diary* (3 vols., Boston, 1862–1866), I, 141.

3. William F. Blackman, *History of Orange County, Florida, Narrative and Biographical* (De Land, Fla., 1927), 37–38.

4. Harriet A. Weed, ed., *Life of Thurlow Weed, Including His Autobiography and Memoirs* (2 vols., Boston, 1884), I, 629.

5. Marsh to Seward, September 4, 1861, Despatches from United States Ministers to the Italian States, 1832–1906, hereafter cited as *DI*.

6. Morgan to William M. Evarts, January 14, 1878, Letters of Application and Recommendation, Department of State, hereafter cited as Applications and Recommendations.

7. S. O. Chase, Sr. and Joshua C. Chase, "Recollections and Reminiscences, 1878–1891," Paper for Sanford Centennial, February 8, 1937, cited in Dorothy P. McMakin, "General Henry Shelton Sanford and His Influence on Florida," (M.A. thesis, Stetson University, 1938), 57.

8. Harriet C. Owsley, *Register: Henry Shelton Sanford Papers* (Nashville, 1960), genealogy tables on second and third unnumbered pages; William Cothren, *History of Ancient Woodbury, Connecticut* (3 vols., Waterbury, Conn., 1854), III, 693; Samuel Orcutt and Ambrose Beardsley, *The History of the Old Town of Derby, Connecticut, 1642–1880* (Springfield, Mass., 1880), 354; Molloy, *Sanford*, 10; Carleton E. Sanford, *Thomas Sanford, the Emigrant to New England, Ancestry, Life and Descendents* (2 vols, Rutland, Vt., 1911), I, 76, 341.

9. Henry Shelton Sanford Journal, June 15, 1845, Henry Shelton Sanford Papers, box 3, folder 4, hereafter cited as SP, 3/4. Henry Shelton Sanford hereafter referred to as HSS.

10. *Ibid.*, HSS to Helen Shelton, April 19, 1846, SP, 93/6.

11. HSS Journal, June 15, 1845, SP, 3/4; "A Description of Derby," SP, 1/8; John W. Barber, *Connecticut Historical Collection* (New Haven, 1856), 196–98; Orcutt and Beardsley, *Derby*, 349, 354.

12. HSS Journal, n.d., SP, 2/7; Orcutt and Beardsley, *Derby*, 643.

13. HSS Journal, n.d., SP, 1/9; George L. Clark, *A History of Connecticut* (New York, 1914), 240; Jarvis M. Morse, *A Neglected Period of Connecticut's History, 1818–1850* (New Haven, 1933), 154; B. C. Steiner, *The History of Education in Connecticut* (Washington, 1893), 37, 56–57.

14. HSS Compositions, SP, 1/8; HSS to Henry S. Sanford, Jr., May 7, [?], SP, 93/2.

15. Washington College Bulletin, n.d., SP, 1/17; Barber, *Connecticut Historical Collection,* 38; Florence S. M. Crofut, *Guide to the History and Historic Sites of Connecticut* (2 vols., New Haven, 1937), I, 252; Morse, *Neglected Period of Connecticut's History,* 163; Steiner, *Education in Connecticut,* 243; Glenn Weaver, *The History of Trinity College* (Hartford, 1967), 17–18, 27, 31–37, 48–50.

16. G. Davis to HSS, November 28, 1840; Statement of Silas Totten, December 5, 1840; A. Brigham to Nehemiah C. Sanford, December 4, 1840; Brigham to HSS, August 5, 1841, SP, 1/10.

17. HSS Journal, June 15, 1845, SP, 3/4.

18. HSS Journal, September 1841, SP, 2/8; June 15, 1845, SP, 3/4.

19. Levita to HSS, September 1, 1871, SP, 124/7.

20. HSS to Janie Howe, September 13, 19 [1846], October 1, 1846, SP, 93/15.

21. HSS Journal, September 5, 6, 17, 1842, SP, 2/9.

22. HSS Passport, December 31, 1846, SP, 19/11.

23. HSS Journal, June 8, 1845, SP, 3/4; Smith to HSS, June 26, 1844, SP, 131/2; S. C. Sanford to HSS, May 4, 1844, SP, 67/15.

24. Smith to HSS, March 19, 1845, SP, 131/3.
25. N. B. Sanford to HSS, March 6, September 18, 1845, SP, 70/3; January 26, 1845, SP, 70/4; October 23, [1848], SP, 70/5.
26. HSS Journal, June 8, 1845, SP, 3/4; November 4, 1846, SP, 3/6.
27. HSS Journal, November 4, 1846, SP, 3/6; Shelton to HSS, January 26, 1846, SP, 73/3; N. B. Sanford to HSS, November 28, [1853], SP, 70/9.
28. HSS "Inventory for 1847," SP, 5/2; Sidney A. Downs to HSS, March 11, 1850, SP, 17/5.
29. HSS Journal, June 8, 14, 15, 1845, June 14, 1846, SP, 3/4; November 1, 1846, SP, 3/6.
30. HSS to Janie Howe, April 18, May 9, [1847], SP, 93/16; HSS to [E. N. Shelton], June 15, SP, 93/7.
31. HSS to J. Howe, October 17, November 12, 1847, SP, 93/16.
32. HSS to William Goddard, February 25, 1849, SP, 104/3.
33. Pennington to HSS, n.d., SP, 94/8.
34. N.B. Sanford to HSS, April 4, November 12, December 25, 1847, January 26, August 2, 1848, SP, 70/4.
35. N. B. Sanford to HSS, June 10, 1847, SP, 70/4.
36. HSS Journal, March 31, 1850, SP, 3/9.
37. *Ibid.;* E. N. Shelton to HSS, December 16, 1848, January 4, April 2, 1849, SP, 73/4; E. N. Shelton to Baldwin, February 23, 1849; Baldwin to Clayton, March 26, 1849; Petition to president of the United States from Connecticut Whigs, June 20, 1849, Applications and Recommendations; Holman Hamilton, *Zachary Taylor* (2 vols., New York, 1941–1951), II, 63, 89, 93–94, 108; Joseph G. Rayback, *Free Soil: The Election of 1848* (Lexington, Ken., 1970), 38, 197.
38. P. S. Shelton to HSS, June 26, July 31, August 27, October 29, 1849, SP, 77/9; P. S. Shelton to Thurlow Weed, June 22, 1849, William Henry Seward Papers, hereafter cited as SeP; Shelton to Weed, June 26, 1849, Thurlow Weed Papers, hereafter cited as WP; Seward to Clayton, July 1, 1849; Weed to Johnson, June 24, 1849; Fillmore to Clayton, August 10, 1849; Taylor to Clayton, June 29, 1849, Applications and Recommendations; C. H. Russell to HSS, July 2, 1849, SP, 129/9. E. N. Shelton was a business associate of Taylor and Russell and probably solicited their aid.
39. Clayton to Rives, June 12, 1859; Rives to Clayton, June 15, 1849, William Cabell Rives Papers, hereafter cited as Rives Papers.
40. Truman Smith to HSS, June 18, 27, 1849, SP, 131/7; HSS Journal, March 31, 1850, SP, 3/9; Rives to Clayton, July 14, 16, 1849; Clayton to Rives, July 9, 1849; Ingersoll to Rives, August 7, 1849, Rives Papers; Rives to HSS, August 17, 1849, SP, 129/5.

Chapter 2

1. HSS to William L. Marcy, January 22, February 8, 1854, Despatches from United States Ministers to France, 1789–1906, hereafter cited as *DF;* HSS to Commodore Engle, September 16, 1850, SP, 142/8; HSS draft, September 10, 1850, SP, 142/2; HSS to Bancroft Davis, n.d., SP, 105/6.
2. Smith to HSS, July 2, 1852, SP, 131/5; HSS draft, SP, 1/7; HSS Journal, March 31, April 1, 1850, SP, 3/9; HSS to N. B. Sanford, January 30, 1851; HSS to Col. [Ingersoll], March 26, 1851, SP, 97/3; E. N. Shelton to HSS, April 25, 1853, SP, 73/8; N. B. Sanford to HSS, April 2, [1853], SP, 70/8. For a subsequent observation on the large number of American tourists in Paris and the high living expenses, see Charles J. Faulkner to James Buchanan, September 1, 1860, James Buchanan Papers, hereafter cited as Buchanan Papers.
3. Bret Harte to Nan Harte, August 11, 1878, in Geoffrey B. Harte, ed., *The Letters of Bret Harte* (Boston, 1926), 87–89; Foster Rhea Dulles, *American's Abroad: Two Centuries of*

European Travel (Ann Arbor, 1964), 73–78; Eugene L. Didier, "The American Colony in Paris," *Lippincott's Magazine,* 24 (1879), 384–86.

4. HSS to N. B. Sanford, November 21, December 19, 1850, SP, 97/3; HSS drafts, SP, 1/7; HSS letters to Bancroft Davis, [1852], SP, 105/7; HSS to C. M. Ingersoll, February 27, 1851, SP, 97/3.

5. HSS to Davis, n.d., SP, 105/7; C. M. Ingersoll to HSS, July 14, 1850, SP, 122/10.

6. N. B. Sanford to HSS, December 7, 1849, SP, 70/5; November 10, [1850], SP, 70/6; May 11 [1851], SP, 70/7; E. N. Shelton to HSS, December 8, 1849, SP, 73/4; November 23, 1851, SP, 73/6; P. S. Shelton to HSS, January 14, 1851, SP, 77/11.

7. HSS to N. B. Sanford, [1851], SP, 93/4; November 21, 1850, SP, 97/3; N. B. Sanford to HSS, March 18, [1850], SP, 70/6; June 21, 1852, SP, 70/8.

8. HSS, *The Different Systems of Penal Codes in Europe; also, A Report on the Administrative Changes in France since the Revolution of 1848* (Washington, 1854). This was U.S. Congress, Senate, *Executive Document* No. 68, 33d Cong., 1st sess.

9. HSS to W. H. Seward, No. 68, May 12, 1862; No. 177, January 14, 1864; No. 311, September 30, 1865, Despatches from United States Ministers to Belgium, 1832–1906, hereafter cited as *DB.* These reports treated Belgium's military recruitment, revenue systems, and public records.

10. Rives to Franklin Pierce, February 3, 1853, Rives Papers; HSS to Bancroft Davis, May 2, [1853], SP, 105/6; HSS to W. L. Marcy, No. 1, May 26, 1853, *DF;* Marcy to Rives, No. 67, April 15, 1853, Diplomatic Instructions of the Department of State, 1801–1906, France.

11. Robert Ralph Davis, Jr., "Diplomatic Plumage: American Court Dress in the Early National Period," *American Quarterly,* 20 (1968), 164–79.

12. U.S. Congress, Senate, *Executive Document* No. 31, 36th Cong., 1st sess., 4–5, hereafter cited as *SED* No. 31, 36th Cong.

13. Davis, "American Court Dress," 174; Ivor D. Spencer, *The Victor and the Spoils: A Life of William L. Marcy* (Providence, 1959), 234–35, *Herald* quote from 235.

14. HSS to Bancroft Davis, January 6, 1853, SP, 105/10; Nelson M. Beckwith to HSS, August 12, 1853, SP, 115/4; HSS to Marcy, No. 24, August 18, 1853; No. 57, January 22, 1854, *DF.*

15. *Washington Daily-Union,* February 2, 1854.

16. Beckles Willson, *America's Ambassadors to France (1777–1927): A Narrative of Franco-American Diplomatic Relations* (London, 1928), 246.

17. William H. Trescot to HSS, September 8, 1853, SP, 132/4; Beckwith to HSS, August 27, 1853, SP, 115/4.

18. Robert L. Scribner, "The Diplomacy of William L. Marcy," (Ph.D. dissertation, University of Virginia, 1949), 104–105; Allan Nevins, *Ordeal of the Union* (8 vols., New York, 1947–1971), II, 59; Beckwith to HSS, June 4, 1854, July 12, 1855, SP, 115/4; Mason to Marcy, January 19, 1854, William Learned Marcy Papers, hereafter cited as Marcy Papers; Mason to Marcy, No. 1, January 28, 1854, *DF.*

19. HSS to Bancroft Davis, January 19, 1854, SP, 105/10; Mason to Marcy, January 19, 1854, Marcy Papers.

20. HSS to Marcy, No. 57, January 22, 1854, *DF;* HSS to Davis, January 19, 23, March 2, 1854, SP, 105/10; HSS to Lewis Cass, January 19, 1860, *SED* No. 31, 36th Cong., 25–27; *Washington Daily-Union,* March 10, 1854.

21. HSS to Davis, March 2, 1854, SP, 105/10; HSS to [E. N. Shelton], n.d., SP, 93/7.

22. Mason to Marcy, January 19, 26, March 15, 1854, Marcy Papers; HSS to Davis, March 20, [1854], SP, 105/5.

23. Rives to HSS, May 12, 1854, SP, 129/6.

24. Marcy to Mason, February 20, 1854, Marcy Papers.

25. HSS to Davis, March 9, [1854], SP, 105/5; Marcy to HSS, February 18, 1854, Marcy Papers.

26. HSS to Marcy, March 12, 1854, *DF;* HSS to Cass, January 19, 1860, *SED* No. 31, 36th Cong., 25–27.

27. On "guano diplomacy" generally, see Roy F. Nichols, *Advance Agents of American Destiny* (Philadelphia, 1956), 157–201. The most detailed examination of the Aves matter is William L. Harris, "The Aves Island Claims: A Study of Claims Technique," (M.A. thesis, Vanderbilt University, 1963); also, William H. Gray, "The Human Aspect of Aves Diplomacy: An Incident in the Relations between the United States and Venezuela," *The Americas,* 6 (1949), 72–84.

28. The account of the discovery and expulsion from Aves is taken from depositions in U. S. Congress, Senate, *Executive Document* No. 10, 36th Cong., 2d sess., 64–66, 85–86, 112–27, 357–66, hereafter cited as *SED* No. 10, 36th Cong.; U. S. Congress, Senate, *Executive Document* No. 25, 34th Cong., 3 sess., 86–92, hereafter cited as *SED* No. 25, 34th Cong.; Mariano de Briceno, *Memoir Justificatory of the Conduct of the Government of Venezuela on the Isle de Aves Question* (Washington, 1858), 3–4; *American Agriculturalist,* November 8, 1854, SP, 41/6; Nichols, *Advance Agents,* 180.

29. Sampson, Tappan, and Shelton to W. L. Marcy, January 15, 29, 1855, *SED* No. 10, 36th Cong., 5–7. Lang and Delano claimed $639,412, of which $500,000 was for potential profits; see B. B. French to Marcy, January 21, 1856, *ibid.,* 94–95.

30. HSS purchased the Lang and Delano claim for $2,500 in 1859, the Sampson and Tappan share for $6,000 in 1862, and Shelton's portion for $6,000 in 1862 (plus an additional $4,000 if more than one-half of the claim was secured); see Lang and Delano to HSS, December 16, 1859, SP, 62/13; E. N. Shelton to HSS, December 26, 1862, SP, 73/15; Agreement with P. S. Shelton, August 15, 1862, SP, 40/15. HSS also paid all the expenses he incurred while prosecuting the claim.

31. Marcy to Eames, No. 12, January 24, 1855; Eames to Marcy, No. 10, April 26, 1855, *SED* No. 25, 34th Cong., 4–10; Marcy to Shelton, June 14, 1855, SP, 35/5.

32. Shelton to Marcy, June 20, 1855, *SED* No. 10, 36th Cong., 26–39; Shelton to Marcy, June 24, 1855, *ibid.,* 40–42; memorial in *ibid.,* 43–64.

33. *New York Times,* May 23, 1855; [HSS], *Venezuelan Outrage upon United States Citizens and Property at Shelton's Isle: Memorandum of Philo S. Shelton, in His Case for State Department* (Derby, Conn., 1855).

34. Shelton to HSS, January 19, 20, February 12, May 5, 14, 15, 1855, SP, 78/1.

35. HSS to Thurlow Weed, February 12, 1856, WP; HSS to Cadwallader, n.d., SP, 37/1.

36. HSS to Pierce, December 24, 1855, January 3, 1856, *SED* No. 10, 36th Cong., 78–83.

37. *SED* No. 10, 36th Cong., 129–31; HSS to A. M. C. Pennington, April 16, 1856, SP, 37/15; HSS to Lafayette S. Foster, n.d., SP, 37/1; HSS to John M. Clayton, May 27, 1856, SP, 37/2; HSS to James M. Mason, May 10, 1856, SP, 37/2; HSS to W. H. Seward, April 17, 19, 1856, SeP.

38. HSS to Samuel L. Barlow, February 26, 1857, SP, 37/4.

39. HSS to Seward, February 25, 1857, SeP; HSS to N. M. Beckwith, September 16, 1857, SP, 104/15; Eames to Jacinto Gutierrez, March 31, May 29, June 11, 1857, *SED* No. 10, 36th Cong., 204–26, 231–32, 234; Gutierrez to Eames, June 2, 1857, *ibid.,* 232–34; *New York Times,* July 9, 1857; Harris, "Aves Island Claims," 90, 92.

40. HSS to Seward, June 20, 1857, SP, 37/18; HSS to Beckwith, September 16, 1857, SP, 104/15; HSS to Cass, August 10, 1857, *SED* No. 10, 36th Cong., 235–40.

41. Philip S. Klein, *President James Buchanan: A Biography* (University Park, Pa., 1962), 313–21; Cass to Florencio Ribas, September 11, 1857; Ribas to Cass, September 4, 1857, *SED* No. 10, 36th Cong., 277–78; *New York Times,* December 14, 1857.

42. HSS to James S. Mackie, January 1, 1858, SP, 37/13; HSS to S. L. Barlow, February 16, 1858, SP, 37/4.

43. Gray, "The Human Aspect of Aves Diplomacy," 81; Robert L. Gilmore, *Caudillism and Militarism in Venezuela, 1810–1910* (Athens, Ohio, 1964), 82–83; W. Urrutia to Eames,

March 24, 1858; Eames to Cass, No. 59, July 7, 1858, *SED* No. 10, 36th Cong., 395–96, 435–37.

44. Shelton to HSS, February 6, 1855, SP, 78/1; April 2, 1857, SP, 78/4; HSS to Cass, August 10, 21, 1858, SP, 37/7; HSS to Marcy, January 26, 1857; Charles U. Cotting and John H. B. Lang to Cass, August 31, 1858; HSS to Cass, September 8, 1858, *SED* No. 10, 36th Cong., 173–79, 443–45.

45. Turpin to HSS, November 7, 1858, February 15, 1859, SP, 36/12; HSS to Cass, December 9, 1858, *SED* No. 10, 36th Cong., 452–53; Harris, "Aves Island Claims," 124–26; William M. Malloy, comp., *Treaties, Conventions, International Acts, Protocols and Agreements between the United States of America and Other Powers: 1776–1909* (2 vols., Washington, 1910), II, 1843–44, hereafter cited as Malloy, *Treaties.*

46. Gilmore, *Caudillism and Militarism in Venezuela,* 83; Guillermo Moron, *A History of Venezuela,* ed. and trans. by John Street (New York, 1963), 168–72; HSS to W. H. Seward, December 29, 1862, *DB;* Erastus D. Culver to HSS, June 8, 1863, SP, 34/9.

47. HSS to Seward, March 20, April 3, 1862, *DB;* Seward to HSS, December 29, 1862, SP, 130/2; January 24, 1863, SP, 130/3; Welles to Seward, January 22, 1863, SP, 36/13; John J. Morse, Jr., ed., *The Diary of Gideon Welles* (3 vols., Boston, 1911), II, 38; Wilkes to Welles, June 9, 1863, SP, 36/15; Culver to Seward, No. 24, June 10, 1863, Despatches from United States Ministers to Venezuela, 1835-1906, hereafter cited as *DV;* Copy of revised payment agreement, June 5, 1863, SP, 39/10; William J. Morgan *et al.,* eds., *Autobiography of Rear Admiral Charles Wilkes, U.S. Navy, 1798–1877* (Washington, 1978), 792–93.

48. Culver to HSS, June 22, August 31, 1863, SP, 34/9; Culver to Seward, No. 29, August 11, 1863, *DV;* Edward B. Eastwick, *Venezuela or Sketches of Life in a South American Republic; with the History of the Loans of 1864* (London, 1868), 101–8; José M. Rojas to HSS, October 25, 1889; Guzmán Blanco to José Andrade, October 22, 1889, Claims: Venezuela, 1866–1888, Envelope 18, Case No. 60, National Archives, RG 76, hereafter cited as Claims, Venezuela, Case No. 60.

49. HSS to Seward, May 26, 1864, Miscellaneous Letters of the Department of State, 1784-1906, hereafter cited as Miscellaneous Letters, State Dept.; HSS to Seward, September 13, 14, 1864, *DB;* Culver to Seward, No. 77, July 25, 1864; No. 86, October 8, 1864, *DV;* José M. Rojas Statement, January 4, 1890; Rojas to HSS, October 25, 1889; Guzmán Blanco to Andrade, October 22, 1889, Claims, Venezuela, Case No. 60; Eastwick, *Venezuela,* 116–19, 121.

50. James R. Hibbs, "Chapters in the Relations of Venezuela and the United States, 1865 to 1889," (Ph.D. dissertation, University of Pennsylvania, 1941), 190–95; John B. Moore, *History and Digest of the International Arbitrations to which the United States Has Been a Party* (6 vols., Washington, 1898), II, 1674–76, 1689; Claims, Venezuela, Case No. 60; *Awards of the Commissioners of the United States of America and the United States of Venezuela under the Convention of December 5, 1885,* 58, National Archives, RG 76; J. S. Mackie to J. J. Foulkrod, September 9, 1890, SP, 126/16.

51. HSS to Squier, October 9, 1857, Ephraim G. Squier Papers, hereafter cited as Squier Papers; *New York Times,* May 22, 23, 1854; Squier, *Notes on Central America; Particularly Honduras and San Salvador . . . and the Proposed Honduras Interoceanic Railway* (New York, 1855), 263–64; Squier, *Honduras: Descriptive, Historical, and Statistical* (London, 1870), 209–10, 214; Charles L. Stansifer, "E. George Squier and the Honduras Interoceanic Railroad Project," *Hispanic American Historical Review,* 46 (1966), 1–22.

52. Squier to HSS, November 17, December 12, 1854, September 4, 1857, SP, 43/8; Sanford drafts to Squier, September 25, October 26, 1857, SP, 43/10.

53. HSS to Squier, October 9, 9 (Private), 26, November 6, 9, 1857, Squier Papers; HSS draft to Squier, December 8, 1857, SP, 43/10; HSS to John C. Trautwine, October 26, 1857, SP, 43/16.

54. HSS drafts to Squier, November 8, 1857, SP, 43/10; November 9, 1857, SP, 43/15; HSS to Squier, November 9, 1857, Squier Papers; HSS to R. R. Morse, April 30, 1858, SP, 43/10;

Squier, *Honduras,* 214–16; Stansifer, "E. George Squier and the Honduras Interoceanic Railroad Project," 23–24.

55. Mackie to HSS, November 26, 1858, SP, 126/3. In addition to his original investment of $2,000, HSS claimed expenses of $3,500 for his trip to Honduras;see Accounts, SP, 43/1.

56. Philip Raine, *Paraguay* (New Brunswick, N.J., 1956), 128–32; *New York Times,* January 9, April 12, June 29, August 1, 1855; June 1, 21, 1858.

57. HSS to Buchanan, n.d., SP, 42/5.

58. Petitions from New York merchants, June 24, 1858; Petition from Connecticut and Rhode Island Democrats, June 25, 1858; Moses Taylor to Buchanan, June 26, August 12, 1858; S. L. Barlow to Buchanan, July 31, 1858, Applications and Recommendations; Brady to HSS, June 19, July 31, 1858, SP, 42/3; Mackie to HSS, June 22, July 6, 8, August 11, 1858, SP, 126/3; August 18, 19, [1858], SP, 126/1.

59. Elijah Ward to HSS, June 21, 1858, SP, 42/3; HSS to Bancroft Davis, July 11, [1858], SP, 105–6.

60. Mackie to HSS, August 18, [1858], SP, 126/1; Brady to HSS, July 23, 1858, SP, 42/3; HSS draft to Buchanan, n.d.; HSS draft to John Appleton, August 2, 1858, SP, 42/5.

61. Mackie to HSS, n.d., SP, 126/1; HSS to P. S. Shelton, March 4, 1858, SP, 37/19; W. V. N. Bay, *Reminiscences of the Bench and Bar of Missouri* (St. Louis, 1878), 462–63; Moore, *History and Digest of International Arbitrations,* II, 1493–94.

62. John M. Dow to HSS, March 17, 1859, SP, 42/10; HSS draft, March 22, [1859], SP, 42/5; Petition to Buchanan on Sanford's behalf, March 17, 1859 (included among the signers were C. H. Russell and J. J. Astor, Jr.); Moses Taylor to Buchanan, March 17, 1859; Gov. Kemble to Buchanan, March 10, 25, 1859; Samuel J. Tilden to Buchanan, March 17, 1859, Applications and Recommendations; John C. Parish, *George Wallace Jones* (Iowa City, 1912), 49–57, 216–20.

63. Hoadley to HSS, January 9, 18, 19, 20, February 29, 1860, SP, 44/3; Fessenden N. Otis, *Illustrated History of the Panama Railroad* (New York, 1861), 17–25; E. Taylor Parks, *Colombia and the United States, 1765–1934* (Durham, 1935), 273–74.

64. HSS to Hoadley, n.d., SP, 44/7; March 21, April 16, 20, June 17, 30, October 22, 1860, SP, 44/9; HSS to G. W. Totten, April 16, 1860, SP, 44/10; George W. Jones to Lewis Cass, No. 24, April 16, 1860; No. 27, May 31, 1860, William R. Manning, *Diplomatic Correspondence of the United States: Inter-American Affairs, 1831–1860* (12 vols., Washington, 1935), V, 960–61; 969–72; HSS Journal, March–April, 1860, SP, 3/14.

65. HSS to Judge Corkery, November 3, [1860], SP, 42/5; HSS to Hoadley, October 22, 1860, SP, 44/9; Statement of trip's expenses, October 31, 1860, SP, 44/1; HSS to Hoadley, [November 14, 1860], SP, 42/7; Hoadley to HSS, December 15, 1860, SP, 44/3.

66. David M. Potter, *Lincoln and His Party in the Secession Crisis* (New Haven, 1962), 46, 69, 78, 113, 116–32, 179; Kenneth M. Stampp, *And the War Came: The North and the Secession Crisis, 1860–61* (Chicago, 1964), 123–24, 180.

67. *Trenton Daily State Gazette and Republican,* January 28, 1861, quoted in Stampp, *Secession Crisis,* 126.

68. Smith to HSS, November 1, 1860, SP, 131/7; Smith to Lincoln, November 7, 1860, Robert Todd Lincoln Collection of the Papers of Abraham Lincoln, hereafter cited as Lincoln Papers.

69. Lincoln to Smith, November 10, 1860, Lincoln Papers; HSS drafts to Rives, n.d., SP, 104/3; Potter, *Lincoln and His Party,* 135.

70. "Free Cotton and Free Cotton States," [Albany, 1860], SP, 104/12; HSS to Weed, December 26, 1860, WP.

71. Hoadley to HSS, January 2, 28, February 20, 21, 25, March 1, 13, 1861, SP, 44/4; W. H. Aspinwall to HSS, March 5, 1861, SP, 42/7; *New York Times,* February 23, 25, 1861; *New York Tribune,* March 13, 20, 1861. When HSS went abroad in April 1861, he assigned the Panama Railroad claim to Samuel S. Cox, who continued the prosecution until its settlement in 1866. The company's judgment was $25,847, with $3,946 going to HSS and $3,808 to Cox;

see Cox to HSS, June 28, 1861, SP, 117/1; May 31, 1866, SP, 117/2; E. N. Shelton to HSS, May 29, 1866, SP, 74/7; July 10, 1866, SP, 74/8; extract from Proceedings of Joint United States—New Granada Commission, April 14, 1866, SP, 44/14.

72. Seward to HSS, January 17, 1861, SP, 130/2; William H. Russell, *My Diary North and South* (Boston, 1863), 31–32, 34, 39; Cassius M. Clay, *The Life of Cassius Marcellus Clay, Writings and Speeches* (2 vols., Cincinnati, 1886), I, 255.

73. Welles to his wife, March 9, 1861, quoted in Frank M. Anderson, *The Mystery of "A Public Man," A Historical Detective Story* (Minneapolis, 1948), 44.

74. Carl Sandburg, *Abraham Lincoln; The War Years* (4 vols., New York, 1939), I, 164.

75. HSS to Bancroft Davis (several letters), n.d., SP, 105/6, 105/11; Davis to HSS, February 25, 27, 1861, SP, 118/8; Davis to Seward, February 27, 1861 (petition from N.Y. merchants enclosed); H. B. Anthony to Seward, March 18, 1861, Applications and Recommendations.

76. HSS to Seward, March 15, 1861; Davis to Seward, February 11, 1861, Applications and Recommendations; Davis to HSS, February 21, 1861, SP, 118/8.

77. *Ibid.;* Glyndon Van Deusen, *William Henry Seward* (New York, 1967), 272; HSS to Davis, March 20, [1861], SP, 105/11; *New York Tribune,* March 21, 1861.

78. William E. Curtis to HSS, March 21, 1861, SP, 117/9; Horatio J. Perry to HSS, June 14, 1861, SP, 128/10; Edward H. Wright to HSS, March 24, 1861, SP, 133/10; Lawrence S. Kaplan, "The Brahmin as Diplomat in Nineteenth Century America: Everett, Bancroft, Motley, Lowell, " *Civil War History,* 19 (1973), 6–8.

79. *New Haven Palladium,* n.d., enclosed in J. J. Babcock to HSS, March 30, 1861, SP, 94/18.

80. *Ibid.*

Chapter 3

1. HSS to Seward, June 18, 1861, SeP.

2. HSS to William Walker, November, 1861, SP, 100/1. Seward is quoted in a pamphlet inspired, if not written, by HSS. Although the quote may be apocryphal, its sense well describes Sanford's activities; see *Some Account of Belair, also of the City of Sanford, Florida, with a Brief Sketch of Their Founder* (Sanford, Fla., 1889), 63.

3. Seward to HSS, No. 2, March 26, 1861, Diplomatic Instructions of the Department of State, 1801–1906, Belgium, hereafter cited as *IB;* Frederick W. Seward, *Seward at Washington as Senator and Secretary of State, a Memoir of His Life, with Selections from His Letters* (2 vols., New York, 1891), II, 532.

4. HSS to Seward, April 19, 25, 1861, *DB;* Faulkner to James Buchanan, September 1, 1860, Buchanan Papers; Lynn M. Case and Warren F. Spencer, *The United States and France: Civil War Diplomacy* (Philadelphia, 1970), 24, 28–29, 49; Donald R. McVeigh, "Charles James Faulkner in the Civil War" *West Virginia History,* 12 (1951), 130–32. Sanford wrote both official, numbered dispatches to Seward (see note 16, this chapter) and unnumbered notes and letters (as cited in this note). If only the date is cited, the correspondence in *DB* falls into this second category.

5. HSS to Seward, April 25, 1861, *DB;* Case and Spencer, *United States and France,* 29–30; Norman B. Ferris, *Desperate Diplomacy: William H. Seward's Foreign Policy, 1861* (Knoxville, 1976), 19.

6. Case and Spencer, *United States and France,* 45–76; Ferris, *Desperate Diplomacy,* 37–41; D. P. Crook, *The North, the South, and the Powers, 1861–1865* (New York, 1974), 75–83.

7. HSS to Seward, May 12, 1861, *DB;* Case and Spencer, *United States and France,* 54–55.

8. *Ibid.,* Ephraim D. Adams, *Great Britain and the American Civil War* (2 vols., London, 1925), I, 98–99; Van Deusen, *Seward,* 294–99.

9. HSS to Seward, May 7, 21, 1861, *DB.*

10. Morse, ed., *The Diary of Gideon Welles,* II, 39.

11. HSS to Seward, October 4, 1861, August 12, 1864, *DB;* Seward to HSS, No. 138, July 30, 1864, *IB.*

12. Seward to HSS, March 5, October 27, 1862, SP, 130/2; November 24, 1863, SP, 130/4; June 15, 1866, SP, 130/7; January 2, 1867, SP, 130/8.

13. HSS to Seward, April 19, 30, May 12, August 6, 1861, *DB;* HSS to Weed, May 18, 1861, WP.

14. Marsh to HSS, October 3, 1861, SP, 128/1; Ferris, *Desperate Diplomacy,* 175–77; Philip Van Doren Stern, *When the Guns Roared: World Aspects of the American Civil War* (Garden City, N.Y., 1965), 56–57; Margaret Clapp, *Forgotten First Citizen: John Bigelow* (Boston, 1947), 150–55, and *passim.*

15. Unidentified newspaper clipping, May 1861, SP, 65/3; HSS to Seward, April 30, May 12, October 18, December 9, 1861, January 23, 1862, *DB;* HSS to Weed, February 12, 1862, WP; Glyndon G. Van Deusen *Thurlow Weed: Wizard of the Lobby* (Boston, 1947), 275–79.

16. HSS to Seward, December 9, 1861, January 23, 1862; No. 229, November 25, 1864; January 26, 1865, *DB;* HSS to Seward, March 27, July 2, 1863, SeP; HSS to Weed, August 29, October 21, 1862, June 12, 25, 1863, WP; HSS to Charles H. Russell, June 12, 1863; HSS to J. V. L. Pruyn, June 25, 1863; HSS to August Belmont, July 3, 1863, SP, 100/4.

17. Seward to HSS, No. 66, October 6, 1862; No. 155, December 21, 1864, *IB.*

18. HSS to Seward, January 23, May 12, 1862, *DB;* Mann to Judah P. Benjamin, No. 26, October 14, 1862, *Official Records of the Union and Confederate Navies in the War of the Rebellion* (31 vols., Washington, 1894–1927), Series 2, vol. III, 553; for selections from the Belgian press, see Belle B. Sideman and Lillian Freedman, *Europe Looks at the Civil War, an Anthology* (New York, 1960), 28–29, 96–97, 105–6, 260, 265.

19. HSS to Seward, November 19, 25, 1862, SeP; HSS to Seward, No. 77, November 19, 1862, *DB.*

20. HSS to Seward, August 28, October 15, 1862, *DB;* HSS to Seward, September 15, November 7, 1862, SeP; HSS to Weed, September 11, October 21, 1862, WP.

21. HSS to Seward, August 28, October 15, 1862, *DB;* J. Bigelow to HSS, July 4, August 4, September 12, 15, October 5, November 10, 1863, SP, 115/12; May 24, 1864, SP, 115/13 and SP, 115/12, 13 *passim;* Malespine to HSS, January 14, August 3, 1863, November 22, 1864, SP, 139/11; William L. Dayton to Malespine, December 4, 1863, William L. Dayton Papers, hereafter cited as Dayton Papers; Serge Gavronsky, *The French Liberal Opposition and the American Civil War* (New York, 1968), 19.

22. HSS to Seward, October 15, 1862, August 26, November 7, 1864, *DB;* HSS to Seward, December 11, 1862, SeP.

23. Seward to HSS, No. 5, May 20, 1861, *IB.*

24. HSS to Seward, July 4, [1861], Lincoln Papers.

25. HSS to James Putnam, October 29, 1861, SP, 139/5; HSS to Seward, June 6, 1861; No. 32, October 31, 1861; No. 40, December 19, 1861, *DB;* HSS to Seward, June 11, 1861, SeP; F. H. Morse to William P. Fessenden, September 28, 1861, March 6, 1869, William Pitt Fessenden Papers; Harriet C. Owsley, "Henry Shelton Sanford and Federal Surveillance Abroad, 1861–1865," *Mississippi Valley Historical Review,* 48 (1961), 220.

26. HSS to Marsh, June 11, 1861, George Perkins Marsh Papers, hereafter cited as Marsh Papers; HSS to Seward, June 11, 1861, SeP; HSS to [Dayton], July 3, 1861, SP, 139/5; Perry to HSS, June 14, 16, 1861, SP, 128/10. Seward sent HSS £625 in May 1861 for use as a "secret service" fund and periodically forwarded additional funds thereafter. HSS employed these funds personally and disbursed them to other Union agents in Europe.

27. HSS to August Francedt, July 31, 1861, SP, 139/5; HSS to Seward, July 4, [1861], Lincoln Papers; HSS to Seward, June 15, 1861, SeP; HSS to Seward, July 11, 1861, *DB.*

28. Morse to HSS, June 29, July 12, 1861, SP, 139/12; HSS to Seward, June 15, 1861, SeP; Pollaky to HSS, September 24, 1861, SP, 139/14.

29. Pollaky to HSS, SP, 139/13, 14, *passim;* Ed Brennan to Pollaky, SP, 139/7, *passim.*

30. Morse to HSS, September 19, 1861, SP, 139/12.

31. Samuel B. Thompson, *Confederate Purchasing Operations Abroad* (Chapel Hill, 1935), 16; Richard I. Lester, *Confederate Finance and Purchasing in Great Britain* (Charlottesville, 1975), 148.

32. HSS to Seward, September 24, 1861, *DB.*

33. HSS to Marsh, October 24, 1861, Marsh Papers; HSS to F. W. Seward, August 12, 1861; HSS to W. H. Seward, July 23, 1861, SeP; HSS to Seward, July 26, 1861; No. 19, August 15, 1861; November 5, 1861, *DB.*

34. HSS to Seward, July 23, 1861, SeP; HSS to Seward, July 26, 1861, *DB;* Frank J. Merli, *Great Britain and the Confederate Navy, 1861–1865* (Bloomington, Ind., 1970), 14–16.

35. James D. Bulloch, *The Secret Service of the Confederate States in Europe* (2 vols., New York, 1959), I, 111–17; Pollaky to HSS, October 14, 1861, SP, 139/14; Brennan to Pollaky, October 4, 5, 8, 9, 10, 11, 1861, SP, 139/7.

36. HSS to William Walker, n.d., SP, 139/5; HSS to Seward, October 10, 1861, *DB.*

37. Charles Francis Adams Diary, June 13, 1861, Adams Papers, hereafter cited as Adams Diary; Adams to Seward, October 18, 1861, Despatches from United States Ministers to Great Britain, 1791–1906, hereafter cited as *DGrB.*

38. *London Express,* n.d., enclosed in Pollaky to HSS, n.d., SP, 139/14; similar reports appeared in the *Manchester Examiner* and *London Evening Star.*

39. Adams to Seward, October 18, November 1, 1861, *DGrB;* Adams Diary, November 2, 1861; Wallace and Gillespie, eds., *Journal of Benjamin Moran,* II, 894, 899, 907–8; Neill F. Sanders, "Lincoln's Consuls in the British Isles, 1861–1865," (Ph.D. dissertation, University of Missouri-Columbia, 1971), 43.

40. Adams Diary, November 2, 1861; for HSS's subsequent dislike of Adams, see HSS to Seward, October 25, 1868, SeP.

41. Seward to HSS, No. 37, November 4, 1861, *IB;* F. W. Seward to Adams, November 18, 1861, Instructions of the Department of State, 1801–1906, Great Britain, hereafter cited as *IGrB;* Sanders, "Lincoln's Consuls," 46, 67, 182; Brainerd Dyer, "Thomas H. Dudley," *Civil War History,* 1 (1955), 404–9.

42. Seward to HSS, January 22, 1862, SP, 130/2; Seward to HSS, No. 41, December 11, 1861; No. 145, September 10, 1864; No. 150, October 15, 1864; No. 161, February 8, 1865, *IB.*

43. HSS to Seward, March 20, April 18, 1862, *DB.*

44. HSS to Seward, July 14, 1863, *DB;* HSS to Thomas H. Dudley, August 27, November 3, 1862, Thomas Haines Dudley Papers.

45. Beckwith to HSS, n.d., SP, 115/5.

46. Merli, *Great Britain and the Confederate Navy,* 59, 163–77, 184–86; Crook, *The North, the South, and the Powers,* 296–98; David F. Kein, "Russell's Decision to Detain the Laird Rams," *Civil War History,* 22 (1976), 158–63.

47. *Ibid.,* HSS to Seward, No. 119, June 9, 1863, *DB.*

48. HSS to Seward, June 15, 1863; No. 125, June [19], 1863; No. 127, June 23, 1863, *DB; New York Times,* May 4, 1890; Douglas H. Maynard, "The Forbes-Aspinwall Mission," *Mississippi Valley Historical Review,* 45 (1958), 67–89.

49. Merli, *Great Britain and the Confederate Navy,* 186; Case and Spencer, *United States and France,* 429–36.

50. Beckwith to HSS, July 9, 1863, SP, 115/6; HSS to Seward, July 10, 14, 1863, *DB.*

51. Bigelow to HSS, July 18, 1863, SP, 115/12; Owsley, "Sanford and Federal Surveillance Abroad," 224.

52. Bigelow to HSS, August 17, 1863, SP, 115/12; Clapp, *Bigelow,* 200–1.

53. Bigelow to HSS, September 12, 15, 24, 1863, SP, 115/12; Bigelow, *France and the Confederate Navy, 1862–1868* (New York, 1888), 1–39; Case and Spencer, *United States and France,* 437–80.

54. *Ibid.;* Clapp, *Bigelow,* 209; HSS to Seward, December 2, 1863, *DB;* HSS to Seward, October 29, December 7, 1863, August 4, 1864, SeP.

55. HSS to Weed, May 31, 1861, WP; HSS to Seward, No. 2, May 12, 1861; No. 4, May 25, 1861; May 12, 28, 1861, *DB;* HSS to Seward, June 18, July 9, 1861, SeP.

56. Seward to Cameron, June 4, 19, 1861, *War of the Rebellion: A Compilation of the Official Records of the Union and Confederate Armies* (130 vols., Washington, 1880–1901), Series 3, I, 247, 277, hereafter cited as *WOR;* Carl L. Davis, *Arming the Union: Small Arms in the Civil War* (Port Washington, N.Y., 1973), 39–53; Nevins, *Ordeal of the Union,* V, 343–45.

57. Robert V. Bruce, *Lincoln and the Tools of War* (Indianapolis, 1956), 43; William Diamond, "Imports of the Confederate Government from Europe and Mexico," *Journal of Southern History,* 6 (1940), 473, *passim;* Clement Eaton, *A History of the Southern Confederacy* (New York, 1965), 132–33; Thompson, *Confederate Purchasing Operations Abroad,* 45.

58. Nevins, *Ordeal of the Union,* V, 352–53; W. L. Dayton to C. F. Adams, May 15, June 6, 1861, Dayton Papers; Seward to HSS, No. 14, July 11, 1861; No. 25, August 30, 1861, *IB;* HSS to Seward, August 6, 10, 1861; No. 21, September 19, 1861, *DB;* George L. Schuyler to S. Cameron, September 5, 1861, *WOR,* Series 3, I, 484–86.

59. James W. Ripley to Schuyler, July 27, 1861, U. S. Congress, House, *Executive Document* No. 67, 37th Cong., 2d sess., 228, hereafter cited as *HED* No. 67, 37th Cong.

60. HSS to G. P. Marsh, October 1861, Marsh Papers; HSS to Seward, No. 21, September 19, 1861, *DB;* HSS to F. W. Seward, September 27, 1861, SeP; A. Howard Meneely, *The War Department, 1861, A Study in Mobilization and Administration* (New York, 1928), 287.

61. Schuyler to HSS, August 13, 1861, SP, 138/11; Cameron to HSS, September 5, 1861, *HED* No. 67, 37th Cong., 77; HSS to Seward, No. 24, September 27, 1861, *DB;* HSS to F. W. Seward, September 27, 1861, SeP.

62. Seward to HSS, No. 33, October 15, 1861, *IB;* Cameron to Seward, August 28, 1861; Thomas A. Scott to Salmon P. Chase, October 14, 1861, *WOR,* Series 3, I, 462, 574–75.

63. Schuyler to HSS, August 8, 13, October 28, 31, 1861, SP, 138/11; HSS to Schuyler, September 30, [1861], SP, 138/3; B. G. Wainwright to HSS, October 17, 1861, SP, 138/16; HSS to Marsh, October 10, 24, 1861, Marsh Papers; Marsh to HSS, September 12, 1861, SP, 128/1.

64. Smith to HSS, July 29, September 5, 1861, SP, 138/13; Gurowski, *Diary,* I, 141; *New York Tribune,* November 9, 1877; *New York World,* November 11, 14, 1877.

65. HSS to Cameron, November 14, 1861, with enclosures Boker & Co. to HSS, November 5, 1861; HSS to Boker & Co., November 11, 1861, Letters Received by the Secretary of War, 1801–1870, National Archives, RG 107, hereafter cited as Letters, Secretary of War; HSS Account of $1 million fund, March 6, 1862, enclosed in HSS to E. M. Stanton, March 6, 1862, SP, 99/2.

66. HSS to Seward, November 12, 1861; HSS to Cameron, November 12, 1861, Letters, Secretary of War; HSS to Cameron, November 19, December 3, 5, 12, 26, 27, 1861, Letters Received by the Ordnance Department, 1862, National Archives, RG 107, hereafter cited as Letters, Ordnance Dept.; HSS to Cameron, November 22, 1861, SP, 99/1; HSS to Seward, November 22, 1861, *DB;* HSS Account of $1 million fund, SP, 99/2.

67. Davis, *Arming the Union,* v, 56; HSS to Schuyler, October 29, 1861, SP, 138/3; HSS to A. Rhulman, December [12], 21, 25, 1861; HSS to James R. McDonald, December 5, 1861; HSS to Marshall Talbott, December 6, 1861, SP, 99/1.

68. HSS to Seward, October 25, 1861, SeP; HSS to Seward, November 12, 1861, Letters, Secretary of War; HSS to Dayton, November, [1861], SP, 139/5; Dayton to HSS, November 4, 1861, Dayton Papers; G. P. Smith to HSS, November 5, 1861, SP, 138/12; HSS to G. P. Smith, November 12, 1861, SP, 100/1.

69. Smith to U. S. Grant, April 13, 1869, Applications and Recommendations; *New York Tribune,* November 9, 1877.

70. HSS to William M. Evarts, May 29, October 26, 1877; Leon Gauchez to Evarts, October 26, 1877, Applications and Recommendations.

71. HSS to Whitelaw Reid, November 21, 1877, WP; HSS to N. B. Sanford, November 8, 1861, SP, 100/1; Wallace and Gillespie, eds., *Journal of Benjamin Moran,* II, 901, 952.

72. HSS to William Walker, November, 1861; HSS to N. M. Beckwith, November 15, 1861; HSS to Uncle [E. N. Shelton], November 14, 1861, SP, 100/1.

73. HSS to W. E. Curtis, November 29, 1861, SP, 100/2; HSS to H. B. Anthony, December 24, 1861, SP, 100/1; HSS to Weed, December 31, 1861, January 3, 1862, WP; HSS to Seward, December 2, 9, 1861, *DB;* Norman B. Ferris, *The Trent Affair: A Diplomatic Crisis* (Knoxville, 1977), 100, 161.

74. HSS to Bigelow, December 7, 1861, SP, 100/1; Clapp, *Bigelow,* 156–59; Case and Spencer, *United States and France,* 190–99.

75. HSS to Seward, December 2, 5, 1861, *DB;* Case and Spencer, *United States and France,* 209–13.

76. HSS to Seward, December 17, 31, 1861, *DB;* HSS to Weed, December 16, 31, 1861, WP.

77. Bruce, *Lincoln and the Tools of War,* 146–47, 150; Kenneth Bourne, *Britain and the Balance of Power in North America, 1815–1908* (Berkeley, 1967), 219.

78. HSS to Seward, December 5, 6, 13, 1861, *DB;* HSS to Weed, December 4, 10, 1861, WP; HSS to Cameron, December 3, 12, 17, 26, 1861, Letters, Ordnance Dept.; HSS to N. M. Beckwith, December 7, 1861, SP, 100/1.

79. *Ibid.;* HSS to Cameron, December 7, 19, 1861, SP, 99/1; HSS to Seward, December 31, 1861, January 3, 1862, *DB.*

80. HSS to Cameron, January 21, 23, 1862, Letters, Ordnance Dept.

81. Benjamin P. Thomas and Harold Hyman, *Stanton: The Life and Times of Lincoln's Secretary of War* (New York, 1962), 142, 156.

82. Adams Diary, September 20, 1861; H. Nelson Gay, "Lincoln's Offer of a Command to Garibaldi: Light on a Disputed Point of History," *Century Magazine,* 75 (1907), 66; Quiggle to Seward, No. 20, July 5, 1861; Quiggle to Garibaldi June 8, 1861; Garibaldi to Quiggle, June 27, 1861, Despatches from United States Consuls in Antwerp, Belgium, 1802–1906, hereafter cited *CDA;* for a brief historiographical comment on this episode, see Joseph A. Fry, "The Messenger to Garibaldi: Henry S. Sanford and the Offer of a Union Command to Giuseppe Garibaldi," *Essays in History,* 12 (1973), 46–47.

83. *New York Herald,* July 31, 1850; Howard R. Marraro, "Lincoln's Offer of a Command to Garibaldi: Further Light on a Disputed Point of History," *Journal of the Illinois State Historical Society,* 36 (1943), 237; *New York Tribune,* June 2, 1861.

84. Seward to HSS, July 27, 1861, *IB;* HSS to Seward, August 16, 1861, SeP.

85. William Hunter to HSS, July 29, 1861, SP, 122/7; HSS to Marsh, August 13, 1861, Marsh Papers; Marsh to HSS, August 19, 1861, SP, 128/1; HSS to Seward, No. 18, August 14, 1861, *DB;* HSS to Seward, August 16, 1861, SeP.

86. *New York Tribune,* August 14, September 23, 24, 26, October 2, 1861; Marsh to HSS, August 30, 1861, SP, 128/1.

87. Quiggle to Garibaldi, August 15, 1861; Quiggle to Seward, August 15, 1861, *CDA;* HSS to Seward, September 12, 1861, *DB.*

88. Joseph Artomi to HSS, August 21, September 3, 1861, SP, 139/1; HSS to Seward, August 21, 1861, SeP; HSS to Seward, August 29, September 18, 1861; HSS to Garibaldi, August 26, 1861, *DB;* George M. Trevelyan, *Garibaldi and the Making of Italy* (London, 1911), 282, 284. Herbert Zettl has recently published a letter (Paris, September 18, 1861) from HSS's friend and confidant in paris, Nelson M. Beckwith, to Paul S. Forbes. Beckwith claimed to have accompanied HSS to Italy and gave his impressions of the trip, see "Garibaldi and the American Civil War," *Civil War History,* 22 (1976), 70–76. Beckwith also told John Bigelow that he had gone with HSS; see Bigelow, *Retrospections of an Active Life* (5 vols., New York, 1909), I, 371–72. Beckwith was actually in Etretat on the Normandy coast on September 1, and in Paris on September 9, when HSS was in Turin; see Beckwith to HSS, September 1,

9, [1861], SP, 115/4. Beckwith's information in the letter to Forbes undoubtedly came from HSS, who arrived back in Paris about September 16, and surely told his old friend the complete story. The two then decided that Beckwith should let the story out privately to help Sanford avoid replying directly to the charges then circulating in the European and American press, and Beckwith subsequently helped Sanford to interpret Garibaldi's character and to write his reports to Seward. See Beckwith to HSS, September 16, 17, 27, 1861, SP, 115/4. For a more extended comment on Beckwith's role, see Fry, "Eyewitness by Proxy: Nelson M. Beckwith's Evaluation of Garibaldi, September 1861," *Civil War History,* 28 (1982), 65–70.

89. HSS to Seward, September 4, 7, 18, 1861, *DB;* Beckwith to HSS, September 1, 9, 1861, SP, 115/4.

90. HSS to Seward, September 4, 7, 12, 18, 1861, *DB;* HSS to Marsh, September 7, 1861, Marsh Papers; HSS to Garibaldi, September 8, 1861, SP, 139/1; Artomi to HSS, September 3, 1861, SP, 139/1.

91. HSS to Seward, September 12, 1861, DB; HSS to Marsh, September 12, 1861, Marsh Papers.

92. HSS to Seward, September 12, 18, 1861, *DB; New York Tribune,* October 9, 1861; Gay, "Lincoln's Offer of a Command to Garibaldi," 71.

93. *New York Tribune,* October 4, 1861; Bigelow to Seward, September 23, 1861, SeP; Dayton to F. Sumner, September 21, 1861, Dayton Papers; W. Reed West, *Contemporary French Opinion of the American Civil War* (Baltimore, 1934), 34.

94. HSS to Marsh, October, 1861, Marsh Papers; HSS to Seward, September 21, 1861, SeP; HSS to Seward, September 27, October 1, 1861, *DB.* See also note 88 above.

95. HSS to Seward, October 1, 1861, *DB;* Beckwith to HSS, September 16, 1861, SP, 115/4; Marsh to HSS, September 23, 26, October 3, 1861, SP, 128/1; HSS to Marsh, October, 1861, Marsh Papers.

96. Hay to Seth Low, April 19, 1904, Hay Papers; Quiggle to Seward, September 30, 1861, *CDA;* Adams Diary, September 20, 1861; Wallace and Gillespie, eds., *The Journal of Benjamin Moran,* II, 881–82.

97. Marsh to Seward, September 4, 1861; No. 19, September 14, 1861, *DI;* Seward to HSS, October 11, 1861, *IB.*

98. HSS to Seward, September 18, 1861, *DB;* HSS to Seward, September 21, 1861, SeP; Marsh to HSS, September 7, 1861, SP, 128/1; Marsh to Seward, No. 19, September 14, 1861, *DI;* David Lowenthal, *George Perkins Marsh: Versatile Vermonter* (New York, 1958), 227; Adams Diary, September 20, 1861; Beckwith to HSS, September 16, 1861, SP, 115/4; Bigelow to Seward, September 23, 1861, SeP; Charles C. Tansill, "A Secret Chapter in Civil War History," *Thought: Fordham University Quarterly,* 15 (1940), 224.

99. Wallace and Gillespie, eds., *The Journal of Benjamin Moran,* II, 861; Adams Diary, June 13, 1861; Lowenthal, *Marsh,* 236; Case and Spencer, *United States and France,* 335.

Chapter 4

1. HSS to Seward, June 18, 1861, SeP; HSS to Seward, October 15, 1861; No. 29, October 25, 1861, *DB;* Burton J. Hendricks, *Statesmen of the Lost Cause: Jefferson Davis and His Cabinet* (Boston, 1939), 400.

2. Leopold to Victoria, October 17, 1861, in Arthur C. Benson, ed., *The Letters of Queen Victoria; A Selection from Her Majesty's Correspondence between the years 1837 and 1861* (3 vols., New York, 1907), III, 579; Leopold to Victoria, November 20, 1862, in George E. Buckle, ed., *The Letters of Queen Victoria: A Selection from Her Majesty's Correspondence and Journal between the Years 1862 and 1878* (3 vols., New York, 1926–1928), I, 47–48.

3. HSS to Seward, No. 1, May 10, 1861; July 18, 1861, *DB.*

4. HSS to L. S. Foster, May 16, 1861, SP, 105/16; HSS to Alexander Ramsey, February 22, 1862, *Correspondence on the Occasion of the Presentation by Major-General Sanford . . . of a Battery of Steel Cannon, to the State of Minnesota for the Use of the First Minnesota Regiment of Volunteers* (St. Paul, 1862), 5–6; William W. Folwell, *A History of Minnesota* (4 vols., St. Paul, 1924), II, 87; Robert Voight, "Defender of the Common Law: Aaron Goodrich, Chief Justice of the Minnesota Territory," (Ph.D. dissertation, University of Minnesota, 1962), 143–44.

5. *New York World,* November 11, 1877.

6. HSS to Seward, July 23, 1867, SeP; HSS to Seward, July 23, 1867, April 23, 1868, *DB;* HSS to Charles Sumner, April 11, 1867, Charles Sumner Papers, hereafter cited as Sumner Papers.

7. HSS to Seward, No. 1, May 10, 1861; No. 69, September 26, 1862; No. 72, October 8, 1862; No. 114, May 23, 1863; July 10, 1863; No. 130, July 14, 1863; No. 145, September 4, 1863; September 15, 1864, *DB;* HSS to Seward, June 20, 1863, SeP.

8. Seward to HSS, No. 4, May 6, 1861, *IB;* Van Deusen, *Seward,* 294–95; Ferris, *Desperate Diplomacy,* 75–76, 82; Case and Spencer, *United States and France,* 79.

9. HSS to Seward, No. 6, May 26, 1861; HSS to de Vriere, June 4, 1861, enclosed in HSS to Seward, No. 8, June 5, 1861; No. 9, June 22, 1861; No. 10, July 2, 1861; No. 16, July 30, 1861, *DB.*

10. Donaldson Jordan and Edwin J. Pratt, *Europe and the American Civil War* (Boston, 1931), 197–98; HSS to Seward, No. 61, April 17, 1862; No. 62, May 1, 1862; No. 67, September 2, 1862, *DB;* HSS to Seward, November 11, 1864, SeP.

11. HSS to Seward, April 10, May 13, 1862, SeP; HSS to Seward, No. 61, April 17, 1862; No. 72, October 8, 1862, *DB;* Seward to HSS, No. 59, May 6, 1862; No. 60, May 23, 1862, *IB;* Case and Spencer, *United States and France,* 291–94; James D. Richardson, *A Compilation of the Messages and Papers of the Presidents 1789–1908* (11 vols., Washington, 1908), VI, 89–90, hereafter cited as Richardson, *Messages of the Presidents.*

12. Eugene A. Brady, "A Reconsideration of the Lancashire 'Cotton Famine,' " *Agricultural History,* 37 (1963), 156–62; Crook, *The North, the South, and the Powers,* 200–1, 205–6; Henry Blumenthal, *A Reappraisal of Franco-American Relations, 1830–1871* (Chapel Hill, 1959), 154–56.

13. HSS to Seward, November 4, 1862, April 24, 1863, SeP; HSS to Seward, No. 90, January 23, 1863; January 23, (private), January 29, April 20, 1863, *DB.*

14. *Ibid.*

15. HSS to Seward, April 16, 1863, January 13, November 10, 1865, SeP; HSS to Seward, No. 195, June 28, 1864; No. 248, March 16, 1865, *DB;* HSS to Marsh, May 17, 1865, Marsh Papers; HSS to Salmon P. Chase, January 20, 1865, Salmon P. Chase Papers.

16. HSS to Seward, No. 253, April 16, 1865; No. 257, April 28, 1865; No. 274, May 19, 1865, *DB;* HSS to Sumner, May 4, 1865, Sumner Papers.

17. HSS to H. B. Anthony, July 5, 1868, SP, 100/4.

18. HSS to Seward, September 5, October 2, 1863, SeP; HSS to Sumner, May 21, 1864, Sumner Papers.

19. HSS to Seward, No. 199, July 6, 1864, *DB;* Arnold Blumberg, *The Diplomacy of the Mexican Empire, 1863–1867* (Philadelphia, 1971), 9, 15, 20–21, 61–63.

20. HSS to Seward, No. 124, September 7, 1864; October 24, 25, 1864; No. 240, February 7, 1865, *DB;* HSS to Seward, March 13, 1865, January 25, 1866, SeP; Seward to HSS, October 4, 1864, *IB;* Blumberg, *Diplomacy of the Mexican Empire,* 34; see also Blumberg, "United States and the Role of Belgium in Mexico, 1863–1867," *The Historian: A Journal of History,* 26 (1964), 206–27.

21. HSS to Seward, June 24, 1865, June 3, 1867, SeP; HSS to Seward, June 7, 1867, *DB;* Van Deusen, *Seward,* 292–94; Crook, *The North, the South, and the Powers,* 367–69; Blumberg, *Diplomacy of the Mexican Empire,* 82–86.

22. HSS to Seward, June 14, August 6, 1867, SeP; HSS to Seward, No. 433, July 5, 1867; No. 447, August 6, 1867, *DB.*

23. Van Deusen, *Seward,* 515; HSS to Seward, No. 35, November 14, 1861; No. 37, November 22, 1861, *DB.*

24. *Ibid.;* HSS to Seward, No. 50, January 24, 1862, *DB.*

25. HSS to Seward, November 22, 1861, *DB;* HSS to Seward, April 10, 1862, SeP; Seward to HSS, No. 58, May 6, 1862; No. 79, December 23, 1862; No. 80, December 29, 1862; No. 85, February 16, 1863, *IB.*

26. Seward to HSS, No. 89, March 9, 1863, *IB;* HSS to Seward, No. 91, January 29, 1863; No. 94, February 9, 1863; May 21, 1863; No. 115, May 28, 1863, *DB;* Malloy, *Treaties,* I, 73–75.

27. HSS to Seward, No. 118, June 9, 1863; No. 124, June 12, 1863; No. 132, July 14, 1863; No. 133, July 20, 1863, *DB;* Seward to HSS, No. 95, May 23, 1863; No. 97, June 12, 1863; No. 101, June 27, 1863; No. 110, August 22, 1863, *IB;* Seward to HSS, June 25, 1863, SP, 130/3; Malloy, *Treaties,* I, 75–79.

28. Pike to W. P. Fessenden, April 6, 1864, James Shepherd Pike Papers; Pike's evaluation of the treaty was colored by his dislike of HSS. Pike had wanted the ministership to Brussels in 1861, and he opposed the Seward wing of the Republican party; see Robert F. Durden, *James Shepherd Pike: Republicanism and the American Negro, 1850–1882* (Durham, 1957), 43, 45, 52, 157, 157n, 158n.

29. David H. Miller, ed., *Treaties and Other International Acts of the United States of America* (8 vols., Washington, 1931), VIII, 946; David Donald, *Charles Sumner and the Rights of Man* (New York, 1970), 142.

30. HSS to Seward, No. 115, May 28, 1863; No. 513, November 16, 1868; No. 523, December 5, 1868; No. 526, December 20, 1868, *DB;* Malloy, *Treaties,* I, 75, 80–87; for a more extended treatment of HSS's work in Brussels generally and these treaty negotiations specifically, see Joseph A. Fry, "An American Abroad: The Diplomatic Career of Henry Shelton Sanford," (Ph.D. dissertation, University of Virginia, 1974), 209–40.

31. George Wurts to G. E. Sanford, September 23, 1864, SP, 81/1. HSS's description is taken from a portrait in the Sanford Memorial Library, Sanford, Florida.

32. HSS to Weed, August 4, 1864, WP; John A. Kasson to HSS, May 27, [1865], SP, 123/8; Martha H. Wurts to G. E. Sanford, March 10, 1866, SP, 81/6; Bigelow to Weed, October 6, 1864, Bigelow, *Retrospections,* II, 218.

33. K. Baedeker, *Belgium and Holland: Handbook for Travellers* (Coblenz, London, Paris, 1869), 59.

34. Descriptions of the legation and Gingelom taken from photographs, Sanford Memorial Library.

35. Kasson to his sisters, May 29, 1867, quoted in William W. Halligan, Jr., "The Berlin West African Conference of 1884–1885 from the Viewpoint of American Participation," (M.A. thesis, University of Virginia, 1949), 18n; Morgan to William M. Evarts, January 14, 1878, Applications and Recommendations; Goodrich to HSS, n.d., SP, 121/8.

36. HSS to N. B. Sanford, November 5, 1868, SP, 102/4.

37. HSS to G. E. Sanford, March 11, 1875, SP, 82/2; G. E. Sanford to HSS, n.d., SP, 88/1; February 25, [1871], SP, 88/2.

38. Donald, *Sumner,* 316. Gertrude lost a child in March 1868; see HSS to Weed, March 27, 1868, WP.

39. Income percentages and totals from stocks taken from Edward N. Shelton letters to HSS, SP, 74/1–16; see especially Shelton to HSS, August 3, 1863, SP, 74/2; May 19, 1864, SP, 74/3; July 20, 1866, SP, 74/8; March 2, 1869, SP, 74/4; HSS in account with E. N. Shelton, 1863, 1864, 1865, 1867, SP, 6/1, 3, 5, and 7/6; Richard J. Amundson, "The American Life of Henry Shelton Sanford," (Ph.D. dissertation, Florida State University, 1963), 74–78.

40. E. N. Shelton letters to HSS, SP, 74/1–16; S. D. Dibble to HSS, December 8, 1864, SP, 63/5; Milo L. Williams to HSS, December 2, 1868, February 26, 1869, SP, 63/17; "Statement

of H. S. Sanford Land and Contracts - 1872," SP, 64/2; HSS in Account with E. N. Shelton, 1863, 1864, 1865, 1867, SP, 6/1, 3, 4 and 7/6; Amundson, "American Life of Henry Sanford," 70–72. HSS also received $11,208 in 1863 for his share of the store owned with E. N. Downs; see E. N. Shelton to HSS, January 22, 1863, SP, 74/1.

41. Charles H. Oakes to HSS, May 16, 1864; Oakes to A. Goodrich, June 23, 1864, SP, 63/10; E. N. Shelton to HSS, January 5, March 23, 1865, SP, 74/5; October 8, 1868, SP, 74/13; David A. Stewart to HSS, May 13, 1868, SP, 131/12.

42. P. S. Shelton to HSS, May 4, 26, 1864, SP, 78/9; May 4, 1869, SP, 78/13; September 28, 1871, SP, 78/14.

43. "Aert's Water-Lubricator," SP, 61/1; Trippel to HSS, May 17, 28, 1867, SP, 18/9; May 18, 1868, SP, 18/11.

44. E. N. Shelton to HSS, February 11, 1866, SP, 74/7; Trippel to HSS, December 20, 1864, February 16, 1866, SP, 18/6; description of tender taken from patent application, November 24, 1863, SP, 61/16; William (?) to P. S. Shelton, October 10, 1865, SP, 61/15.

45. Patent application, November 8, 1864, SP, 61/18; "Estimated Profits from working Mr. Haeck's Still," SP, 61/7; Trippel to HSS, November 7, 1867, SP, 18/10; April 23, 1868, SP, 18/6; February 5, June 29, October 19, 1868, March 2, September, 1869, SP, 18/11; "H. S. Sanford in Account with Alex Trippel," SP, 29/7; E. N. Shelton to HSS, January 10, May 6, 1867, SP, 74/9; December 19, 1867, SP, 74/10; June 9, 1868, SP, 74/12; September 15, 24, 1868, SP, 74/13; January 15, 1869, SP, 74/14.

46. E. N. Shelton to HSS, April 22, 1861, SP, 73/10; May 5, 1865, SP, 74/5; Robert H. Lamborn to HSS, June 20, 1870, SP, 62/3; A. Goodrich to E. N. Shelton, April 22, 1861, SP, 73/10; April 26, 1865, SP, 74/5; Lester B. Shippee, "The First Railroad between the Mississippi and Lake Superior," *Mississippi Valley Historical Review,* 5 (1918), 127, 134, 140–41.

47. HSS to Banning, June 2, 1865; HSS to E. N. Shelton, May 25, 1865; HSS to D. A. Stewart, June 2, August 21, 1865; HSS to Goodrich, June 2, 1865, SP, 100/4; Goodrich to HSS, May 10, 1865, SP, 121/7.

48. Stewart to HSS, May 7, 1867, SP, 131/12; HSS to Banning, September 15, 1866; HSS to Goodrich, n.d., SP, 100/4; Goodrich to HSS, May 31, 1866, SP, 121/8; January 31, 1867, SP, 121/9.

49. Contract between Banning *et al.* and Edgar Thompson and Thomas A. Scott, November 2, 1867, SP, 64/7; E. N. Shelton to HSS, April 13, 17, 19, May 11, 1868, SP, 74/12; October 26, 1869, SP, 74/15; HSS to Uncle [E. N. Shelton], n.d., SP, 100/4; Robert H. Lamborn to HSS, March 18, 1869, SP, 64/10; Henrietta M. Larson, *Jay Cooke: Private Banker* (New York, 1968, rep. of 1936 ed.), 249–50.

50. HSS to Uncle [E. N. Shelton], March 26, 1869, SP, 102/4; E. N. Shelton to HSS, May 30, 1869, SP, 74/14; September 28, 1869, SP, 74/15; Jay Cooke to HSS, November 22, 1870, SP, 63/3; P. S. Shelton to HSS, March 25, 1871, SP, 78/14; Charles S. Hincham to HSS, April 6, 1870, SP, 62/17; D. A. Stewart to HSS, June 1, 1870, SP, 131/13. HSS invested in one final transportation area, a sailing ship named the *Henry S. Sanford.* He took a one-eighth interest for $8,000. The ship operated with small profits from 1869 through 1873 and yielded HSS nearly $1,500 in a damage suit, but it is unclear if and when the vessel was sold. It seems unlikely that he recouped his investment; see E. N. Shelton to HSS, October 14, 1869, SP, 74/5; William H. Dunphy to HSS, August 13, 27, 1871, December 7, 1872, SP, 17/6.

51. HSS to Seward, No. 162, November 20, 1863, *DB;* HSS to Weed, December 1, 1863, WP; Anthony to HSS, December 21, 1863, SP, 114/3. For a subsequent U.S. minister's similar view on the need to elevate the mission, see, Lambert Tree to Thomas F. Bayard, April 24, July 24, 1886, Thomas F. Bayard Papers, hereafter cited as Bayard Papers.

52. Anthony to HSS, December 21, 1863, March 16, 1864, SP, 114/3; *Congressional Globe,* 38th Cong., 1st sess., 1864, Part II, 1093–96, 1109–14.

53. Anthony to HSS, March 16, June 17, 1864, SP, 114/3; *Congressional Globe,* 38th Cong., 1st sess., 1864, Part II, 1095–96, 1110, 1114; *Some Account of Belair,* 64.

54. *New York World,* April 11, June 4, 1864.

55. HSS to Seward, June 4, 1864, SeP; Gurowski, *Diary,* I, 141; LeRoy H. Fischer, *Lincoln's Gadfly, Adam Gurowski* (Norman, Okla., 1964), 75–76, 86, 221, 263, 265–68.

56. Hunter to HSS, March 11, 15, 1867, SP, 122/8; Anthony to HSS, May 7, November 27, 1867, SP, 114/5; HSS to Sumner, April 5, 1867, Sumner Papers.

57. HSS to Weed, June 28, 1862, April 14, 1863, WP; HSS to Seward, No. 400, December 24, 1866, *DB;* HSS to Seward, March 19, August 7, 1866, SeP; P. S. Shelton to HSS, March 20, 1867, SP, 78/12; E. N. Shelton to HSS, March 11, 1867, SP, 74/9; Van Deusen, *Seward,* 474.

58. HSS to Seward, December 6, 1864, SeP.

59. Seward to HSS, December 28, 1864, SP, 130/5; HSS to Weed, December 6, 1864, WP; Foster to HSS, December 27, 1864, SP, 120/12; Hunter to HSS, April 10, 1865, SP, 122/7; P. S. Shelton to HSS, January, [5], 24, 1865, SP, 78/11; Van Deusen, *Seward,* 373.

60. HSS to Seward, January 29, 1869, SeP; Seward to HSS, February 20, 1869, SP, 130/10; Anthony to HSS, February 14, March 18, 24, April 4, 1869, SP, 114/7; Weed to HSS, April 27, 1869, SP, 132/15.

61. Donald, *Sumner,* 373; Allan Nevins, *Hamilton Fish: The Inner History of the Grant Administration* (New York, 1936), 118; *New York Tribune,* April 13, 14, 1869; *New York World,* April 13, 14, 1869; List of Appointments dated March 17, 1869, Hamilton Fish Papers, hereafter cited as Fish Papers; Davis to HSS, April 23, June 1, 1869, SP, 118/8.

62. *New York World,* April 13, 14, 22, 1869; *New York Times,* April 24, 1869.

63. *New York Times,* April 15, 22, 23, 1869; *New York World,* April 15, 16, 22, 23, 1869; *New York Tribune,* April 20–24, 1869; Anthony to HSS, April 19, 23, 1869, SP, 114/7; Davis to HSS, April 23, 1869, SP, 118/8. Sanford believed that he had alienated Cameron by refusing to deal through middlemen and contractors in 1861 and 1862; see HSS to D. A. Stewart, January 26, 1869, SP, 102/4.

64. HSS to Fish, May 19, 1869, *DB;* HSS to Sumner, May 3, 1869, Sumner Papers; HSS to Tuckerman, May 19, 1869; HSS to Hunter, May 19, 1869, SP, 102/4. Tuckerman's laudatory editorial appeared in the *New York Times,* June 5, 1869; see Tuckerman to HSS, June 5, 1869, SP, 132/5.

65. HSS to Seward, May 7, 1869, June 27, 1870, SeP; HSS to Weed, August 15, 1869, WP.

Chapter 5

1. Curtis to HSS, April 3, 1866, SP, 117/9; HSS to E. N. Shelton, March 15, 1869, SP, 102/4. I have found Richard J. Amundson, "The American Life of Henry Shelton Sanford," (Ph.D. dissertation, Florida State University, 1963) and the articles derived therefrom (see bibliography) helpful in the writing of Chapters 5 and 6.

2. Richard N. Current, "Carpetbaggers Reconsidered," in *Reconstruction: An Anthology of Revisionist Writings,* eds., Kenneth M. Stampp and Leon Litwack (Baton Rouge, 1969), 227–28, 231; Charlton W. Tebeau, *A History of Florida* (Coral Gables, 1971), 268.

3. T. Frederick Davis, "A Narrative History of the Orange in the Floridian Peninsula," (typescript, Jacksonville, 1941, 19–20, P. K. Yonge Library of Florida History, University of Florida, Gainesville). Yonge Library hereafter cited as PKY. George W. Smith, "Carpetbag Imperialism in Florida 1862–1868," *Florida Historical Quarterly,* 27 (1949), 229; Jerry W. Weeks, "Florida Gold: The Emergence of the Florida Citrus Industry, 1865–1895," (Ph.D. dissertation, University of North Carolina, 1977), 231. Weeks' dissertation provided invaluable background for evaluating Sanford's involvement in the citrus industry.

4. Maurice M. Vance, "Northerners in Late Nineteenth Century Florida: Carpetbaggers or Settlers?" *Florida Historical Quarterly,* 38 (1958), 14.

5. HSS to F. W. Seward, January 10, 1868, SeP; Memorandum on lease of Barnwell Island, January 6, 1868, SP, 33/11; Trescot to HSS, January 28, 1868, SP, 33/8.

6. Lawrence N. Powell, *New Masters: Northern Planters During the Civil War and Reconstruction* (New Haven, 1980), xii, xiii, 8, 10, 13, 18, 24, 57.

7. Trescot to HSS, March 9, May 8, 1868, SP, 33/8; HSS to Weed, May 8, 186[8], WP; Powell, *New Masters,* 146.

8. Trescot to HSS, May 8, 22, July 15, October 7, November 8, December 9, 1868, SP, 33/8; HSS to Uncle [E. N. Shelton], June 16, 1869, SP, 102/4; HSS in "account with Clark, Dodge, & Co. to Trescot," SP, 8/2.

9. Patterson to HSS, October 14, 1869, SP, 33/6; Patterson to Trescot, May 2, 1869, SP, 33/9; Trescot to HSS, August 29, 1869, SP, 33/9.

10. HSS to Trescot, March 12, April 23, 1869, SP, 102/3; Trescot to HSS, n.d., May 22, December 14, 1868, April 15, 1869, May 13, 1870, SP, 33/8; HSS to Weed, November 10, 1870, WP.

11. Rogers to HSS, January 14, [1869], SP, 59/5.

12. HSS to Rogers, October 20, [1868], March 26, April 2, 1869, SP, 102/4; HSS to Uncle [E. N. Shelton], March 19, 1869, SP, 102/4; Rogers to HSS, March 26, April 20, 1869, SP, 59/5.

13. HSS to Seward, April 13, 1869, SeP.

14. Partnership Agreement, HSS and S. Rogers, April 15, 1869, SP, 60/10; Rogers to HSS, April 20, June 1, July 13, 1869, SP, 59/5; September 29, 1870, SP, 59/6.

15. HSS to Rogers, August 4, 1876, SP, 60/1; Rogers to HSS, June 22, August 26, 1869, SP, 59/5; May 4, July 19, 1871, SP, 59/7; F. R. Shelton to HSS, December 9, 1876, SP, 72/5; Oakley Accounts, SP, 57/1.

16. Oakley Accounts, SP, 57/1, 9; Rogers letters to HSS, SP, 59/4–12; HSS to Rogers, August 4, 1876, SP, 60/1; R. Milliken to F. R. Shelton, February 12, 1880, SP, 59/1; J. Carlyle Sitterson, *Sugar Country: The Cane Sugar Industry in the South, 1753–1950* (Lexington, Ken., 1953), 251, 294, 301–4; Charles P. Roland, *Louisiana Sugar Plantations during the American Civil War* (Leiden, Netherlands, 1957), 137–39, *passim.*

17. Memorandum, Transfer of 1/3 C. A. Rogers' share of Oakley to HSS, May 4, 1874, SP, 60/10; Rogers to HSS, July 15, 17, 1876, SP, 59/12; HSS to Rogers, August 4, 1876, SP, 60/1.

18. HSS to G. E. Sanford, January 17, 1876, SP, 82/4; F. R. Shelton to HSS, December 9, 1876, SP, 72/5; Rogers to HSS, August 24, November 29, December 11, 1876, SP, 59/12; Rogers to F. R. Shelton, December 4, 14, 1876, SP, 59/12; R. Milliken to HSS, December 9, 1876, January 23, 27, March 26, 1877, SP, 59/1.

19. Williams to F. R. Shelton, May 25, July 7, September 25, 1879, SP, 60/5; Williams to HSS, July 16, 1879, SP, 60/5; Oakley Accounts, SP, 57/9, 10.

20. HSS to G. E. Sanford, December 28, 29, 1878, SP 82/8.

21. Oakley Accounts, SP 57/1.

22. R. Milliken to HSS, October 18, November 12, December 2, 1881, January 27, April 24, June 16, 1884; Milliken to J. J. Foulkrod, June 28, 1883; July 17, 1884, SP, 59/1; Williams to HSS, February 24, April 22, 1881, SP, 60/6; April 26, 1882, SP, 60/7; May 29, July 2, 1883, SP, 60/8; F. R. Shelton to HSS, June 9, 1886, SP, 72/6; HSS to G. E. Sanford, April 18, 1888, SP, 87/6; Legal Memorandum: Dupuy v. Sanford, SP, 60/11.

23. HSS to G. E. Sanford, December 6, 1886, SP, 86/3; April 18, 1888, SP, 87/6; Oakley Accounts, SP, 57/3, 4, 10; Oakley Payrolls, SP, 57/12–15; T. Mann Gage to HSS, July 7, August 11, 1888, SP, 58/3; Gage to F. R. Shelton, November 5, 1888, SP, 58/3; Maes to HSS, January 10, February 2, 1885, SP, 58/14; May 8, 1890, SP, 58/18; Maes to F. R. Shelton, September 8, 1885, SP, 58/14; January 31, May 7, 1888, SP, 58/17; Maes to J. J. Foulkrod, December 21, 1889, SP, 58/18; H. D. Forsyth to HSS, April 4, 10, 12, 20, 1889, SP, 58/8.

24. HSS to G. E. Sanford, December 6, 1886, SP, 86/3; Sitterson, *Sugar Country,* 13, 251, 257–64, 268–86, 294, 304–306.

25. Weeks, "Florida Gold," 231.

26. Jerrell H. Shofner, *Nor Is It Over Yet: Florida in the Era of Reconstruction, 1863–1877* (Gainesville, 1974), 202.

27. James H. Foss, comp., *Florida: Its Climate, Soil, Productions, and Agricultural Capabilities* (Washington, 1882), 76; J. O. Matthews, "A New Enterprize! The Florida Orange Grove Company," (promotional pamphlet, 1876), PKY.

28. E. N. Shelton to HSS, September 5, 16, 1867, SP, 74/10; E. K. Foster to HSS, November 4, 22, 1867, November 22, 1868, March 16, April 4, 1869, SP, 48/1.

29. G. E. Sanford to N. B. Sanford, February 21, April 19, 1870, SP, 80/10.

30. George W. Parsons Diary, May 21, 1875, PKY, hereafter cited as Parsons Diary; J. S. Adams, *Florida: Its Climate, Soil, and Productions, with A Sketch of Its History, Natural Features and Social Condition* (New York, 1870), 13; Ledyard Bill, *A Winter in Florida* (New York, 1870), 79–80, 82; Samuel A. Drake, *Florida: Its History, Condition, and Resources* (Boston, 1878), 10–11; D. H. Jacques, *Florida as a Permanent Home* (Jacksonville, 1877), 7–8; George W. Nichols, "Six Weeks in Florida," *Harpers New Monthly Magazine*, 41 (1870), 657.

31. Parsons Diary, May 26, 1875; Bill, *A Winter in Florida*, 109, 111–12.

32. G. E. Sanford to N. B. Sanford, February 21, 1870, SP, 80/10; Bill, *A Winter in Florida*, 112–19, 123–25; Nichols, "Six Weeks in Florida," 665–66; Henry Lee, *The Tourists' Guide of Florida and the Winter Resorts of the South* (New York, 1886), 137.

33. E. K. Foster to HSS, May 12, 1870, SP, 48/1; HSS to Seward, April 10, 1870, SeP; Gifford A. Cochran, "Mr. Lincoln's Many-Faceted Minister and Entrepreneur Extraordinary," (unpublished typescript, n.d.), 291, PKY; "The Sanford Grant, A Fine Chance for Investment," (Broadside, Sanford, Fla., 1877, University of Virginia Library).

34. Shelton to HSS, December 4, 1870, SP, 78/14.

35. Shelton to HSS, September 16, 1870, SP, 78/14; Eastman to HSS, June 8, 1871, SP, 119/14; Mackie to G. E. Sanford, December 28, 1875, SP, 82/3.

36. HSS to G. E. Sanford, December 23, 1875, SP, 82/3; December 6, [1878], SP, 82/7; February 16, 1879, SP, 83/2.

37. HSS to G. E. Sanford, December 22, 1875, SP, 82/3; January (?), January 27, [1879], SP, 83/1.

38. Blackman, *History of Orange County Florida*, 37–38; E. H. Gore, *History of Orlando* (Orlando, 1951), 247.

39. HSS to G. E. Sanford, December 8, [1878], SP, 82/7; HSS to Weed, December 20, 1871, WP.

40. Eastman to E. N. Shelton, December 6, 1870, SP, 119/13.

41. Eastman to HSS, December 10, 1870, SP, 119/13; Eastman to E. N. Shelton, December 22, 1870, SP, 119/13; Edgar Ashby to J. S. Mackie, September 17, 1876, SP, 46/11; Henry L. De Forest to HSS, October 7, 1872, SP, 47/9.

42. HSS to G. E. Sanford, December 7, 1875, SP, 82/3; January 15, 1876, SP, 82/4.

43. HSS to G. E. Sanford, January 14, 1879, SP, 83/1; HSS to Ingraham, July 26, 1879, SP, 51/8; Ingraham to HSS, September 18, November 1, 1879, SP, 50/3; January 20, 1880, SP, 50/4; Ingraham to F. R. Shelton, November 3, 1879, SP, 50/3; January 16, 1880, SP, 50/4.

44. Joseph W. Tucker to HSS, November 9, 1870, SP, 51/11; Marks to HSS, June 14, 1870, SP, 51/15; Haight to HSS, April 15, 1871, SP, 48/6.

45. Tucker to HSS, November 9, 11, 1870, SP, 51/11; Whitner and Marks to HSS, September 13, 1870; B. F. Whitner to HSS, November 1, 1870, SP, 51/15.

46. W. A. Henschen to HSS, February 15, 1871, SP, 53/1; De Forest to HSS, June 7, 1871, SP, 47/6; Evasusane Amelung, "History of Economic Development of the Sanford, Florida Area," (M.A. thesis, University of Florida, 1971), 22.

47. Tucker to HSS, August 14, 1871, SP, 51/11; De Forest to HSS, June 17, 1872, SP, 47/9.

48. De Forest to HSS, June 7, 12, July 16, 19, 23, 27, 1871, SP, 47/6; L. M. Tucker to E. N. Shelton, June 12, 1871, SP, 46/2.

49. De Forest to HSS, November 8, December 26, 1871, SP, 47/7; January 11, 21, March 7, 29, April 11, 25, May 13, 1872, SP, 47/8.

50. Six Italians were brought to Sanford in 1873, and several more Italians went to Oakley in 1881; three adult Swedes and one child came to Belair in 1880, and HSS's Florida Land and Colonization Company (FLCC) sponsored fifty-three Swedes for the company and nine adults and six children for HSS in 1882. In each case problems similar to those described arose. See De Forest to HSS, January 5, 1873, SP, 47/10; Ingraham to F. R. Shelton, October 29, 1879, SP, 50/3; Ingraham to HSS, January 20, 1880, SP, 50/4; M. L. Williams to HSS, January 15, February 5, 9, 17, March 14, 1881, SP, 60/6; E. R. Trafford to Board of Directors, FLCC, August 21, October 23, 1883; FLCC Board Minutes #102, October 11, 1883, SP, 56/6; Shofner, *Reconstruction,* 259–61; Powell, *New Masters,* 74; C. Vann Woodward, *Origins of the New South, 1877–1913* (Baton Rouge, 1951), 297–99; Rowland T. Berthoff, "Southern Attitudes Toward Immigration, 1865–1914," *Journal of Southern History,* 27 (1951), 328–60.

51. De Forest to HSS, June 25, July 4, 15, 1872, SP, 47/9; E. K. Foster to HSS, July 21, 1872, SP, 48/1.

52. HSS-Tucker Agreement, May 18, 1870, SP, 51/11; Statement, cost of slaughter house, SP, 45/15; Tucker to HSS, December 20, 1870, May 30, 1871, SP, 51/1; Eastman to E. N. Shelton, December 22, 1870, SP, 119/13.

53. Tucker to HSS, July 18, September 5, 1870, SP, 51/11; De Forest to HSS, August 20, 28, 1871, SP, 47/6; December 25, 1871, SP, 47/7; Wharf Accounts, SP, 45/14; Statement, cost of wharf, SP, 45/15.

54. Ferguson to HSS, April 22, 1870, SP, 46/2; Ferguson to E. N. Shelton, November 15, 1870, SP, 46/2; Whitner and Marks to HSS, August 9, September 13, 1870, SP, 51/15; Sawmill Accounts, SP, 45/9–11.

55. Eastman to E. N. Shelton, December 6, 1870; Eastman to HSS, December 22, 1870, SP, 119/13; De Forest to HSS, April 10, August 20, 1871, SP, 47/6; November 16, 1871, SP, 47/7; December 4, [1872], SP, 47/9; January 14, 1873, SP, 47/10; F. R. Shelton to HSS, February 7, 1879, SP, 72/5; Store Accounts, SP, 45/12.

56. Ingraham to F. R. Shelton, October 3, 1878, SP, 50/1; Ingraham to HSS, March 27, 1879, SP, 50/2; HSS to G. E. Sanford, January 14, 1879, SP, 83/1.

57. Sanford House Accounts, SP, 45/8; Sawmill Accounts, SP, 45/11; "Sanford House," (advertising flyer, n.d.), PKY.

58. Sidney Lanier, *Florida: The Scenery, Climate, and History* (Gainesville, 1973, rep. of 1875 ed.), 130n; Ingraham to HSS, April 28, 1879, SP, 50/2; March 26, 1880, SP, 50/4; Ingraham to F. R. Shelton, December 22, 30, 1879, SP, 50/3; March 25, 1880, SP, 50/4.

59. Parsons Diary, May 21, 1875; M. A. Williams, "Lands of East and South Florida," *The Semi–Tropical,* 2 (1876), 609; Shofner, *Reconstruction,* 132, 261–62; "The Sanford Grant," Memorandum, SP, 55/19; De Forest to HSS, March 11, 1873, SP, 47/10; HSS to G. E. Sanford, December 15, 1875, SP, 82/3; January 15, 1876, SP, 82/4; January 9, [1879], SP, 83/1; February 10, [1879], SP, 83/2.

60. *Some Account of Belair,* 17; Weeks, "Florida Gold," 227–28; Davis, "Narrative History of the Orange in the Floridian Peninsula," 5–21; Louis W. Ziegler and Herbert S. Wolfe, *Citrus Growing in Florida* (Gainesville, 1971), 6.

61. Weeks, "Florida Gold," 36–100.

62. Whitner and Marks to HSS, May 25, September 27, 1870, SP, 51/15; Tucker to HSS, November 9, 1870, SP, 51/11.

63. Thomas Rivers and Sons to HSS, August 3, 1870, SP, 14/3; August 17, 1870, SP, 45/7; HSS to Seward, November 10, 1870, SeP.

64. Whitner and Marks to HSS, September 27, 1870, SP, 51/15; Tucker to HSS, December 20, 1870, SP, 51/11; Ziegler and Wolfe, *Citrus Growing in Florida,* 101, 104.

65. HSS to William G. De Luce, September 19, 1877, SP, 51/18; Eastman to HSS, December 3, 1870, SP, 119/13; George to HSS, December 8, 1870, SP, 46/2.

66. De Forest to HSS, October 7, 1872, SP, 47/9; August 4, 1873, SP, 47/10; J. A.

MacDonald to HSS, August 28, 1871, SP, 51/2; S. O. Chase, "Belair," 2-3 (biographical boxes: "Henry Shelton Sanford"), PKY.

67. HSS to Weed, November 8, 1877, WP; Chase, "Belair," 3; *Some Account of Belair,* 5, 17ff.; Ziegler and Wolfe, *Citrus Growing in Florida,* 31-32; H. Harold Hume, *Citrus Fruits* (New York, 1957), 51-57, 106.

68. *The Semi-Tropical,* 2 (1876), 623, quoted in Morita M. Clark, "The Development of the Citrus Industry in Florida before 1895," (M. A. thesis, Florida State University, 1947), 33n; HSS to De Luce, September 19, 1877, SP, 51/18; Swingle quoted in Weeks, "Florida Gold," 132; Branch Cabell and A. J. Hanna, *The St. Johns: A Parade of Diversities* (New York, 1943), 271; Davis, "Narrative History of the Orange in the Floridian Peninsula," 19-20.

69. F. G. Sampson, "Pioneering in Orange and Lemon Culture in Florida," *Proceedings of the Florida State Horticultural Society* (April 17-20, 1923), 193; Edgar Ashby to J. S. Mackie, September 17, 1876, SP, 46/11; Ingraham to HSS, October 3, 22, 1878, SP, 50/1; June 10, 17, 1879, SP, 50/2; HSS to G. E. Sanford, December 8, 13, [1878], SP, 82/7.

70. F. G. Lindberg to HSS, July 25, 1879, SP, 46/4; HSS to G. E. Sanford, October 27, 1878, SP, 82/5; December 6, [1878], SP, 82/7.

71. HSS to G. E. Sanford, January 17, [1879], SP, 83/1.

72. G. E. Sanford to HSS, October 28, 1872, SP, 88/2; HSS to G. E. Sanford, October 27, 1878, SP, 82/5.

73. G. E. Sanford to HSS, May 18, [1877], SP, 88/3; HSS to G. E. Sanford, November 3, 1878, SP, 82/5; December 20, [1878], SP, 82/8; February 16, 1879, SP, 83/2; n.d., SP, 83/4.

74. HSS to G. E. Sanford, December 7, 1875, SP, 82/3; November 21, 1878, SP, 82/6; December 31, [1878], SP, 82/8.

75. HSS to G. E. Sanford, October 27, November 3, 15, 1878, SP, 82/5; November 18, 21, 1878, SP, 82/6; December 29, 30, 1878, SP, 82/8; February 10, 21, [1879], SP, 83/2; March 6, 1879, SP, 83/3.

76. HSS to G. E. Sanford, November 28, [1878], SP, 82/6.

77. G. E. Sanford to HSS, January 20, 1876, SP, 88/3; October 30, 1879, SP, 88/4; n.d., SP, 88/3; G. E. Sanford to N. B. Sanford, August 6, 1864, SP, 80/6.

78. G. E. Sanford to N. B. Sanford, April 19, 1870, SP, 80/10; May 19, 1876, SP, 80/11; September 27, 1876, SP, 80/12. HSS had purchased a house in Jacksonville in 1871 for $5,300; see Eastman to HSS, August 4, 1871, SP, 119/14.

79. G. E. Sanford to HSS, May 18, [1877]; n.d., SP, 88/3.

80. G. E. Sanford to HSS, May 18, [1877], SP, 88/3; January 17, [1878], SP, 88/4.

81. HSS to G. E. Sanford, November 3, 1878, SP, 82/5; December 6, 18, 1878, SP, 82/7; [December 25, 1878], SP, 82/8.

82. HSS to G. E. Sanford, n.d., SP, 83/4; November 7, 15, 1878, SP, 82/5; November 18, [1878], SP, 82/6; G. E. Sanford to HSS, May 18, [1877], SP, 88/3.

83. HSS to G. E. Sanford, n.d., SP, 83/4; [December 1, 1878], SP, 82/8.

Chapter 6

1. "Memorandum," 1876, SP, 55/18; Jules Levita to HSS, June 24, July 7, September 19, 1876, SP, 124/10; Mackinnon to HSS, March 22, October 9, 1880, SP, 127/3; SP, 127/2-3, *passim.*

2. "Agreement between Hon. H. S. Sanford and the Florida Land & Colonization Company Limited," September 7, 1880, SP, 55/12; "Prospectus: The Florida Land and Colonization Company Limited," SP, 53/6; A. W. Macfarlane to HSS, December 23, 1884, SP, 54/1; Statement FLCC holdings, June 30, 1882, SP, 53/1; FLCC Annual Reports, SP, 53/2.

3. HSS to G. E. Sanford, January 5, 188[1], SP, 83/5; Dawes to HSS, December 8, 1881, SP, 53/7; G. A. Thomson to HSS, July 30, 1881, SP, 54/16. Nancy B. Sanford died on December 21, 1880.

4. Thomson to HSS, October 2, November 23, 1880, January 27, February 5, 1881, SP, 54/16; Waller to HSS, October 26, 1880, SP, 54/19.

5. Thomson to G. E. Sanford, February 11, 1881, SP, 54/16; *Minutes of the Board of Trustees Internal Improvement Fund of the State of Florida (1783–1881)* (Tallahassee, 1904), 435–36, 438–39, 441–42, 444, 452, 455–56, 480, 492–93; Samuel A. Swann to HSS, June 16, November 18, 29, 1880; Hugh A. Corley to Swann, February 2, March 14, 31, 1881; M. A. Williams to Swann, April 12, 1881; Swann to James Hastings, March 18, 1881, Samuel A. Swann Papers.

6. Thomson to HSS, March 8, July 30, 1881, SP, 54/16.

7. "H. S. Sanford, Appellant, vs. A. St.-Clair Abrams, Appellee," *Cases Argued and Adjudicated in the Supreme Court of Florida, during the Year 1888* (vol. XXIV, Tallahassee, 1889), 181–97; HSS to G. E. Sanford, May 23, 28, 30, 1884, SP, 84/3; Thomson to HSS, June 12, 21, 1884, SP, 54/17, E. K. Foster to G. E. Sanford, March 30, 1891, SP, 48/3. HSS also involved the FLCC in legal difficulties over a second land title; see "Henry S. Sanford, Appellant, vs. Aaron Cloud, Appellee," *Cases Argued and Adjudicated in the Supreme Court of Florida, during the Year 1880* (vol. XVII, Part II, Tallahassee, 1880), 557–75. For additional HSS legal problems not involving the FLCC, see "The Orange County High School et al., Appellant, vs. Henry S. Sanford, Appellee," and "The Trustees of the Wylly Academy, Appellants, vs. Henry S. Sanford, et als., Appelles," *Cases Argued and Adjudicated in the Supreme Court of Florida, during the Years, 1878–9* (vol. XVII, Part I, Tallahassee, 1879), 120–21, 162–68; Ingraham to HSS, November 24, 1879, SP, 50/3; November 18, 20, December 13, 1880, SP, 50/5; Foster to HSS, August 9, 1879; Foster to F. R. Shelton, November 7, 28, 1879, SP, 48/2.

8. HSS to FLCC Board of Directors, November 7, 1881, SP, 55/2; Thomson to HSS, November 28, 1881, SP, 54/16.

9. HSS to FLCC Board of Directors, [November 1881], SP, 55/1; HSS to Mackinnon, December 3, 9, 1881, January 12, 1882, SP, 127/10; Dawes to HSS, March 14, 1884, SP, 53/7.

10. HSS to G. E. Sanford, August 21, October 31, 1883, SP, 83/6; HSS to Mackinnon, n.d., SP, 55/1; October 15, [1883], SP, 127/10; HSS to J. Levita, October 24, [1883], SP, 55/4; Thomson to HSS, October 4, 1882, SP, 54/16; July 26, 1883, SP, 54/17; FLCC Report, June 30, 1884, SP, 53/2.

11. HSS to FLCC Board of Directors, n.d., SP, 55/1; HSS to Mackinnon, October 15, 1883, SP, 127/10; n.d., SP, 55/1; HSS to G. E. Sanford, [October, 1883], [November, 1883], SP, 83/6.

12. Mackinnon to HSS, October 9, 20, 29, 30, 1883, SP, 127/5; HSS to G. E. Sanford, October 31, 1883; n.d., SP, 83/6.

13. HSS to Mackinnon, May 5, 1884, SP, 127/10; HSS to J. Levita, February 15, April 1, May 5, 1884, SP, 55/4; Gray & Dawes Co. to HSS, January 24, 1882, March 14, 1884; Gray & Dawes Co. to [J. Levita], April 15, 1884, SP, 53/7; Levita to HSS, March 14, April 19, 22, 23, 1884, SP, 125/4.

14. FLCC Annual Reports, 1884–1890, SP, 53/2; A. W. Macfarlane to HSS, SP, 54/1–6, *passim.*

15. FLCC Annual Reports, 1883–1887, SP, 53/2; FLCC Agent's Annual Reports, 1883–1887, SP, 56/5–9; Agent's Minutes, September 14, 1887, SP, 56/9; March 10, 1889, SP, 56/10; Sanford Memorandum, n.d., SP, 55/1; Statement of Waterworks Expenses to June 30, 1886, SP, 53/1; FLCC Financial Statement, November 16, 1887, enclosed in Macfarlane to HSS, November 17, 1887, SP, 54/2; F. H. Rand to HSS, May 6, 1890, SP, 54/12.

16. FLCC Agent's Annual Report, June 30, 1884, SP, 56/6; Macfarlane to HSS, February 4, 1887, SP, 54/2.

17. Minutes of FLCC Board Meeting, June 26, 1883, SP, 56/5; for examples of the pamphlets and broadsides, see "Sanford and Beyond," (n.d.), SP, 54/1; "The Sanford Grant, (Orange County) Florida," (1881); Frederick H. Rand, "Florida," [1887]; E. R. Trafford, "The Sanford Grant! (Orange County) Florida," [1883], SP, 56/3; "Sanford House," (New York, n.d.); "Sanford House, Sanford Florida," (n.d.), PKY; Cabell and Hanna, *The St. Johns,* 272.

18. Ingraham to F. R. Shelton, January 3, February 9, 16, 1880; Ingraham to HSS, January 26, 1880, SP, 50/4; George W. Pettengill, Jr., *The Story of the Florida Railroads, 1834–1903* (Boston, 1952), 41; FLCC Agent's Annual Report, June 30, 1885, SP, 56/7.

19. "Florida Land and Colonization Co.," (Sanford, n.d.), PKY; Lee, *Tourists' Guide of Florida*, 148–50, 238; Oliver M. Crosby, *Florida Facts Both Bright and Blue: A Guide Book to Intending Settlers, Tourists and Investors from a Northerner's Standpoint* (New York, 1887), 91–93.

20. HSS to G. E. Sanford, May 23, 1884, SP, 84/3; December 8, 1886, SP, 86/3; *Some Account of Belair*, 55–57.

21. HSS to G. E. Sanford, August 2, [1885], SP, 85/10; Mackinnon to HSS, July 13, 1888, SP, 127/8; Statement of HSS's indebtedness to Mackinnon and Dawes Co., September 5, 1890, SP, 53/4.

22. *Dayton Journal, Southern Sun,* and Saunders all quoted in *Some Account of Belair*, 4, 32–33, 36, 39–43; *Jacksonville Daily Florida Union,* January 28, 1882; U. S. Department of Agriculture, Division of Pomology, *Bulletin* No. 1, "Report on the Condition of Tropical and Semi-Tropical Fruits in the United States in 1887," (Washington, 1888); Foss, *Florida Facts: Found after a Six Years' Search* (Boston, 1882); Foss, comp., *Florida: Its Climate, Soil, Productions and Agricultural Capabilities* (Washington, 1882); Lyman Phelps to HSS, April 11, 1882, SP, 51/6.

23. HSS to G. E. Sanford, June 8, 1885, SP, 85/7; HSS to Mackinnon, January 18, 1888, SP, 127/10.

24. Donald Houston to HSS, January 15, 19, July 16, 1886, SP, 48/9; May 14, July 11, 1888, SP, 48/11; December 17, 1889, SP, 48/13; T. F. Huggins to HSS, April 7, 23, May 7, 1888, SP, 49/7; April 17, May 11, 1889, SP, 49/10; HSS to G. E. Sanford, May 18, [1884], SP, 84/2; Amelung, "Economic Development of the Sanford, Florida Area," 30–31; Ziegler and Wolfe, *Citrus Growing in Florida*, 92, 96–97, 99–101.

25. Huggins to HSS, April 9, 1886, SP, 49/3; August 31, November 18, 1887, SP, 49/6; Houston to HSS, April 2, 18, May 15, 1890, SP, 48/14; Lyman Phelps, "The Lemon," *Florida Dispatch* (August 8, 1887), 656–57; H. D. Kedney, "The Lemon in Florida," *Florida Agriculturist* (April 10, 1889), 226–27; U.S. Department of Agriculture, "Report on Condition of Tropical and Semi-Tropical Fruits," 81–84.

26. Clark, "Development of the Citrus Industry in Florida before 1895," 93; Theophilus W. Moore, *Treatise and Hand-Book of Orange Culture in Florida* (New York, 1881), 150.

27. HSS to Mackinnon, January 18, 1888, SP, 127/10; Huggins to HSS, March 12, 1888, SP, 49/7; May 11, 1889, SP, 49/10; Belair Accounts, SP, 45/3–5.

28. Weeks, "Florida Gold," 180–89; Clark, "Development of the Citrus Industry in Florida before 1895," 48, 106; Allison C. Kistler, "The History and Status of Labor in the Citrus Industry of Florida," (M.A. thesis, University of Florida, 1939), 23.

29. Phelps to HSS, June 10, August 12, 1884, SP, 51/8.

30. Huggins to HSS, May 20, 1887, SP, 49/5; September 27, 1887, SP, 49/6; October 19, November 6, 20, 21, December 6, 14, 18, 1888, SP, 49/9.

31. Haight to HSS, April 15, 1871, SP, 48/6; Huggins to F. R. Shelton, January 9, 1886; Huggins to HSS, January 9, 11, 13, 19, 1886, SP, 49/3; August 26, September 19, 26, 1888, SP, 49/8; Houston to HSS, August 16, September 24, 29, 1888, SP, 48/12; HSS to G. E. Sanford, January 10, 1887, SP, 86/6; HSS to Mackinnon, January 18, 1888, SP, 127/10.

32. E. S. Dawes to HSS, July 5, 1889, SP, 53/9; Houston to G. E. Sanford, September 7, 1897, SP, 48/16; Chase, "Belair," 6.

33. Shofner, *Reconstruction,* 290.

34. HSS to G. E. Sanford, January 17, 26, 1879, SP, 83/1.

35. Shofner, *Reconstruction,* 167–76, 194–95, 223–24.

36. *Ibid.,* 188–224; Jerrel H. Shofner, "Florida: A Failure of Moderate Republicanism," in *Reconstruction and Redemption in the South,* ed., Otto H. Olsen (Baton Rouge, 1980), 23–24, 26–28, 42.

37. Eastman to HSS, March 8, 1871, SP, 119/14; Foster to HSS, January 8, 10, 1872, SP, 48/1; N. W. Van Ness to HSS, January 12, 1872, SP, 136/16; HSS to James J. Daniel, September 20, 1872, SP, 136/4; Shofner, *Reconstruction,* 276.

38. Jonathan C. Greeley to HSS. December 7, 1872, SP, 136/10; Knight to HSS, February 9, 1873, SP, 136/2; "Too Thin," (broadside, [1873]), SP, 136/19; Shofner, *Reconstruction,* 295–96.

39. HSS, "Possible Results of the Election upon the South: Letter to Thurlow Weed from Henry S. Sanford," (Sanford, Fla., 1876), SP, 105/19.

40. Edward C. Williamson, *Florida Politics in the Gilded Age, 1877–1893* (Gainesville, 1976), 43–45, 67–69; Allan Peskin, *Garfield* (Kent, Ohio, 1978), 511.

41. Martin to HSS, March 12, 1878, SP, 136/2; James Bell to HSS, December 26, 1879, SP, 136/6.

42. HSS draft, December 31, 1877, SP, 136/4; Edward C. Williamson, ed., "Florida Politics in 1881: A Letter of Henry S. Sanford," *Florida Historical Quarterly,* 31 (1953), 279–81, hereafter cited as HSS to Arthur, November 19, 1881, Williamson, ed., *FHQ* (1953), 279–81.

43. *Ibid.;* HSS to J. G. Blaine, June 4, 1889, James G. Blaine Papers, hereafter cited as Blaine Papers; HSS to Garfield, August 3, September 10, December 21, 1880, James A. Garfield Papers, hereafter cited as Garfield Papers; HSS to Wm. Astor, April 25, 1884, SP, 136/4; Harrison Reed to HSS, May 9, 1884, SP, 136/15.

44. Long and Conant to HSS, January 18, 1881, SP, 136/14; Vincent P. DeSantis, *Republicans Face the Southern Question—The New Departure Years, 1877–1897* (Baltimore, 1959), 73–74, 87, 99.

45. HSS to G. E. Sanford, January 14, 15, 19, 1881, SP, 83/5; HSS to Weed, January 29, 1881, WP; William Gillette, *Retreat from Reconstruction, 1869–1879* (Baton Rouge, 1979), 348–49.

46. HSS to W. Astor, October 27, 1880, SP, 136/4; HSS to G. E. Sanford, January 15, [1881], SP, 83/5; HSS to Garfield, August 3, September 10, December 21, 1881, Garfield Papers; Julian Westcott to HSS, February 28, 1881, SP, 136/2; M. Jewell to HSS, August 6, September 29, 1880, SP, 123/2.

47. Hamilton Jay to HSS, March 11, April 5, 1881, SP, 136/13; Oscar Hart to HSS, March 30, 1881, SP, 136/2; Letters from Executive Committee and Republican senators enclosed in Long and Conant to HSS, January 18, 1881, SP, 136/14; Long to HSS, February 28, 1881, SP, 136/14.

48. HSS to G. E. Sanford, January 5, [1881], SP, 83/5; HSS to Garfield, March 24, 1881; G. E. Sanford to Garfield, May 17, 1881, Garfield Papers; Long to HSS, [April] 24, 1881, SP, 136/14; Peskin, *Garfield,* 514–32.

49. HSS to Arthur, November 19, 1881, Williamson, ed., *FHQ* (1953), 279–81; HSS to William E. Chandler, May 9, 1883, William E. Chandler Papers, hereafter cited as Chandler Papers.

50. Reed to HSS, December 21, 1883, January 8, 188[4], SP, 136/15; Williamson, *Florida Politics,* 96–99, 104–5; Arnold M. Pavolovsky, " 'We Busted Because We Failed': Florida Politics, 1880–1908," (Ph.D. dissertation, Princeton University, 1973), 40–44.

51. HSS to W. Astor, April 25, 1884, SP, 136/4; Reed to HSS, March 7, 1884, SP, 136/15.

52. *Ibid.;* Reed to HSS, December 21, 1883, January 8, March 7, 15, 30, May 6, 1884, SP, 136/15; HSS to G. E. Sanford, May 25, 30, 1884, SP, 84/3; June 2, 1884, SP, 84/4.

53. Hawley to HSS, March 15, 29, 1884; Disston to HSS, March 19, 1884, SP, 136/3; HSS to W. Astor, April 25, 1884, SP, 136/4; Williamson, *Florida Politics,* 99.

54. Reed to HSS, December 21, 1883, March 15, April 8, 22, 24, 1884, SP, 136/15; Williamson, *Florida Politics,* 100.

55. Williamson, *Florida Politics,* 102, 106.

56. HSS to G. E. Sanford, May 25, 1884, SP, 84/3; Adams to HSS, May 3, 21, 26, June 12, 1884, SP, 136/5; Reed to HSS, April 9, 16, 18, May 6, 1884, SP, 136/15.

57. Long to HSS, June 21, 1884, SP, 136/14; C. A. Boardman to HSS, August 13, 1884, SP, 46/15; Reed to HSS, May 14, 1884, SP, 136/15; Williamson, *Florida Politics,* 102.

58. HSS to G. E. Sanford, May 25, 30, 1884, SP, 84/3; June 2, [1884], June 2, 1884, SP, 84/4.

59. HSS to G. E. Sanford, [July 15, 1884], SP, 84/7; Williamson, *Florida Politics,* 109.

60. Williamson, *Florida Politics,* 105, 114, 191; Pavolovsky, "Florida Politics, 1880–1908," 6, 68–69, 274; De Santis, *Republicans Face the Southern Question,* 164.

61. De Santis, *Republicans Face the Southern Question,* 28–29, 31; Gillette, *Retreat from Reconstruction,* 360–61.

62. Weed to HSS, December 14, 1880, SP, 132/16.

Chapter 7

1. Jean Stengers, "King Leopold and Anglo-French Rivalry, 1882–1884," in *France and Britain in Africa: Imperial Rivalry and Colonial Rule,* eds., Prosser Gifford and Wm. Roger Louis (New Haven, 1971), 145.

2. Baron Greindl to HSS, November 28, 1877, SP, 24/16; Barbara Emerson, *Leopold II of the Belgians: King of Colonialism* (New York, 1979), 63.

3. Morse, ed., *The Diary of Gideon Welles,* II, 39; HSS Memo, n.d., SP, 29/2; Lysle E. Meyer, "Henry S. Sanford and the Congo: A Reassessment," *African Historical Studies,* 4 (1971), 20–22, 28–30, hereafter cited as "Sanford: A Reassessment." Meyer's dissertation, "Henry Shelton Sanford and the Congo," (Ph.D. dissertation, Ohio State University, 1967), from which this article is derived is a solid and thoughtful study, and I profited from reading it. For the influence of economic considerations in late-nineteenth-century American diplomacy, see Walter LaFeber, *The New Empire: An Interpretation of American Expansion, 1860–1898* (Ithaca, 1963) and William A. Williams, *The Roots of the Modern American Empire: A Study of the Growth and Shaping of Social Consciousness in a Marketplace Society* (New York, 1969).

4. HSS to Fish, July 11, 18, September 14, 15, 21, 28, October 7, 1870, January 26, February 25, March 15, June 23, 1876, Fish Papers; HSS to G. E. Sanford, March 8, 10, 1875, SP, 82/2; Jewell to HSS, October 11, 20, 1875, SP, 123/2; Anthony to HSS, March 1, 1875, March 24, 1876, SP, 114/10.

5. HSS to Weed, March 15, 1877, WP; James A. Garfield Diary, February 19, 1877, Garfield Papers; G. E. Sanford to William M. Evarts, [April 1877], William Maxwell Evarts Papers, hereafter cited as Evarts Papers; *New York Sun,* March 19, 1877; unidentified newspaper clipping, January 1, 1885, SP, 65/1.

6. HSS to Evarts, May 29, 1877, Applications and Recommendations; Weed to HSS, April 8, July 5, 1877, SP, 132/16; Anthony to HSS, August 16, October 20, 1877, SP, 114/11; "Index to Letters Received, 1877–1881," Evarts Papers. Although the index summarizes the contents of these eight letters from Sanford to Evarts, I could not locate them in either the Evarts Papers or the Miscellaneous Letters of the Department of State.

7. Smith to Hayes, April 13, 1877, Rutherford B. Hayes Papers; Smith to Webb C. Hayes, June 19, 22, 1877, Webb C. Hayes Papers; *New York Tribune,* November 9, 1877; *New York World,* November 11, 1877; *New York Times,* November 6, 1877; *New York Evening-Telegraph,* n.d., SP, 65/14; HSS to Evarts, October 26, 1877, with enclosure Leon Gauchez to Evarts, October 26, 1877, Applications and Recommendations; HSS to Weed, October 27, 1877, WP.

8. Weed to HSS, December 3, 10, 1877, April 11, 1878, SP, 132/16; Anthony to HSS, December 10, 11, 24, 1877, January 15, 25, February 25, 1878, SP, 114/11; Bancroft Davis to Fish, November 26, 1877, Fish Papers; Anthony to Evarts, December 29, 1877, Evarts Papers; Truman Smith to James G. Blaine, May 20, 1878, Blaine Papers; *New York Tribune,* November 24, 1877; February 16, March 5, 1878.

9. Weed to HSS, December 10, 1877, SP, 132/16; HSS to G. E. Sanford, October 27, November 3, [10–11], 1878, SP, 82/5; December 20, 1878, SP, 82/8.

10. Anthony to Blaine, March 23, 1881, Blaine Papers; Fish to Bancroft Davis, March 15, 1881, Fish Papers; Weed to Garfield, March 11, 1881, Applications and Recommendations; Weed to HSS, April 29, 1881, SP, 132/16; G. E. Sanford to Chester A. Arthur, March 2 [1884], Chester A. Arthur Papers, hereafter cited as Arthur Papers; HSS to Garfield, August 3, September 10, November 4, December 21, 1880, January 1, 19, 1881, Garfield Papers; *Some Account of Belair,* 68.

11. G. E. Sanford to Arthur, March 2, [1884], Arthur Papers; Weed to Arthur, October 18, 1881; Morgan to Arthur, March 2, 1882, Applications and Recommendations; Davis to HSS, January 1, 1882, SP, 118/8; Anthony to HSS, December 19, 1881, January 22, April 19, May 5, 1882, SP, 114/12; Thomas C. Reeves, *Gentleman Boss: The Life of Chester Alan Arthur* (New York, 1975), 401.

12. Stengers, "Leopold and Anglo-French Rivalry," 121–25; Robert S. Thomson *Fondation de L'Etat Indépendant du Congo* (Brussels, 1933), 42–47.

13. Harold E. Hammond, "American Interest in the Exploration of the Dark Continent," *The Historian: A Journal of History,* 18 (1956), 202–19; Milton Plesur, *America's Outward Thrust: Approaches to Foreign Affairs, 1865–1890* (De Kalb, Ill., 1971), 144–47; Emerson, *Leopold II,* 80.

14. *New York Times,* June 3, 1877; Daly to HSS, June 3, 1877, SP, 24/8; Latrobe to W. Coppinger, May 8, 1877, American Colonization Society Papers; HSS to Latrobe, July 30, 1877, SP, 29/16; Hammond, "American Interest," 218–19.

15. HSS, "Report of the Hon. Henry Shelton Sanford, U.S. Delegate from the American Branch to the Annual Meeting of the African International Association, in Brussels, in June 1877," *Bulletin of the American Geographical Society* 9 (1877): 103–8; HSS to Daly, June 22, 1877, Charles P. Daly Papers, hereafter cited as Daly Papers; Thomson, *Fondation de L'Etat Indépendant du Congo,* 56.

16. HSS, "Report," 103, 108; HSS to Daly, August 15, 1877, Daly Papers; Latrobe to HSS, September 22, 1877, SP, 25/8.

17. HSS to Daly, October 22, 1877, Daly Papers; Greindl to HSS, September 27, 1877, SP, 24/16; Stengers, "Leopold and Anglo-French Rivalry," 125–26.

18. HSS to Bennett, [Fall, 1877], SP, 29/2; Greindl to HSS, October 5, December 12, 1877, SP, 24/16.

19. HSS to Bennett, January 17, 1878, SP, 29/2; Henry M. Stanley, *The Congo and the Founding of Its Free State: A History of Work and Exploration* (2 vols., New York, 1885), I, 21; Greindl to HSS, January 31, February 4, March 8, 16, 1878, SP, 24/17; Frank Hird, *H. M. Stanley: The Authorized Life* (London, 1935), 168.

20. HSS, "American Interests in Africa," *The Forum,* 9 (1890), 411; HSS to Greindl, [September 1878], SP, 29/12; Greindl to HSS, June 4, 11, 17, September 18, November 18, December 10, 1878, SP, 24/18; Stanley, *Congo,* I, 24–28; Stanley to HSS, December 20, 1878, SP, 27/2; February 27, 1879, SP, 27/3; Robert S. Thomson, "Leopold II et le Congo: Révélés par les Notes Privées de Henry S. Sanford," *Congo Revue Générale de la Colonie Belge,* 12 (1931), 178, 192; Ruth Slade, *King Leopold's Congo: Aspects of the Development of Race Relations in the Congo Independent State* (New York, 1962), 37–39; Emerson, *Leopold II,* 87–90.

21. HSS to Stanley, August 4, 1879, SP, 29/15; HSS to Leopold, June 1, 1879, SP, 29/12; n.d., 29/4.

22. HSS to Evarts, January 25, 1879, SP, 105/15; Greindl to HSS, May 31, 1878, SP, 24/18; Evarts to Richard Thompson, February 3, 1879; Thompson to Shufeldt, February 25, 1879; Shufeldt to Thompson, June 3, 1879, all in Francois Bontinck, *Aux Origines L'Etat Indépendant du Congo: Documents tirés d'Archives Américaines* (Louvain and Paris, 1966), 65–66, 71–73.

23. HSS to Daly, April 25, December 16, 1879, Daly Papers; HSS to G. E. Sanford, March 6, 1879, SP, 83/3; HSS address before N. Y. Chamber of Commerce, March 6, 1879, SP, 30/4.

24. Stanley, *Congo,* I, 79–449; Stengers, "Leopold and Anglo-French Rivalry," 127–41; Emerson, *Leopold II,* 91–100; Henri Burnschwig, *French Colonialism, 1871–1914* (New York, 1966), 43–49, 68–70; Roger Anstey, *Britain and the Congo in the Nineteenth Century* (Oxford, 1962), 40–53, 100–7, 139–50.

25. Thomson, *Fondation de L'Etat Indépendant du Congo,* 148–49; for a historiographical discussion of the genesis of the appeal to the U. S., see Bontinck, *Origines L'Etat Indépendant du Congo,* 133, n.44.

26. HSS to Blaine, June 27, 1881; HSS to Frelinghuysen, December 30, 1882, Miscellaneous Letters, State Dept.; HSS to Chandler, January 2, 7, April 4, May 9, June 13, August 1, 1883, January 20, 1884, Chandler Papers; HSS to Arthur, June 13, 1883, SP 105/1; Frelinghuysen to HSS, August 4, 1883, SP, 24/11; Kenneth J. Hagan, *American Gunboat Diplomacy and the Old Navy, 1877–1889* (Westport, Conn., 1973), 73–74.

27. HSS draft of Leopold to Arthur, November 7, 1883, SP, 105/1; HSS to Baron Beyens, October 26, 1883; Beyens to HSS, October 28, 1883, SP, 29/12; HSS to Col. Maximilien Strauch, [December 2, 1883], SP, 29/16; HSS to G. E. Sanford, November 27, 28, 1883, SP, 83/7.

28. *Ibid.,;* Richardson, *Messages of the Presidents,* VIII, 175–76.

29. HSS to G. E. Sanford, November 27, 30, 1883, SP, 83/7; *New York Times,* January 2, 1884; *New York Herald,* December 30, 1883.

30. A. A. Low to HSS, December 7, 1883, January 10, 11, 1884, SP, 125/15; Daly to HSS, January 2, 3, 9, 1884, SP, 24/8; HSS to Daly, January 4, [1884], Daly Papers; *New York Herald,* January 11, 1884; George Wilson to Arthur, January 11, 1884, U. S. Congress, Senate, *Report* No. 393, 48th Cong., 1st sess., 37; N. Y. Chamber Resolutions, *ibid.,* 37–38, hereafter cited as *SR* No. 393, 48th Cong.

31. Latrobe to HSS, February 19, 22, March 5, 6, 16, April 1, 3, 1884, SP, 25/8; Latrobe to Coppinger, March 5, 1884, American Colonization Society Papers.

32. August C. Radke, Jr., "John Tyler Morgan, An Expansionist Senator, 1877–1907," (Ph.D. dissertation, University of Washington, 1953), *passim;* O. Lawrence Burnette, "John Tyler Morgan and Expansionist Sentiment in the New South," *Alabama Review,* 18 (1965), 163–82; Morgan to HSS, February 1, 7, 24, March 5, 22, 1884, SP, 26/5; Latrobe to HSS, March 16, 1884, SP, 25/8; Latrobe, *Maryland in Liberia* (Baltimore, 1885), 90–91; Trescot to HSS, April 15, 1884, SP, 33/10; G. Wilson to HSS, February 25, 1884, SP, 22/2; HSS to G. E. Sanford, May 16, [1884], SP, 84/2.

33. HSS to Daly, December 3, [1883], Daly Papers; Frelinghuysen to Morgan, January 18, 1884, *SR* No. 393, 48th Cong., 9–10; U.S. *Congressional Record,* 48th Cong., 1st sess., 1884, XV, Part I, 520.

34. Morgan to HSS, February 7, 1884, SP, 26/5; HSS to Frelinghuysen, February 9, 1884, Miscellaneous Letters, State Dept.

35. Frelinghuysen to Morgan, March 13, 1884, *SR* No. 393, 48th Cong., 10–11; Jules Devaux to HSS, December 12, 1883, SP, 25/19.

36. Morgan to HSS, February 24, 1884, SP, 26/5; U.S. *Congressional Record,* 48th Cong., 1st sess., 1884, XV, Part II, 1339, 1378.

37. *SR* No. 393, 48th Cong., *passim;* U.S. *Congressional Record,* 48th Cong., 1st sess., 1884, XV, Part III, 2275; *New York Times,* April 11, 1884.

38. Malloy, *Treaties,* I, 327–28, emphasis added.

39. Roustan to Ferry, No. 230, April 4, 1884, in R. J. Gavin and J. A. Betley, eds., *The Scramble for Africa: Documents on the Berlin West African Conference and Related Subjects 1884/1885* (Ibadan, Nigeria, 1973), 308–9; Jean Stengers, "The Congo Free State and the Belgian Congo before 1914," in *Colonialism in Africa, 1870–1960,* eds., L. H. Gann and Peter Duignan (3 vols., London, 1969), I, 264; Willard P. Tisdel to J. T. Morgan, November 25, 1884, John Tyler Morgan Papers, hereafter cited as Morgan Papers.

40. Ernest R. May, *American Imperialism: A Speculative Essay* (New York, 1968), 35–36.

41. David M. Pletcher, *The Awkward Years: American Foreign Relations under Garfield*

and Arthur (Columbia, Mo., 1962), 308, 314; Reeves, *Arthur,* 393; James L. Roark, "American Expansionism vs. European Imperialism: Henry S. Sanford and the Congo Episode, 1883–1885," *Mid-America: An Historical Review,* 15 (1978), 33.

42. *New York Herald,* April 13, 1884; Pletcher, *Awkward Years,* 314; M. Strauch to HSS, April 12, 1884, SP, 27/12; G. E. Sanford to HSS, n.d., SP, 88/7; [April 1884], SP, 88/11.

43. J. Devaux to HSS, April 27, 1884, SP, 25/19; Thomson, *Fondation de L'Etat Indépendant du Congo,* 163–69; Henry A. Turner, Jr., "Bismarck's Imperialist Venture: Anti-British in Origin?" in *Britain and Germany in Africa: Imperialist Rivalry and Colonial Rule,* eds., Prosser Gifford and Wm. Roger Louis (New Haven, 1967), 51; Wm. Roger Louis, "The Berlin Congo Conference," *Ibid.,* 190, 195; Sybil Crowe, *The Berlin West African Conference, 1884–1885* (London, 1942), 20–70.

44. *Ibid.*

45. Baron Von Alvensleben to Frelinghuysen, October 10, 1884; Frelinghuysen to Von Alvensleben, October 17, 1884, U. S. Congress, Senate, *Executive Document* No. 196, 49th Cong., 1st sess., 7–8, 10, hereafter cited as *SED* No. 196, 49th Cong.

46. Edward Younger, *John A. Kasson: Politics and Diplomacy from Lincoln to McKinley* (Iowa City, 1955), 329; Halligan, "Berlin West African Conference," 78; HSS to G. E. Sanford, June 11, 1884, SP, 84/5; June 26, 1884, SP, 84/6.

47. Kasson to HSS, October 21, 1884, SP, 25/4; Baron Borchgrave to HSS, August 18, 31, October 24, 25, November 9, 1884, SP, 25/16; Emerson, *Leopold II,* 112.

48. HSS to G. E. Sanford, [August 29, 30, 1884], SP, 84/8; October 24, 1884, SP, 84/10.

49. HSS to G. E. Sanford, [November 16, 18, 1884], SP, 84/11; [February 28], 1885, SP, 85/3; Tisdel to Morgan, November 25, 1884, Morgan Papers.

50. Kasson to Frelinghuysen, No. 77, November 20, 1884, Despatches from United States Ministers to Germany, 1835–1906, hereafter cited as *DG.*

51. Kasson to Frelinghuysen, No. 79, November 24, 1884; No. 83, November 26, 1884; No. 88, December 1, 1884, *DG;* Crowe, *Berlin West African Conference,* 107–15; Louis, "Berlin Congo Conference," 196–97; for an HSS memo almost identical to Kasson's proposal, see SP, 27/4.

52. Borchgrave to HSS, December 4, 1884, SP, 29/12; Mackinnon to HSS, December 12, 1884, SP, 127/5; Kasson to Frelinghuysen, No. 95, December 8, 1884; No. 100, December 15, 1884; No. 181, February 23, 1885, *DG.*

53. Banning, *Mémoires Politiques et Diplomatiques* (Paris, 1927), 25–26; HSS to Leopold, December 10, 1884, SP, 29/2; Borchgrave to HSS, December 4, 6, 1884, SP, 29/12; January 16, 1885, SP, 25/17; Thomson, *Fondation de L'Etat Indépendant du Congo,* 229; Crowe, *Berlin West African Conference,* 130–31.

54. Courcel to Ferry, No. 475, December 3, 1884, Gavin and Betley, eds., *Scramble for Africa,* 358; Crowe, *Berlin West African Conference,* 143–55.

55. HSS to G. E. Sanford, [November 26, 1884], SP, 84/12; Borchgrave to HSS, January 13, 1885, SP, 25/17; Stanley to HSS, December 24, 1884, SP, 27/4; Banning, *Mémoires,* 38; Crowe, *Berlin West African Conference,* 158–64.

56. HSS to Mackinnon, December 24, 1884, SP, 127/10.

57. Borchgrave to HSS, December 24, 1884, SP, 29/12; Banning, *Mémoires,* 38; Bontinck, *Origines de L'Etat Indépendant du Congo,* 261; Morton to Frelinghuysen, December 30, 1884, *ibid.,* 264–65; Morton to HSS, December 31, 1884, SP, 22/3.

58. Borchgrave to HSS, January 13, 15, 1885, SP, 25/17; Banning, *Mémoires,* 41–42, 53–54; Crowe, *Berlin West African Conference,* 165–68.

59. HSS to Baron [Borchgrave], January 8, [1885], Robert S. Thomson, "Leopold II et la Conference de Berlin: Documents inédits Provenant de la Correspondence Particulière de l'Hon. Henry S. Sanford," *Congo Revue Général de la Colonie Belge,* 12 (1931), 347; HSS to Leopold, January 14, [1885], SP, 29/2.

60. Borchgrave to HSS, January 13, 1885, SP, 25/17; Crowe, *Berlin West African Conference,* 168–74; Louis, "Berlin Congo Conference," 205.

61. Younger, *Kasson,* 335; Mackinnon to HSS, February 10, 23, 1885, SP, 127/6; Stanley to G. E. Sanford, October 31, 1895, SP, 27/6.

62. *New York Times,* January 11, 1885; *New York Herald,* December 10, 1884, January 30, 1885; Fish quoted in Younger, *Kasson,* 343. For more extensive comment on reaction to the agreement, see Pletcher, *Awkward Years,* 320–24.

63. Perry Belmont, *An American Democrat* (New York, 1940), 311, 325, 331–34; U. S. *Congressional Record,* 48th Cong. 2d sess., 1885, XVI, Part I, 446, 464; U. S. Congress, House, *Executive Document* No. 247, 48th Cong., 2d sess.; U. S. Congress, House, *Report* No. 2655, 48th Cong., 2d sess. For a "Draft of Resolution for U.S. House of Reps. Repudiating Congo Conference," [February 26, 1885], see Manton M. Marble Papers. Marble was Belmont's confidant and adviser.

64. Younger, *Kasson,* 331, 343.

65. HSS interviews in *New York Times,* May 26, 1885, February 14, April 28, 1889; HSS, "American Interests in Africa," 414–15; HSS to Thomas F. Bayard, March 25, 1885, Bayard Papers; HSS to E. M. Halford, July 20, [1889], Benjamin Harrison Papers, hereafter cited as Harrison Papers.

66. HSS to G. E. Sanford, [February 16, 1885], SP, 85/2; HSS Memo, [March 1885], SP, 31/14.

67. Taunt's report, "Journey on the River Congo," was printed as U.S. Congress, Senate, *Executive Document* No. 77, 49th Cong., 2d sess.; Taunt to HSS, January 2, 1886, SP, 28/1.

68. SEE Organization Papers, SP, 32/1, 7, 11; Amos A. Lawrence to HSS, May 17, June 25, 1886, SP, 25/11; SEE "Confidential Memorandum," SP, 32/5. The original investors put in another $30,000 in 1888.

69. SEE "Confidential Memorandum," SP, 32/5; Taunt to Camille Janssen, July 28, 1886, SP, 28/1.

70. SEE Reports, SP, 32/9, 13; HSS to Bayard, June 14, 1886, Bayard Papers.

71. Taunt to HSS, January 10, 1887, SP, 28/3; Swinburne to HSS, November 17, 1886, SP, 27/14.

72. Taunt to HSS, August 22, 1886, SP, 28/1; Parminter to HSS, October 14, 1886, SP, 26/7; Glave to HSS, October 31, 1886, SP, 24/13.

73. SEE Reports, SP, 32/9; Taunt to HSS, February 15, 1887, SP, 28/3; Stanley to HSS, August 17, 1886, SP, 27/6; Parminter to HSS, September 14, December 8, 1886, SP, 26/7; Swinburne to HSS, November 17, 1886, SP, 27/14.

74. C. Janssen to Strauch, July 22, 1886, SP, 25/3; Taunt to HSS, July 11, August 4, 22, 1886, SP, 28/1; Glave to HSS, August 27, 1887, SP, 24/13; Stengers, "Congo Free State and the Belgian Congo before 1914," 265–67; L. H. Gann and Peter Duignan, *The Rulers of Belgian Africa, 1884–1914* (Princeton, 1979), 96, 125.

75. Taunt to HSS, September 7, 12, 21, November 28, 1886, SP, 28/2; Parminter to HSS, September 14, October 14, December 2, 3, 1886, SP, 26/7; Swinburne to HSS, November 17, 1886, SP, 27/14; HSS drafts to Taunt, n.d., SP, 29/18.

76. Montefiore-Levi to HSS, July 11, 1887, SP, 26/4.

77. SEE Reports, SP, 32/9; Swinburne to HSS, n.d., SP, 27/14; Taunt to HSS, August 22, 1886, SP, 28/1; Weber to HSS, October 27, 1886, SP, 23/8; HSS to Weber, October 27, 1886, July 13, 1887, SP, 29/19; HSS draft, n.d., SP, 29/2.

78. HSS to Weber, September 25, [1887], SP, 29/19; Swinburne to HSS, September 29, 1887, SP, 27/14; Weber to HSS, September 30, 1887, SP, 23/10.

79. Taunt to HSS, September 21, 1886, SP, 28/2; Parminter to HSS, March 8, 1887, SP, 26/7; Weber to HSS, April 23, June 22, 1887, SP, 23/9; Levita to HSS, April 29, May 4, 1887, SP, 125/7.

80. Taunt to HSS, October 12, [1886], SP, 28/2; February 15, 1887, SP, 28/3; Weber to HSS, August 13, 1886, SP, 23/8; Baron Rothkirch to Parminter, March 10, 1887, SP, 24/14.

81. Swinburne to HSS, March 31, 1887, SP, 27/14; William J. Davy Affidavit, SP, 32/2; Hird, *Stanley,* 215–27; John S. Galbraith, *Mackinnon and East Africa* (Cambridge, 1972),

111–23; H. M. Stanley, *In Darkest Africa; or the Quest, Rescue, and Retreat of Emin, Governor of Equatoria* (2 vols., New York, 1891), I, 95–96.

82. Weber to HSS, August 22, 1889, SP, 23/11; Francis De Winton to HSS, June 11, 1889, SP, 32/3; Levita to HSS, September 5, 1889, SP, 125/10; May 10, 1890, SP, 125/11; Mackinnon to HSS, March 14, 1890, SP, 127/9.

83. SEE "Confidential Memorandum," SP, 32/5; Montifiore-Levi to HSS, November 27, 1887, SP, 26/4; HSS to Swinburne, October 8, 1887, SP, 29/17; De Winton to HSS, March 4, 1887, SP, 24/10; Parminter to Weber, January 27, 1888, SP, 23/11; Lysle E. Meyer, Jr., "Henry Shelton Sanford and the Congo," (Ph.D. dissertation, Ohio State University, 1967), 201.

84. Weber to HSS, October 27, 1886, SP, 23/8; July 16, 1887, SP, 23/10; Levita to HSS, August 26, November 10, 1886, SP, 125/6; June 1, 21, 1887, SP, 125/7.

85. HSS to G. E. Sanford, June 9, 1888, SP, 87/9; Levita to HSS, October 9, 1886, SP, 125/6; July 24, 1887, SP, 125/8; April 28, 1888, SP, 125/9.

86. HSS to G. E. Sanford, April 12, [1888], SP, 87/6; Levita to HSS, January 2, 1888, SP, 125/9; HSS to A. H. Rice, n.d., SP, 29/2; SEE "Confidential Memorandum," SP, 32/5.

87. HSS to G. E. Sanford, March 25, 27, 1888, SP, 87/4; April 14, 1888, SP, 87/6; G. A. Alden to HSS, June 25, 1888; Charles R. Flint to HSS, October 12, 1888; H. M. Flagler to HSS, May 7, 1888, SP, 22/4.

88. Mackinnon to HSS, January 28, October 26, 1888, SP, 127/8; Hutton to HSS, September 19, 25, 1888, SP, 23/3.

89. Levita to HSS, September 9, 16, 1888, SP, 125/9; "Société Anonyme Belge pour le Commerce du Haut-Congo," (Brussels, 1888), SP, 30/15.

90. Georges Brugman to HSS, January 19, 1890, SP, 24/5; Mackinnon to G. E. Sanford, December 11, 1891, SP, 127/9; Gann and Duignan, *Rulers of Belgian Africa*, 40–51; Paul A. Varg, "The Myth of the China Market, 1890–1914," *American Historical Review*, 73 (1968), 742–58; "Société Anonyme Belge pour le Commerce du Haut-Congo," SP, 30/15.

Chapter 8

1. HSS to G. E. Sanford, March 9, 1889, SP, 87/15.

2. HSS to Blaine, June 4, 1889, Blaine Papers; HSS to Harrison, June 14, 1889, Harrison Papers; E. M. Halford to HSS, March 12, 13, 25, May 25, June 17, September 28, November 5, 1889, SP, 122/3.

3. Halford to HSS, September 28, 1889, SP, 122/3; Latrobe to HSS, October 9, 1889, SP, 25/9; Blaine to HSS, November 22, 23, December 4, 7, 1889, *IB;* HSS to Blaine, November 27, 1889, *DB.* Problems subsequently arose concerning HSS's position at the conference, and Blaine made him a "Delegate Plenipotentiary" in April 1890; see Fry, "Diplomatic Career of Henry Shelton Sanford," 351–53.

4. Suzanne Miers, "The Brussels Conference of 1889–1890: The Place of the Slave Trade in the Policies of Great Britain and Germany," in *Britain and Germany in Africa,* eds., Gifford and Louis, 83, 89–100; Henry S. Wilson, *The Imperial Experience in Sub-Saharan Africa since 1870* (Minneapolis, 1977), 120–22.

5. Wilson, *Imperial Experience in Sub-Saharan Africa,* 122.

6. Miers, "Brussels Conference," 103–13; for a copy of the conference's final act, see Malloy, *Treaties,* II, 1964–92.

7. Terrell to Blaine, No. 72, March 19, 1890; HSS to Blaine, March 14, 1890, *DB;* Miers, "Brussels Conference," 111–13.

8. HSS to Blaine, April 3, 1890, *DB;* Blaine to HSS, April 18, 25, 1890, *IB.*

9. Blaine to HSS, April 25, 1890, *IB;* Terrell to Blaine, No. 80, May 2, 1890; No. 82, May 5, 1890, *DB.*

10. HSS to Blaine, May 24, 27, June 6, 1890, *DB;* Terrell to Blaine, No. 94, May 24, 1890; No. 100, June 3, 1890; No. 102, June 6, 1890, *DB.*

11. HSS to Blaine, May 14, 1890; Terrell to Blaine, No. 88, May 10, 1890, *DB;* Miers, "Brussels Conference," 117.

12. HSS to Blaine, January 3, May 27, June 3, 1890; HSS to Baron Lambermont, June 2, 1890, enclosed in HSS to Blaine, June 3, 1890, *DB;* HSS to E. M. Halford, January 3, 1890, SP, 29/3.

13. HSS interview in *New York Times,* April 28, 1889; HSS, "American Interests in Africa," 413.

14. HSS to G. E. Sanford, March 8, 1885, SP, 85/4; [February 6, 1886], SP, 86/1.

15. Grenfell to HSS, November 23, 1889, June 23, 26, 1890, SP, 24/19; Meyer, "Sanford: A Reassessment," 37–38; Emerson, *Leopold II,* 64.

16. Terrell to Blaine, No. 88, May 10, 1890; No. 89, May 14, 1890; No. 104, June 16, 1890, *DB;* Blaine to Terrell, June 10, 16, 1890, *IB.*

17. Banning, *Mémoires,* 140; Mackinnon to HSS, May 27, 1890, SP, 127/9; HSS to Blaine, n.d., SP, 28/5; HSS to Blaine, June 20, July 1, 3, 1890; Terrell to Blaine, No. 93, May 22, 1890; No. 95, May 28, 1890; No. 99, June 2, 1890; No. 108, June 19, 1890; June 20, 1890; No. 109, June 27, 1890; No. 113, July 2, 1890, *DB;* Malloy, *Treaties,* II, 1964–92.

18. HSS to Blaine, n.d., SP, 28/5; HSS to Blaine, June 20, 1890, *DB.*

19. HSS to G. E. Sanford, [August 25, 1884], SP, 84/8; February 11, [1885], SP, 85/2; August 1, [1887], SP, 86/9; August 27, 30, 1887, SP, 86/10; November 1, 1887, SP, 86/11; Levita to HSS, October 25, 1890, SP, 125/12; HSS to Mackinnon, n.d., SP, 127/10; Mackinnon to HSS, December 1, 1890, SP, 127/9.

20. G. E. Sanford to HSS, n.d., SP, 88/9; n.d., SP, 88/9; n.d., SP, 88/14.

21. HSS to G. E. Sanford, June 11, 1884, SP, 84/5; May 27, 1885, SP, 85/6; January 10, 1887, SP, 86/6; June 15, 1888, SP, 87/10; G. E. Sanford to HSS, n.d., SP, 88/9; W. F. Astor to HSS, May 3, 1887, SP, 46/12; Gray Dawes & Co. to HSS, September 5, 1890, SP, 53/10; A. A. Lawrence to G. E. Sanford, April 25, 1892, SP, 11/5; A. A. Low to G. E. Sanford, May 25, 1892, SP, 11/7; E. De Mot to G. E. Sanford, n.d., August 3, 1892, SP, 11/2; "Stocks and Other Property," February 20, 1892, SP, 11/20.

22. HSS to G. E. Sanford, [February 19, 1888], SP, 87/2; July 20, 1888, SP, 87/11.

23. HSS to G. E. Sanford, February 11, 1885, SP, 85/2; December 18, 1886, SP, 86/4; December 6, 1887, SP, 86/11; April 14, 1888, SP, 87/6; June 6, 1888, SP, 87/9; June 15, 1888, SP, 87/10.

24. G. E. Sanford to HSS, n.d., SP 88/8–10.

25. G. E. Sanford to HSS, n.d., SP, 88/8.

26. HSS to G. E. Sanford, June 8, 1885, SP, 85/7; January 10, 1887, SP, 86/6; HSS, Jr., to HSS, December 12, 1886, SP, 68/2; April 28, 1888, SP, 68/3; Clement L. Smith to HSS, December 27, 1886, SP, 68/7.

27. HSS to G. E. Sanford, March 21, 1888, SP, 87/3; May 1, 1888, SP, 87/7; May 21, 1888, SP, 87/8; Frank Bolles to HSS, April 27, 1888; F. W. Taussig to HSS, June 6, 1888, SP, 68/7; HSS, Jr., to HSS, April 20, 28, May 8, 1888, SP, 68/3; John Hay to HSS, Jr., March 31, May 28, 1888, SP, 68/8.

28. HSS to G. E. Sanford, March 8, 1888, SP, 87/4; May 21, 23, 1888, SP, 87/8; June 8, [1888], SP, 87/9.

29. HSS, Jr., to HSS, May 7, 20, 22, 1888, SP, 68/3; HSS, Jr., to G. E. Sanford, February 17, 1888, December 28, 1890, [December 1890], [January 17, 1891], SP, 68/6; G. E. Sanford to HSS, Jr., March 3, 1889, December 11, [1890], SP, 80/5.

30. Description from 1887 photograph, Sanford Memorial Library.

31. HSS to Mackinnon, July 3, [1890], SP, 127/10; Levita to HSS, July 12, 1890, SP, 125/12; January 7, 1891, SP, 125/13; Prospectus for phosphate co., SP, 52/13. HSS had invested £1,000 in the Electro-Mechanical Development Co., a London–based company dealing in electrical patents; see James M. Ormes to HSS, April 17, 1885, SP, 16/7.

BIBLIOGRAPHY

I. PRIMARY SOURCES

A. Manuscripts

Archives of the American Geographical Society, New York City.
  Charles P. Daly Papers
Rutherford B. Hayes Presidential Center, Fremont, Ohio.
  Rutherford B. Hayes Papers.
  Webb C. Hayes Papers.
Historical Society of Pennsylvania, Philadelphia.
  James Buchanan Papers.
Houghton Library, Harvard University.
  Charles Sumner Papers.
Huntington Library, San Marino, California.
  Thomas Haines Dudley Papers.
Manuscripts Division, Library of Congress.
  American Colonization Society Papers.
  Chester A. Arthur Papers.
  Thomas F. Bayard Papers.
  James G. Blaine Papers.
  William E. Chandler Papers.
  Salmon P. Chase Papers.
  William Pitt Fessenden Papers.
  Hamilton Fish Papers.
  James A. Garfield Papers.
  Benjamin Harrison Papers.
  John Hay Papers.
  Robert Todd Lincoln Collection of the Papers of Abraham Lincoln.
  Manton M. Marble Papers.
  William Learned Marcy Papers.
  John Tyler Morgan Papers.
  James Shepherd Pike Papers.
  William Cabell Rives Papers.
  Ephraim G. Squier Papers.
Massachusetts Historical Society, Boston.
  Adams Papers.
Princeton University Library.
  William Lewis Dayton Papers.

Henry Shelton Sanford Memorial Library and Museum, Sanford, Florida.
Henry Shelton Sanford Papers.
University of Rochester Library.
William Henry Seward Papers.
Thurlow Weed Papers.
University of Vermont Library.
George Perkins Marsh Papers.
University of Virginia Library.
"The Sanford Grant, A Fine Chance for Investment." Sanford, 1877.
P. K. Yonge Library of Florida History, University of Florida.
[Chase, S. O.]. "Belair."
"Florida Land and Colonization Co." Sanford, [1885 or 1886].
Matthews, J. O. "A New Enterprise! The Florida Orange Grove Company." N.p., n.d.
George W. Parsons Diary.
"Sanford House." New York, n.d.
Samuel A. Swann Papers.

B. DIPLOMATIC CORRESPONDENCE,
NATIONAL ARCHIVES, RECORD GROUP 59

Despatches from U.S. Ministers to Belgium, France, Germany, Great Britain, Italy, and Venezuela.
Despatches from U.S. Consuls to Antwerp.
Instructions from Department of State to United States Ministers to Belgium, France, Germany, Great Britain, Italy, and Venezuela.
Miscellaneous Letters of the Department of State, 1784–1906.
Letters of Application and Recommendation, Department of State.

C. RECORDS OF BOUNDARY AND CLAIMS
COMMISSIONS AND ARBITRATIONS,

NATIONAL ARCHIVES, RECORD GROUP 76

Awards of the Commissioners of the United States of America and the United States of Venezuela Under the Convention of December 5, 1885.
Claims, Venezuela, 1866–1888, Envelope 18, Case No. 60

D. RECORDS OF THE OFFICE OF THE
SECRETARY OF WAR,

NATIONAL ARCHIVES, RECORD GROUP 107

Letters Received by the Ordnance Department, 1862.
Letters Received by the Secretary of War.

E. U.S. GOVERNMENT DOCUMENTS

United States Department of Agriculture. Division of Pomology.
Bulletin No. 1. *Report on the Condition of Tropical and Semi-Tropical Fruits in the United States in 1887.* Washington, 1888.
United States Congress. House. *Executive Document.* No. 156. 48th Cong., 2d sess.
_____. *Executive Document.* No. 247, 48th Cong. 2d sess.
_____. *Report.* No. 2655. 48th Cong. 2d sess.

United States Congress. Senate. *Executive Document.* No. 25. 34th Cong. 3rd sess.
——. *Executive Document.* No. 31. 36th Cong. 1st sess.
——. *Executive Document.* No. 10. 36th Cong. 2d sess.
——. *Report.* No. 393. 48th Cong. 1st sess.
——. *Executive Document.* No. 196. 49th Cong. 1st sess.
——. *Executive Document.* No. 77. 49th Cong. 2d sess.
Congressional Globe.
Congressional Record.
Official Records of the Union and Confederate Navies in the War of the Rebellion. 31 vols. Washington, 1894–1927.
War of the Rebellion: A Compilation of the Official Records of the Union and Confederate Armies. 130 vols. Washington, 1880–1901.

F. FLORIDA STATE DOCUMENTS

Cases Argued and Adjudicated in the Supreme Court of Florida, During the Year 1878–79, Vol. XVII. Tallahassee, 1879.
Cases Argued and Adjudicated in the Supreme Court of Florida, During the Year 1880, Vol. XVIII. Tallahassee, 1880.
Cases Argued and Adjudicated in the Supreme Court of Florida, During the Year 1888, Vol. XXIV. Tallahassee, 1889.
Minutes of the Board of Trustees Internal Improvement Fund of the State of Florida (1783– 1881). Tallahassee, 1904.

G. PRINTED DOCUMENTS AND COLLECTIONS

Benson, Arthur C., ed. *The Letters of Queen Victoria: A Selection from Her Majesty's Correspondence between the Years 1837 and 1861.* 3 vols. New York, 1907.
Bontinck, François. *Aux Origines L'Etat Indépendant du Congo: Documents tirés d'Archives Américaines.* Louvain and Paris, 1966.
Buckle, George E., ed. *The Letters of Queen Victoria: A Selection from Her Majesty's Correspondence and Journal between the Years 1862 and 1878.* 3 vols. New York, 1926–1928.
Correspondence on the Occasion of the Presentation by Major-General Sanford . . . of a Battery of Steel Cannon, to the State of Minnesota for the Use of the First Minnesota Regiment of Volunteers. St. Paul, 1862.
Gavin, R. J. and Betley, J. A., eds. *The Scramble for Africa: Documents on the Berlin West African Conference and Related Subjects 1884/1885.* Ibadan, Nigeria, 1973.
Harte, Geoffrey, ed. *The Letters of Bret Harte.* Boston, 1926.
Malloy, William M., comp. *Treaties, Conventions, International Acts, Protocols, and Agreements between the United States of America and other Powers: 1776–1909.* 2 vols. Washington, 1910.
Manning, William R., ed. *Diplomatic Correspondence of the United States: Inter-American Affairs, 1831–1860.* 12 vols. Washington, 1935.
Miller, David H., ed. *Treaties and Other International Acts of the United States of America.* 8 vols. Washington, 1931.
Richardson, James D. *A Compilation of the Messages and Papers of the Presidents 1789–1908.* 11 vols. Washington, 1908.

H. NEWSPAPERS

American Agriculturalist
Jacksonville Daily Florida Union
London Express
New Haven Palladium

New York Evening-Telegraph
New York Herald
New York Sun
New York Times
New York Tribune
New York World
Washington Daily-Union

I. Sanford Writings

Sanford, Henry S. "American Interests in Africa." *The Forum,* 9 (June 1890), 409–29.

_____. *The Aves Island Case, with the Correspondence Relating Thereto and Discussions of Law and Facts, Being the Official Documents Published by Order of the Senate of the United States.* Washington, 1861.

_____. *The Different Systems of Penal Codes in Europe; Also a Report on the Administrative Changes in France Since the Revolution of 1848.* Washington, 1854.

_____. "Free Cotton and Free Cotton States." [Albany, 1860].

_____. *The Law of Special Reprisals.* [Washington, 1858].

_____. "Possible Results of the Election Upon the South: Letter to Thurlow Weed from Henry S. Sanford." Sanford, Fla., 1876.

_____. "Report of the Hon. Henry Shelton Sanford, U.S. Delegate from the American Branch to the Annual Meeting of the African International Association, in Brussels, in June 1877." *Bulletin of the American Geographical Society,* 9 (1877), 103–108.

_____. *Venezuelan Outrage Upon United States Citizens and Property at Shelton's Isle: Memorandum of Philo S. Shelton, in His Case for State Department.* Derby, Conn., 1855.

J. MEMOIRS, AUTOBIOGRAPHIES, DIARIES,
AND FIRST-HAND ACCOUNTS

Banning, Emile. *Mémoires Politiques et Diplomatiques.* Paris, 1927.

Bay, W. V. N. *Reminiscences of the Bench and Bar of Missouri.* St. Louis, 1878.

Belmont, Perry. *An American Democrat.* New York, 1940.

Bigelow, John. *France and the Confederate Navy, 1862–1868.* New York, 1888.

_____. *Retrospections of an Active Life.* 5 vols. New York, 1909.

Briceno, Mariano. *Memoir Justificatory of the Conduct of the Government of Venezuela on the Isle de Aves Question.* Washington, 1858.

Bulloch, James D. *The Secret Service of the Confederate States in Europe.* 2 vols. New York, 1959.

Clay, Cassius M. *The Life of Cassius Marcellus Clay, Writings and Speeches.* 2 vols. Cincinnati, 1886.

Didier, Eugene L. "The American Colony in Paris." *Lippincott's Magazine,* 24 (1879), 384–86.

Eastwick, Edward A. *Venezuela or Sketches of Life in a South American Republic; with the History of the Loans of 1864.* London, 1868.

Gurowski, Adam. *Diary.* 3 vols. Boston, 1862–1866.

Kedney, H. D. "The Lemon in Florida." *Florida Agriculturalist,* April 10, 1889, 226–27.

Latrobe, Benjamin H. B. *Maryland in Liberia.* Baltimore, 1885.

Morse, John J., Jr., ed. *The Diary of Gideon Welles.* 3 vols. Boston, 1911.

Morgan, William J.; Tyler, David B.; Leonhart, Joyce L; and Loughlin, Mary F., eds. *Autobiography of Charles Wilkes, U.S. Navy, 1798–1877.* Washington, 1978.

Phelps, Lyman. "The Lemon." *Florida Dispatch,* August 8, 1887, 656–57.

Russell, William H. *My Diary North and South.* Boston, 1863.

Sampson, F. G. "Pioneering in Orange and Lemon Culture in Florida." *Proceedings of the Florida State Horticultural Society* (April 17–20, 1923), 190–97.

Seward, Frederick W. *Seward at Washington as Senator and Secretary of State, a Memoir of His Life, with Selections from His Letters.* 2 vols. New York, 1891.

Some Account of Belair, also of the City of Sanford, Florida, with a Brief Sketch of Their Founder. Sanford, 1889.

Squier, Ephraim G. *Honduras; Descriptive, Historical, and Statistical.* London, 1870.

———. *Notes on Central America; Particularly Honduras and San Salvador . . . and the Proposed Honduras Interoceanic Railway.* New York, 1855.

Stanley, Henry M. *The Congo and the Founding of Its Free State: A Story of Work and Exploration.* 2 vols. New York, 1885.

———. *In Darkest Africa; or the Quest, Rescue, and Retreat of Emin, Governor of Equatoria.* 2 vols. New York, 1891.

Wallace, Sarah A. and Gillespie, Frances E., eds. *The Journal of Benjamin Moran.* 2 vols. Chicago, 1948.

Weed, Harriet A., ed. *Life of Thurlow Weed, Including His Autobiography and a Memoir.* 2 vols. Boston, 1884.

Williams, M. A. "Lands of East and South Florida." *The Semi-Tropical,* 2 (1876), 609–12.

K. GUIDE BOOKS AND TOURIST ACCOUNTS

Adams, J. S. *Florida: Its Climate, Soil, and Productions, with a Sketch of Its History, Natural Features and Social Conditions.* New York, 1870.

Bill, Ledyard. *A Winter in Florida.* New York, 1870.

Baedeker, K. *Belgium and Holland: Handbook for Travellers.* Coblenz, London, Paris, 1869.

Crosby, Oliver M. *Florida Facts Both Bright and Blue: A Guide Book to Intending Settlers, Tourists, and Investors from a Northerner's Standpoint.* New York, 1887.

Drake, Samuel A. *Florida: Its History, Condition, and Resources.* Boston, 1878.

Foss, James H. *Florida Facts: Found after a Six Years' Search.* Boston, 1882.

———. comp. *Florida: Its Climate, Soil Productions and Agricultural Capabilities.* Washington, 1882.

Jacques, D. H. *Florida As a Permanent Home.* Jacksonville, 1877.

Lanier, Sidney. *Florida: The Scenery, Climate, and History.* Gainesville, 1973; reprint of 1875 ed.

Lee, Henry. *The Tourists' Guide of Florida and the Winter Resorts of the South.* New York, 1886.

Moore, Theophilus W. *Treatise and Handbook of Orange Culture in Florida.* New York, 1881.

Nichols, George W. "Six Weeks in Florida." *Harper's New Monthly Magazine,* 41 (1870), 555–67.

II. SECONDARY SOURCES

A. BOOKS

Adams, Ephraim D. *Great Britain and the American Civil War.* 2 vols. London, 1925.

Anderson, Frank M. *The Mystery of "A Public Man," A Historical Detective Story.* Minneapolis, 1948.

Anstey, Roger. *Britain and the Congo in the Nineteenth Century.* Oxford, 1962.

Barber, John W. *Connecticut Historical Collection.* New Haven, 1856.

Beisner, Robert L. *From the Old Diplomacy to the New, 1865–1900.* New York, 1975.

Blackman, William F. *History of Orange County, Florida, Narrative and Biographical.* DeLand, Fla., 1927.

Blumberg, Arnold. *The Diplomacy of the Mexican Empire 1863–1867.* Philadelphia, 1971.

Blumenthal, Henry. *A Reappraisal of Franco-American Relations, 1840–1871.* Chapel Hill, 1959.

Bourne, Kenneth. *Britain and the Balance of Power in North America, 1815–1908.* Berkeley, 1967.

Bruce, Robert V. *Lincoln and the Tools of War.* Indianapolis, 1956.

Brunschwig, Henri. *French Colonialism, 1871–1914.* New York, 1966.

Cabell, Branch and Hanna, A. J. *The St. Johns: A Parade of Diversities.* New York, 1943.

Case, Lynn M. and Spencer, Warren F. *The United States and France: Civil War Diplomacy.* Philadelphia, 1970.

Clapp, Margaret. *Forgotten First Citizen: John Bigelow.* Boston, 1947.

Clark, George L. *A History of Connecticut.* New York, 1914.

Cothren, William. *History of Ancient Woodbury Connecticut.* 3 vols. Waterbury, Conn., 1854.

Crofut, Florence S. M. *Guide to the History and Historic Sites of Connecticut.* 2 vols. New Haven, 1937.

Crook, D. P. *The North, the South, and the Powers, 1861–1865.* New York, 1974.

Crowe, Sybil. *The Berlin West African Conference, 1884–1885.* London, 1942.

DeSantis, Vincent P. *Republicans Face the Southern Question-The New Departure Years, 1877–1897.* Baltimore, 1959.

Donald, David. *Charles Sumner and the Rights of Man.* New York, 1970.

Dulles, Foster R. *Americans Abroad: Two Centuries of European Travel.* Ann Arbor, 1964.

Durden, Robert F. *James Shepherd Pike: Republicanism and the American Negro, 1850–1882.* Durham, 1957.

Eaton, Clement. *A History of the Southern Confederacy.* New York, 1965.

Emerson, Barbara. *Leopold II of the Belgians: King of Colonialism.* New York, 1979.

Ferris, Norman B. *Desperate Diplomacy: William H. Seward's Foreign Policy, 1861.* Knoxville, 1976.

———. *The Trent Affair: A Diplomatic Crisis.* Knoxville, 1977.

Fischer, LeRoy H. *Lincoln's Gadfly, Adam Gurowski.* Norman, Okla., 1964.

Folwell, William M. *A History of Minnesota.* 4 vols. St. Paul, 1924.

Galbraith, John S. *Mackinnon and East Africa.* Cambridge, 1972.

Gann, L. H. and Duignan, Peter. *The Rulers of Belgian Africa, 1884–1914.* Princeton, 1979.

Gavronsky, Serge. *The French Liberal Opposition and the American Civil War.* New York, 1968.

Gillette, William. *Retreat from Reconstruction, 1869–1877.* Baton Rouge, 1979.

Gilmore, Robert L. *Caudillism and Militarism in Venezuela, 1880–1910.* Athens, Ohio, 1964.

Gore, E. H. *History of Orlando.* Orlando, 1951.

Hagan, Kenneth J. *American Gunboat Diplomacy and the Old Navy, 1877–1889.* Westport, Conn., 1973.

Hamilton, Holman. *Zachary Taylor.* 2 vols. New York, 1941–1951.

Hendricks, Burton J. *Statesmen of the Lost Cause: Jefferson Davis and His Cabinet.* Boston, 1939.

Hird, Frank. *H. M. Stanley: The Authorized Life.* London, 1935.

Hume, H. Harold. *Citrus Fruits.* New York, 1950.

Jordan, Donaldson and Pratt, Edwin J. *Europe and the American Civil War.* Boston, 1931.

Klein, Philip S. *President James Buchanan: A Biography.* University Park, Pa. 1962.

LaFeber, Walter. *The New Empire: An Interpretation of American Expansion, 1860–1898.* Ithaca, 1963.

Larson, Henrietta M. *Jay Cooke: Private Banker.* New York, 1968, reprint of 1936 ed.

Lester, Richard I. *Confederate Finance and Purchasing in Great Britain.* Charlottesville, 1975.

Lowenthal, David. *George Perkins Marsh; Versatile Vermonter.* New York, 1958.

May, Ernest R. *American Imperialism: A Speculative Essay.* New York, 1968.

Meneely, A. Howard. *The War Department 1861, A Study in Mobilization and Administration.* New York, 1928.

Molloy, Leo T. *Henry Shelton Sanford, 1823–1891: A Biography.* Derby, Conn., 1952.

Moore, John B. *History and Digest of International Arbitrations to which the United States Has Been a Party.* 6 vols. Washington, 1898.

Moron, Guillermo. *A History of Venezuela.* John Street, ed. and trans. New York, 1963.

Morse, Jarvis M. *A Neglected Period of Connecticut's History, 1818–1850.* New Haven, 1933.

Nevins, Allan. *Hamilton Fish: The Inner History of the Grant Administration.* New York, 1936.

——. *Ordeal of the Union.* 8 vols. New York, 1947–1971.

Nichols, Roy F. *Advance Agents of American Destiny.* Philadelphia, 1956.

Otis, Fessenden N. *Illustrated History of the Panama Railroad.* New York, 1861.

Orcutt, Samuel and Beardsley, Ambrose. *The History of the Old Town of Derby, Connecticut, 1642–1880.* Springfield, Mass., 1880.

Owsley, Harriet C. *Register: Henry Shelton Sanford Papers.* Nashville, 1960.

Parish, John C. *George Wallace Jones.* Iowa City, 1912.

Parks, Taylor. *Colombia and the United States, 1765–1934.* Durham, 1935.

Peskin, Allan. *Garfield.* Kent, Ohio, 1978.

Pettengill, George W., Jr. *The Story of the Florida Railroads, 1834–1903.* Boston, 1952.

Plesur, Milton. *America's Outward Thrust: Approaches to Foreign Affairs, 1865–1890.* DeKalb, Ill., 1971.

Pletcher, David M. *The Awkward Years: American Foreign Relations Under Garfield and Arthur.* Columbia, Mo., 1962.

Potter, David M. *Lincoln and His Party in the Secession Crisis.* New Haven, 1962.

Powell, Lawrence N. *New Masters: Northern Planters During the Civil War and Reconstruction.* New Haven, 1980.

Raine, Philip. *Paraguay.* New Brunswick, N.J., 1956.

Raybeck, Joseph G. *Free Soil: The Election of 1848.* Lexington, 1970.

Reeves, Thomas C. *Gentleman Boss: The Life of Chester Alan Arthur.* New York, 1975.

Roland, Charles P. *Louisiana Sugar Plantations During the American Civil War.* Leiden, Netherlands, 1957.

Sandburg, Carl. *Abraham Lincoln; The War Years.* 4 vols. New York, 1939.

Sanford, Carleton E. *Thomas Sanford, the Emigrant to New England, Ancestry, Life and Descendents.* 2 vols. Rutland, Vt., 1911.

Shofner, Jerrell H. *Nor Is It Over Yet: Florida in the Era of Reconstruction.* Gainesville, 1974.

Sideman, Belle B. and Freedman, Lillian. *Europe Looks at the Civil War, an Anthology.* New York, 1960.

Sitterson, J. Carlyle. *Sugar Country: The Cane Sugar Industry in the South, 1753–1950.* Lexington, 1953.

Slade, Ruth. *King Leopold's Congo: Aspects of the Development of Race Relations in the Congo Independent State.* New York, 1962.

Spencer, Ivor D. *The Victor and the Spoils: A Life of William L. Marcy.* Providence, 1959.

Stampp, Kenneth M. *And the War Came: The North and the Secession Crisis, 1860–61.* Chicago, 1964.

Steiner, B. C. *The History of Education in Connecticut.* Washington, 1893.

Stern, Philip Van D. *When the Guns Roared: World Aspects of the American Civil War.* Garden City, N.Y. 1965.

Tebeau, Charlton W. *A History of Florida.* Coral Gables, 1971.

Thomas, Benjamin P. and Hyman, Harold. *Stanton: The Life and Times of Lincoln's Secretary of War.* New York, 1962.

Thompson, Samuel B. *Confederate Purchasing Operations Abroad.* Chapel Hill, 1935.

Thomson, Robert S. *Fondation de L'Etat Indépendant du Congo.* Brussels, 1933.

Trevelyan, George M. *Garibaldi and the Making of Italy.* London, 1911.

Van Deusen, Glyndon G. *Thurlow Weed: Wizard of the Lobby.* Boston, 1947.

——. *William Henry Seward.* New York, 1967.

Weaver, Glenn. *The History of Trinity College.* Hartford, 1967.

214 *Bibliography*

West, W. Reed. *Contemporary French Opinion of the American Civil War.* Baltimore, 1924.
Williams, William A. *The Roots of Modern American Empire: A Study of the Growth and Shaping of Social Consciousness in a Marketplace Society.* New York, 1969.
Williamson, Edward C. *Florida Politics in the Gilded Age, 1877–1893.* Gainesville, 1976.
Willson, Beckles. *America's Ambassadors to France (1777–1927): A Narrative of Franco-American Diplomatic Relations.* London, 1928.
Wilson, Henry S. *The Imperial Experience in Sub-Saharan Africa since 1870.* Minneapolis, 1977.
Woodward, C. Vann. *Origins of the New South, 1877–1913.* Baton Rouge, 1951.
Younger, Edward. *John A. Kasson: Politics and Diplomacy from Lincoln to McKinley.* Iowa City, 1955.
Ziegler, Louis W. and Wolfe, Herbert S. *Citrus Growing in Florida.* Gainesville, 1971.

B. ARTICLES

Amundson, Richard J. "The Florida Land and Colonization Company." *Florida Historical Quarterly,* 44 (1966), 153–68.
_____. "Henry S. Sanford and Labor Problems in Florida Orange Industry." *Florida Historical Quarterly,* 43 (1965), 229–43.
_____. "Oakley Plantation: A Post-Civil War Venture in Louisiana Sugar." *Louisiana History,* 9 (1968), 21–42.
_____. "Sanford and Garibaldi." *Civil War History,* 14 (1968), 40–45.
_____. "Trescot, Sanford, and Sea Island Cotton." *The South Carolina Historical Magazine,* 68 (1967), 31–36.
Berthoff, Rowland T. "Southern Attitudes Toward Immigration, 1865–1914." *Journal of Southern History,* 27 (1951), 328–60.
Blumberg, Arnold. "United States and the Role of Belgium in Mexico, 1863–1867." *The Historian: A Journal of History,* 26 (1964), 206–27.
Brady, Eugene A. "A Reconsideration of the Lancashire 'Cotton Famine.' " *Agricultural History,* 37 (1963), 156–62.
Burnette, O. Lawrence. "John Tyler Morgan and Expansionist Sentiment in the New South." *Alabama Review,* 18 (1965), 163–182.
Current, Richard N. "Carpetbaggers Reconsidered." In *Reconstruction: An Anthology of Revisionist Writings,* 223–40. Edited by Kenneth M. Stampp and Leon Litwack. Baton Rouge, 1969.
Davis, Robert R., Jr. "Diplomatic Plumage: American Court Dress in the Early National Period." *American Quarterly,* 20 (1968), 164–79.
Diamond, William. "Imports of the Confederate Government from Europe and Mexico." *Journal of Southern History,* 6 (1940), 470–503.
Dyer, Brainerd. "Thomas H. Dudley." *Civil War History,* 1 (1955), 401–13.
Fry, Joseph A. "Eyewitness by Proxy: Nelson M. Beckwith's Evaluation of Garibaldi, September 1861." *Civil War History,* 28 (1982), 65–70.
_____. "The Messenger to Garibaldi: Henry S. Sanford and the Offer of a Union Command to Giuseppe Garibaldi," *Essays In History* (Corcoran Dept. of History, University of Virginia), 17 (1973), 37–50.
Gay, H. Nelson. "Lincoln's Offer of a Command to Garibaldi: Light on a Disputed Point of History." *Century Magazine,* 75 (1907), 63–74.
Gray, William H. "The Human Aspect of Aves Diplomacy: An Incident in the Relations between the United States and Venezuela." *The Americas,* 6 (1949), 72–84.
Hammond, Harold E. "American Interest in the Exploration of the Dark Continent." *The Historian: A Journal of History,* 18 (1956), 202–29.
Kaplan, Lawrence S. "The Brahmin as Diplomat in Nineteenth Century America: Everett, Bancroft, Motley, Lowell." *Civil War History,* 19 (1973), 5–28.

Kein, David F. "Russell's Decision to Detain the Laird Rams." *Civil War History*, 22 (1976), 158–63.

Louis, Wm. Roger, "The Berlin Congo Conference.' In *France and Britain in Africa: Imperial Rivalry and Colonial Rule*, 167–230. Edited by Prosser Gifford and Wm. Roger Louis. New Haven, 1971.

McVeigh, Donald R. "Charles James Faulkner in the Civil War." *West Virginia History*, 12 (1951), 129–41.

Marraro, Howard R. "Lincoln's Offer of a Command to Garibaldi: Further Light on a Disputed Point of History." *Journal of the Illinois State Historical Society*, 36 (1943), 237–70.

Maynard, Douglas A. "The Forbes-Aspinwall Mission." *Mississippi Valley Historical Review*, 45 (1958), 67–89.

Meyer, Lysle E. "Henry S. Sanford and the Congo: A Reassessment." *African Historical Studies*, 4 (1971), 19–39.

Miers, Suzanne. "The Brussels Conference of 1889–1890: The Place of the Slave Trade in the Policies of Great Britain and Germany." In *Britain and Germany in Africa: Imperial Rivalry and Colonial Rule*, 83–118. Edited by Prosser Gifford and Wm. Roger Louis. New Haven, 1967.

Owsley, Harriet C. "Henry Shelton Sanford and Federal Surveillance Abroad, 1861–1865." *Mississippi Valley Historical Review*, 48 (1961), 211–28.

Roark, James L. "American Expansionism vs European Imperialism: Henry S. Sanford and the Congo Episode, 1883–1885." *Mid-America: An Historical Review*, 60 (1978), 21–33.

Shippee, Lester B. "The First Railroad between the Mississippi and Lake Superior." *Mississippi Valley Historical Review*, 5 (1918), 121–42.

Shofner, Jerrel H. "Florida: A Failure of Moderate Republicanism." In *Reconstruction and Redemption*, 13–66. Edited by Otto H. Olsen. Baton Rouge, 1980.

Smith, George W. "Carpetbag Imperialism in Florida, 1862–1868." *Florida Historical Quarterly*, 27 (1949), 269–99.

Stansifer, Charles L. "E. George Squier and the Honduras Interoceanic Railroad Project." *Hispanic American Historical Review*, 46 (1966), 1–27.

Stengers, Jean. "The Congo Free State and the Belgian Congo before 1914." In *Colonialism in Africa, 1870–1960*, I, 261–92. Edited by L. H. Gann and Peter Duignan. London, 1969.

_____. "King Leopold and Anglo-French Rivalry, 1882–1884." In *France and Britain in Africa: Imperial Rivalry and Colonial Rule*, 121–66. Edited by Prosser Gifford and Wm. Roger Louis. New Haven, 1971.

Tansill, Charles C. "A Secret Chapter in Civil War History." *Thought: Fordham University Quarterly*, 15 (1940), 215–24.

Thomson, Robert S. "Léopold II et la Conférence de Berlin: Documents inédits Provenant de la Correspondence Particulière de l'Hon. Henry S. Sanford." *Congo Revue Générale de la Colonie Belge* 12, (1931), 325–52.

_____. "Léopold II et le Congo: Révélé par les Notes Privées de Henry S. Sanford." *Congo Revue Générale de la Colonie Belge*, 12 (1931), 168–96.

_____. "Léopold II et Henry S. Sanford; Papiers inédits concernant le Rôle Joué par un Diplomate Americain dans la Création de l'E. I. du Congo." *Congo Revue Générale de la Colonie Belge*, 11 (1930), 295–329.

Turner, Henry A., Jr. "Bismarck's Imperialist Venture: Anti-British in Origin?" In *Britain and Germany in Africa: Imperial Rivalry and Colonial Rule*, 47–82. Edited by Prosser Gifford and Wm. Roger Louis. New Haven, 1967.

Vance, Maurice M. "Northerners in Late Nineteenth Century Florida: Carpetbaggers or Settlers?" *Florida Historical Quarterly*, 38 (1959), 1–14.

Varg, Paul A. "The Myth of the China Market, 1890–1914." *American Historical Review*, 73 (1968), 742–58.

White, James P. "The Sanford Exploring Expedition." *Journal of African History,* 13 (1967), 291–302.
Williamson, Edward C., ed. "Florida Politics in 1881: A Letter of Henry S. Sanford." *Florida Historical Quarterly,* 31 (1953), 279–81.
Zettl, Herbert. "Garibaldi and the American Civil War." *Civil War History,* 22 (1976), 70–76.

C. UNPUBLISHED THESES, DISSERTATIONS,
AND TYPESCRIPTS

Amundson, Richard J. "The American Life of Henry Shelton Sanford." Ph.D. dissertation, Florida State University, 1963.
Amelung, Evasusanne. "History of Economic Development of the Sanford, Florida Area." M.A. thesis, University of Florida, 1971.
Clark, Morita M. "The Development of the Citrus Industry in Florida before 1895." M.A. thesis, Florida State University, 1947.
Cochran, Gifford A. "Mr. Lincoln's Many-Faceted Minister and Entrepreneur Extraordinary." Typescript, n.d., P. K. Yonge Library of Florida History, University of Florida.
Davis, T. Frederick. "A Narrative History of the Orange in the Floridian Peninsula." Typescript, Jacksonville, 1941, P. K. Yonge Library of Florida History.
Fry, Joseph A. "An American Abroad: The Diplomatic Career of Henry Shelton Sanford." Ph.D. dissertation, University of Virginia, 1974.
Halligan, William W., Jr. "The Berlin West African Conference of 1884–1885 from the Viewpoint of American Participation." M.A. thesis, University of Virginia, 1949.
Harris, William L. "The Aves Island Claims: A Study of Claims Technique." M.A. thesis, Vanderbilt University, 1963.
Heppner, Francis J. "Henry S. Sanford, United States Minister to Belgium, 1861–1869." M.A. thesis, Georgetown University, 1955.
Hibbs, James R. "Chapters in the Relations of Venezuela and the United States 1865 to 1889." Ph.D. dissertation, University of Pennsylvania, 1941.
Kistler, Allison C. "The History and Status of Labor in the Citrus Industry of Florida." M.A. thesis, University of Florida, 1939.
McMakin, Dorothy P. "General Henry Shelton Sanford and His Influence on Florida." M.A. thesis, Stetson University, 1938.
Meyer, Lysle E., Jr. "Henry Shelton Sanford and the Congo." Ph.D. dissertation, Ohio State University, 1967.
Pavolovsky, Arnold M. " 'We Busted Because We Failed': Florida Politics, 1880–1908." Ph.D. dissertation, Princeton University, 1973.
Radke, August C., Jr. "John Tyler Morgan, An Expansionist Senator, 1877–1907." Ph.D. dissertation, University of Washington, 1953.
Sanders, Neill F. "Lincoln's Consuls in the British Isles." Ph.D. dissertation, University of Missouri– Columbia, 1971.
Scribner, Robert L. "The Diplomacy of William L. Marcy." Ph.D. dissertation, University of Virginia, 1949.
Voight, Robert C. "Defender of the Common Law: Aaron Goodrich, Chief Justice of Minnesota Territory." Ph.D. dissertation, University of Minnesota, 1962.
Weeks, Jerry W. "Florida Gold: The Emergence of the Florida Citrus Industry, 1865–1895." Ph.D. dissertation, University of North Carolina, 1977.

INDEX

Abrams, Alexander St. Clair, 114
Adams, Charles Francis, 37–38, 64, 173;
  objects to HSS's secret service work in
  Great Britain, 45; characterizes HSS,
  45; HSS's opinion of, 52, 65; evaluation
  of HSS and Garibaldi affair, 63
Adams, Solon A., 129–130
Africa, 134, 137–39, 141, 151, 155–56, 160,
  165–66
Afrikaanche Handelsvereeniging, 140
Alabama (C.S.S.), 47–48
Albany Evening Journal, 32
Albert, Prince (England), 57
Alden, A. H., 162
Alden, George A., 162
Alexandria (C.S.S.), 47
Allen, Philip, 28
Allison, William B., 136
American Colonization Society, 137–38,
  144, 165
American Geographical Society, 137
Anderson, Edward C., 43
Anglo-Portuguese Treaty (1884), 141, 143,
  148–49, 168; HSS denounces, 145–46
Anthony, Henry B., 32–33, 84, 85, 135–36;
  supports upgrading U.S. mission to
  Belgium, 81–83
Antietam, 40
Appleton, John, 28–29
Arman, Lucien, 48–49
Arthur, Chester A., 126, 136–37, 142–44,
  146, 155; administration of, 128–29,
  131, 148, 174; refuses to aid HSS in
  Florida politics, 129, 131
Artomi, Joseph, 61–62
Aspinwall, William H., 33, 47
*Association Africaine Internationale du
  Congo* (AIC), 140–41, 146, 148–54,
  168

Association Internationale Africaine (AIA),
  112, 137–40, 142–46, 148, 150, 156, 162,
  174; American branch of, 138, 140, 144
Astor, J. J., Jr., 33
Astor, William, 129
Atlantic Monthly, 34
Aves Island, 20–26, 29–30, 78, 82, 161
Aves Island Convention (Jan. 14, 1859), 24

Babcock, Orville E., 84
Baker, Edward D., 33
Baldwin, Roger J., 10
Banana Point (Congo), 157–58, 160
Bank of Belgium, 58
Banning, Emile, 152–53
Banning, William L., 139
Baring Brothers, 30, 51–52, 57–58
Barnwell Island Plantation, 88–90, 94–96
Beckwith, Nelson M., 16; aids HSS's
  surveillance work in Paris, 46, 48;
  advises HSS during Garibaldi affair, 63,
  187–88 n. 88
Belair Grove, 95, 97, 99–100, 105, 109,
  112–13; 173–74; location, soil type, and
  size of, 106; experimentation at,
  106–107; unprofitability of, 107–108,
  119–23; sold, 123
Belgium, 1, 12, 24, 33–35, 38, 41, 43, 46,
  56–57, 73–75, 81, 83, 85, 95, 108, 122,
  133–35, 137–38, 143, 146, 165, 171, 173;
  and the American Civil War, 39–40,
  65–71; and the Brussels Antislavery
  Conf., 166
Belmont, Perry, 155
Bennett, James Gordon, 139
Berlin, Germany, 9, 150–51, 153, 155–56,
  169–70
Berlin West African Conference, 156, 174;
  background to, 148–49; U.S. invited to,